America's Most Haunted Encyclopedia Series | Vol. III

By US Ghost Adventures

Photo on Cover: Welty House of Brickhouse Inn in Gettysburg, PA.

Copyright @ 2024 US Ghost Adventures LLC

All rights reserved. No part of this publication may be reproduced, distributed, or transmitted in any form or by any means, including photocopying, recording, or other electronic or mechanical means, without the prior written permission of the publisher, except in the case of brief quotations in critical reviews and certain other non-commercial uses permitted by copyright law. For permission requests, write to the publisher, at the address below.

ISBN: 979-8-9890835-1-0

Although the author and publisher have made every effort to ensure that the information in this book was correct at press time, the author and publisher do not assume and hereby disclaim any liability to any party for any loss, damage, or disruption caused by errors or omissions, whether such errors or omissions result from negligence, accident, or any other cause.

Cover design: Draftive Digital Agency
Book design: Studio de Mel, studiodemel.com

Printed by Amazon on demand

First printed edition, March 2024

US Ghost Adventures Books
The Lizzie Borden House 230 2nd St, Fall River, MA 02721
usghostadventures.com

America's Most Haunted Encyclopedia Series | Vol. III

The Ghosts of Maryland, New Jersey, New York & Pennsylvania:

Annapolis, Baltimore, Atlantic City, New York City, Gettysburg, Philadelphia, Pittsburgh, and The Welty House

By US Ghost Adventures

America's Most Haunted Encyclopedia Series | Vol. III

The Ghosts of Maryland, New Jersey, New York & Pennsylvania:

Annapolis, Baltimore, Atlantic City, New York City, Gettysburg, Philadelphia, Pittsburgh, and The Welty House

By US Ghost Adventures

CONTENTS

Acknowledgements 16
About US Ghost Adventures 17
Introduction 18

CHAPTER I
The Ghosts of Annapolis 20
Middleton's Tavern 22
Governor Calvert House Inn 26
The James Brice House 30
The Little Brice House 34
Galway Bay Irish Pub and Restaurant 36
Reynolds Tavern 40
The Maryland Inn 44
The Brooksby Shaw House 48
The Shiplap House 52
Dock Street Bar and Grill 56
The U.S. Naval Academy 60

CHAPTER II
The Ghosts of Baltimore 66
Max's Taphouse 68
807 S. Broadway 70
Eat Bertha's Mussels 74
Fell Family Cemetery 76
The Horse You Came in On Saloon 78
Admiral Fell Inn 80
Waterfront Hotel 82
Cat's Eye Pub 84
Alexander Thompson House 86
Sticky Rice 88
Bar Vasquez 90
Blue Moon Cafe 92

Maryland's Most Haunted Continued 94
The Witch's Grave at Truxton Park, Annapolis 96
Fletchertown Road, Bowie 100
U.S. Coast Guard Ship Taney, Baltimore 104
Antietam National Battlefield, Sharpsburg 108
Dr. Samuel Mudd's House, Waldorf 112

CHAPTER III
The Ghosts of Gettysburg 118
Rupp House 120
Jennie Wade House 124
Farnsworth House 128

Gettysburg Battlefield, East Cemetery Hill...132
Gettysburg Battlefield, Devil's Den...136
Sachs Covered Bridge..138
Evergreen Cemetery...140
Gettysburg College...144
Tillie Pierce House..148
National Soldiers' Orphans' Homestead...150
Lincoln Train Museum..152

CHAPTER IV
The Ghosts of The Welty House..**156**
The Texas Room..160
The Illinois Room...162
The Basement..165
The Brickhouse..168

CHAPTER V
The Ghosts of Philadelphia..**172**
Washington Square..174
Independence Hall...178
American Philosophical Society Library...180
First Bank of the United States...182
Bishop White House..184
St. Peter's Church..186
Old St. Joseph's Church..188
St. Mary's Church and Cemetery..190
Thaddeus Kosciuszko National Memorial..192
Todd House..194
The Hill-Physick House..196

CHAPTER VI
The Ghosts of Pittsburgh..**202**
U.S. Steel Tower..204
Clayton...206
Cindy Esser's Floral Shop...208
Omni William Penn Hotel..210
Pittsburgh University..214
Allegheny County Health Department..218
The Old Allegheny Jail Museum...220
Extra Space Storage..224
S.W. Randall Toyes & Giftes...226
The Pennsylvania Apartments...228

Pennsylvania's Most Haunted Continued...**232**
Eastern State Penitentiary, Philadelphia..234
The Devil's Elbow, Altoona..238
Penn's Cave & Wildlife Park, Centre Hall...240
Hotel Bethlehem, Bethlehem..242

CHAPTER VII
The Ghosts of Atlantic City **248**
Playground Pier 250
Warner Theater 254
Caesars Atlantic City 256
The Colosseum Parking Garage 260
Jim Whelan Boardwalk Hall 262
Atlantic City Beach 266
The Absecon Lighthouse 270
The Claridge Hotel 272
Resorts Casino Hotel 274
The Psychic Shop 278

New Jersey's Most Haunted Continued **282**
The Pine Barrens, Pemberton Township 284
The Devil's Tree, Bernards Township 290
Union Hotel, Flemington 292
The Cranbury Inn, Cranbury 296
Emlen Physick Estate, Cape May 300

CHAPTER VIII
The Ghosts of New York City **306**
Washington Square Park 308
House of Death 314
Emma Lazarus House 320
Jefferson Market Library 324
12 Gay Street 328
Marie's Crisis Café 332
One if by Land, Two if by Sea 336
Brown Building 340
Fire Patrol No. 2 344
Edgar Allan Poe House 346

New York's Most Haunted Continued **350**
The Dakota, New York City 352
Sleepy Hollow, Sleepy Hollow 356
Belhurst Castle and Winery, Geneva 360
Utica State Hospital, Utica 364
The New York State Education Building, Albany 368

"The boundaries which divide life from death are at best shadowy and vague. Who shall say where the one ends, and where the other begins?"

- Edgar Allan Poe

For the US Ghost Adventures staff, who work tirelessly to bridge the realms of the living and the departed.

Here's to the spirits who offer up their stories, and the curious souls who are brave enough to listen.

Acknowledgements

This volume is one part of a larger encyclopedia series devoted to unveiling the most iconic haunted places across the US. The series is the result of countless hours of research. Most importantly, it is from talking to the people of the cities whose stories we tell here. Ghosts live among us in one form or fashion, and they form a part of the heritage and history of our cities. We are privileged to share the stories of some of our greatest cities here, with you.

To the team who made this book possible we extend our gratitude.
The hours of research, proofing and fact checking have elevated this from a collection of stories to a true encyclopedia of the best stories of hauntings and history.

To you, the reader, whose curiosity and quest for knowledge about the ghosts of your hometowns, and of haunted towns far away, sustains our enthusiasm for sharing these stories.

May you never stop wondering and wandering.

About US Ghost Adventures

What makes a place haunted? What ties the supernatural to a location and attracts, entices, or binds spirits, ghosts, energy, and otherworldly phenomenon in such a way that a haunted place becomes known as a hotspot for the unexplained?

No matter the reason, effect, or consequences—US Ghost Adventures researches, explores, and attempts to uncover the hidden truths and authenticity behind the science of hauntings and tries to reveal exactly why these locations have secured their place in history as… America's Most Haunted.

US Ghost Adventures is the leading provider of haunted house and ghost tours in America — we even own some of the most haunted properties in America, like the Lizzie Borden House! Every tour is hosted by an experienced, knowledgeable local guide. You'll hear firsthand accounts from people who have witnessed the unexplained — sometimes even a guest's eerie encounter or the guide's own!

US Ghost Adventures offers an authentic experience that strives to make sense of the unexplainable. These ghost tours are based on real-world portrayals of hauntings and well-documented history. Whether you're just visiting Massachusetts and Rhode Island, or looking to learn more about your hometown's haunted past, US Ghost Adventures offers a ghostly experience that you won't forget.

You can find all of our tours and services at **usghostadventures.com**

usghostadventures.com

- facebook.com/usghostadventures
- usghostadv
- usgadventures
- usghostadvntrs
- pinterest.com/usghostadventures
- usghostadventures

Introduction

Welcome to America's Most Haunted Places: Volume III. You're about to plunge into the most haunted corners of the Mid-Atlantic, from Greenwich Village down to the Annapolis harbor. But be warned: Once you know what lurks in the shadows, you may never feel safe in the light again.

These spine-chilling tales have been passed down for generations, terrifying wide-eyed children at bedtime and forcing the most skeptical adults to sleep with the lights on. They've been whispered around campfires and retold at the dinner table, and now we're passing them on to you.

It begins with Annapolis, a colonial port city that's preserved more than just historic buildings. The ghosts of mariners, slaves, and bootleggers roam the harbor — and what they have to say may shock you. Did a medium reveal the truth about a cold-blooded murder at the U.S. Naval Academy? And what went on behind the walls of the famous James Brice House? Archeology is finally catching up to what the ghosts have been trying to tell us all along.

Next, we dive into the charming city of Baltimore, where hip Fells Point bars are embroiled in a war with the spirits of the past. Ghostly prostitutes and murdered sailors wreak havoc behind historic brick walls. You may even run into Edgar Allan Poe. His tortured spirit is said to breeze into the "Horse You Came In On Saloon" for a final drink in the city that ended his life.

From there, you'll visit Gettysburg, where over 40,000 men lay wounded or dead after a bloody Civil War battle. Today, the bullet-riddled buildings hold the spirits — and secrets — of those harrowing three days. Cannonfire echoes in the night. Hotel guests are jolted awake by phantom soldiers. In the midst of it all are the ghostly civilians who sacrificed everything when the war came knocking.

And then it's on to Philadelphia, where America's founders poured their blood, sweat, and tears into a new nation. It seems some of them never left. Ben Franklin, Alexander Hamilton, and Benedict Arnold meddle in the hallowed halls of the historic district, but there's more to the "Cradle of Liberty" than ghostly politicians. War, betrayal, and violent epidemics have littered the streets with spirits, and some of them only want one thing: Revenge.

After that, you'll explore the shadows of "Steel City." Pittsburgh may have boomed under industrialism, but it came at a high cost. The cursed steel magnate Henry Clay Frick claimed he was saved by the ghost of his five-year-old daughter, and his former home is still one of the most haunted locations in the city. At the Pennsylvania Apartments, residents are constantly barraged by the specters of a bloody railroad strike… and a mysterious trunk tied to a Chicago murder. Living in a historic building is all fun and games until the history wakes you up at night.

From there, you'll stroll down the haunted boardwalk of Atlantic City, where the neon lights of hotels and casinos hide a dark web of mob violence, war, and suicide. Once a World War II base, the city has absorbed the trauma of "combat fatigue." Ghostly airmen walk the halls of old hotels, where their brothers succumbed to diseases and horrific injuries. Even the sun-soaked beaches become a nightmare when the sun disappears… when the postcard-blue ocean becomes a black mass, and its victims are turned loose.

Finally, you'll dive into New York's Greenwich Village, an artists' haven that began as a graveyard. Disease, corruption, murder, and a deadly factory fire have scattered restless souls through the historic, cobblestone streets — but the houses are even more chilling. The infamous House of Death is plagued by 22 spirits, including American icon Mark Twain. But not all of the spirits are as docile as the mustachioed author. Some are so violent the nation's leading ghost hunter washed his hands of it.

So pull the blankets close and prepare to be spooked. These stories may haunt you long after the last page is turned.

GHOSTS OF ANNAPOLIS

CRABTOWN GHOSTS

CHAPTER I

The Ghosts of Annapolis

Three centuries ago Annapolis was a thriving, colonial city. Salt-drenched sailors poured into local taverns for a hearty meal; merchants built elaborate Georgian mansions; and the spirit of revolution was in the air. You could find George Washington and Thomas Jefferson dancing in gaslit ballrooms as shipbuilders constructed sloops and schooners that would soon stare down the Royal Navy.

Thanks to historic preservation, those taverns, mansions, and inns have been restored to their 18th-century glory — but the city's restored more than just architecture. Phantom footsteps echo in the night. Shadows dart through empty rooms. Poltergeists kick and slam to terrify the living. And crews have uncovered secrets that have been hidden for centuries…

The following chapters unveil the most spine-chilling ghost stories Annapolis has to offer — legendary, first-hand accounts you won't find in any history textbook. From the cigar-smoking ghost of Middleton's Tavern to a murder victim at the U.S. Naval Academy, these stories prove the past is never truly dead, and — sometimes — the only people who know what truly happened are the ghosts who lived it…

usghostadventures.com/annapolis

Middleton's Tavern

A true Annapolis staple, Middleton's Tavern is famous for three things: Its iconic red exterior, its one-of-a-kind oyster shooter, and its resident ghost.

When Horatio Middleton bought the tavern in 1750, the tagline was an "Inn for seafaring men," but it soon attracted a more high-brow crowd. George Washington, Thomas Jefferson, and Benjamin Franklin ate there when they were in town for business.

Washington likely dined at Middleton's in 1783, in the days leading up to his resignation from the Continental Army. He arrived in town on December 19th and didn't address Congress until December 23rd. That day, he gave a teary, heart-felt speech at the Old Senate Chamber. When he was through, he bowed to Congress and rode off into the sunset, believing he was going to live out the rest of his years in peace at Mount Vernon. Wrong.

America dragged him right back into politics. He became the first president of the United States in 1789 and served until 1797. After that, he had two peaceful years at Mount Vernon before he died — but it's very sweet that he thought his Annapolis speech would be his last.

Middleton's housed a few different businesses after Horatio died in 1770. It was a hotel, a general store, a meat market, and a bar. In the mid-twentieth century, it became a Greek diner called "Mandris." The tavern we know today got its start in 1968 when Jerry Hardesty bought it at the age of 26.

Hardesty restored it to its former glory, changed the name back to "Middleton Tavern," and introduced the famous "Middleton Oyster Shooter" (a shot glass filled with a freshly shucked oyster, cocktail sauce, and vodka).

He was as much a fixture of Annapolis as his business. He used to sit at the bar for hours and talk to every customer. He would stuff a rockfish right in the middle of the dining room just for the entertainment value.
He knew Middleton's better than anyone, and he firmly believed the place was haunted...

For decades, the top-floor bar has been haunted by a shadowy figure in colonial clothing. He often appears on Sundays, always filling the room with the thick smell of cigar smoke. When he isn't smoking, he's pushing glasses off shelves, knocking over wine bottles, and causing electronics to go haywire.

When Mike Conroy was first hired, he was a firm skeptic. He figured people were imagining things. After all, Middleton's is an old tavern, and it's fun to be able to say it's haunted by the spirits of the past. He didn't believe a word of it… until he saw the ghost with his own eyes.

In 2019, Conroy told the chilling story on a podcast called "The Ghost in my Room."

It was a Sunday night around 10:30 p.m. He had just yelled out, "Last call!" so the only person left at the bar was his manager, Josh, who was nursing a stiff drink after a long shift. Mike was completely sober, wiping down bottles and cleaning up for the night.

As he chatted with Josh, he noticed a man walk into the room. Customers often wander upstairs looking for the bathrooms. He thought the guy was lost, so he tried to get his attention. But as he rounded the bar, the figure kept moving. It was unnatural, like he was floating, or moving on wheels… and he wasn't looking at Mike. He just stared straight ahead. Without stopping, the figure moved to the other end of the room and disappeared.

Just then, Josh jumped up from his barstool and grabbed the back of his neck, saying he could feel the hair standing up. They searched everywhere for the man. He was nowhere to be found — not upstairs, not downstairs,

Middleton's Tavern, Annapolis, MD.

not outside. He was gone. Josh looked at Mike and said, "Oh my God, you just saw Roland."

Roland has haunted Middleton's for decades, but the staff didn't know his name until the 1990s, when Jerry Hardesty held a seance and invited a medium to speak with the spirits of the tavern. She said she felt a man's presence. His name was Roland Johnson, and he had been a regular at Middleton's in the 18th century. He dressed well, smoked cigars, and annoyed everyone who worked and dined there. It seems he continued that practice well into the afterlife.

Roland doesn't usually interact with the living, but his appearance is still terrifying. At least once a month, a server will come down the stairs and say they're never going back up there again. Multiple employees have quit. If Roland isn't enough to freak them out, the tavern's *other* spirits usually are.

Shadowy figures move across the dining room. Tables and chairs have been moved by phantom hands.

On a hot summer day a few years back, one of the servers spotted a man in colonial dress sitting by the window looking out at the water. He thought it was a reenactor. Knowing how hot those costumes are, he left the room to bring the man a glass of water... but when he got back, he was gone.

It's like the spirits of the past are still dining there — right alongside the living.

Jerry Hardesty may be there too. He died in 2021 at the age of 79, after running Middleton Tavern for over 50 years. He was known to be a showman, and what greater show is there than coming back to life as a ghost?

Middleton's Tavern, Annapolis, MD.

Governor Calvert House Inn

Governor Calvert House Inn, Annapolis, MD.

The story of the Governor Calvert House Inn is filled with unexpected twists. It involves murder, war, oranges, and — of course — ghosts.

The inn is named for Captain Charles Calvert, who ruled over the Province of Maryland from 1720 to 1727. At the end of his term, Calvert purchased the property at 58 State Circle and built a one-story brick house. That might seem modest for a royal governor, but he spent all of his money on one major amenity: A greenhouse for growing oranges.

Under the greenhouse, he installed an ancient Roman heating system called a "hypocaust," which allowed him to heat the orange plants to tropical temperatures. He was rich enough to create a little piece of Florida in northern Maryland.

In 1734, Calvert died of early senility and the greenhouse was immediately demolished. It's since been dug up, and the hotel displays it under a glass floor.

The house changed hands several times after Calvert's death. It was struck by lightning in 1752 and destroyed by a fire in 1764. After that, it was rebuilt into a two-story, Georgian-style house that was used for everything under the sun, including a barracks. British officers captured during the Revolutionary War were held there until 1784.

In 1854, the house was sold to the Mayor of Annapolis, Abram Claude. After Claude's death it was split into apartments, which remained until the late 70s. Time eventually caught up with the colonial house. By 1977, the apartments were abandoned and crumbling. That's when Paul Pearson stepped in.

Pearson had visited Annapolis on a sailing trip in 1968, when the historic district was marked by boarded-up buildings and empty streets, and he desperately wanted to bring it back to life. He started with the Maryland Inn in the 1970s, then moved on to the Calvert House, Reynolds Tavern, Robert Johnson House, and State House Inn.

Restoring historic buildings may be satisfying work, but it isn't lucrative work. Pearson once said if he wanted to make money, he would have built Pizza Huts, not historic hotels.

By the early 90s, he was divorced and bankrupt. Friends held a benefit concert for him in 1994, which kept him afloat for a few years. But his health ended his preservation career. He died of complications from a stroke in 2001. His memorial service was held here at the Calvert House.

With such a long and storied history, the Governor Calvert House could be haunted by anyone. Maybe British officers are still sitting in their cells? Maybe Charles Calvert is still tending to his oranges?

Every so often, a guest will wander into the room where the hypocaust used to be. They'll peer down at the glass, studying the brickwork underneath. After a few seconds, faces will appear — as if they're surrounded by people... but there's no one else in the room.

Paranormal investigators believe the house is still occupied by the spirits of the past. Some are content to linger in the shadows and watch... Some like to interact with the living...

In August of 2020, an Ohio couple had a horrifying experience in Room 3202. This was during the COVID-19 pandemic, so they had the entire wing to themselves. As they stayed up late reading on their iPads, they heard weird noises — bumps, footsteps — but thought nothing of it.

Maybe employees were cleaning the rooms, or another guest had checked in late. They finished reading and switched off the light.

That's when the nightmares began.

They both dreamt of a violent murder and a demonic creature. Each time they woke up, sweat-soaked and screaming, they felt a presence in the room, like someone was watching them. This happened over and over until they both bolted awake for the last time at 8 a.m. on the dot. They were both self-proclaimed skeptics, yet they had the exact same thought: Their room was *haunted*. They packed their bags and left.

The hauntings don't end there. Several guests have woken up to the TV turning on by itself — the remote perched on the table, untouched. The clerk has had to warn people that there's a prankster spirit who likes to switch it on in the middle of the night.

It could be "Dominic," the hotel's resident ghost. When a medium spoke to him years back, they discovered he likes to spy on people… especially when they're getting undressed. The eerie presence the Ohio couple felt in their room could have been Dominic… or someone far more sinister.

In the 1940s, a gruesome murder occurred in the apartments. The details have been lost to history, but the spirits haven't. The victim still wanders the halls at night — her bloody dress hanging loosely around her pale form. Maybe she was projecting the details of her grisly murder on that poor Ohio couple. But then… who was looming over them when they woke up? Was it her? Or the killer?

The James Brice House

Lauded as the most pristine example of Georgian architecture in the country, James Brice's mansion has been the pride of Annapolis for over two centuries. But the facade of this esteemed estate — and the family who lived there — is starting to crumble. Centuries-old secrets have been unearthed, and what they've revealed is downright chilling.

It all began in 1766, when 20-year-old James Brice inherited two plantations and two Annapolis lots from his father, Judge John Brice. Almost immediately, he began planning a grand, five-part mansion. It would take seven years and 326,000 bricks to build, but — by the time it was completed in 1774 — it was the most elegant home in the entire city.

Brice went on to serve as a colonel in the Revolutionary War, an alderman, mayor of Annapolis, and acting governor of Maryland. He's been celebrated as a war hero and influential politician, as well as a master architect. Brice was meticulous about the building process. He kept a detailed ledger of every transaction: The exact number of shingles, the exact number of bricks... Lucky for Historic Annapolis, the ledger was found in a local masonic lodge in 1971. It's currently being used to restore the house to its 1774 state — with one important change:

They're going to highlight the work of the enslaved African Americans who built and maintained the Brice House.

While James was away at war or working long hours at the State House, his wife, Julianna, managed their five children and a staff of eight to thirteen slaves. They cooked, cleaned, gardened, and served guests.

Inside the home, there's a narrow, hidden staircase separate from the main stairs. Wealthy slave owners would build these features into their homes so their slaves were rarely seen or heard. The richer the slave owner, the more secret staircases, tunnels, and rooms they would have.

At Monticello in Charlottesville, Thomas Jefferson installed a hidden dumbwaiter that connected the dining room fireplace to the basement. When he ran out of wine, he would put the empty bottle in the fireplace and send it down to the basement, where a slave would be waiting to replace it with a new one. Jefferson would pull a fresh bottle out, as if he'd conjured it by "magic."

Slavery at Monticello has been well-documented over the years, but the Brice family's slaves are more of a mystery. What we do know about them has been pieced together by historians, and it isn't a pretty picture...

In 1998, archeologists were given the chance to dig through the Brice House. They probably expected to find old documents, tools — maybe some extra building materials. Instead, they found a hidden stash of Hoodoo charms.

Hoodoo is a form of folk magic that branched off of Voodoo, which is a blend of West African and Christian beliefs. When slaves were brought to the colonies, they had their own religion, but anything other than Christianity was unacceptable to white Europeans, so they were forced to convert.

In New Orleans, where slaves were allowed to congregate and celebrate their culture, Voodoo was eventually accepted by the white population. They tried to use it for their own gain, seeking out the magic of Marie Laveau, known as the "Queen of Voodoo." In Maryland, slaves weren't given the same freedoms. The Brice family's slaves would have had to hide any aspect of their former religion. That's where Hoodoo comes in.

Hoodoo takes all of the magical elements of Voodoo — the spell bags,

The James Brice House, Annapolis, MD.

the dolls, the charms — and leaves the religious aspects behind. Basically, Hoodoo practitioners ask the spirits for favors. They don't worship them.

So, what did archeologists find? The slaves had to use whatever they found around the house: Coins, buttons, beads, old doll parts, seashells, matchsticks… They would hide these items until the family left or fell asleep, and then use them for hoodoo rituals.

The stashes were deliberately placed: One by each fireplace and one under a doorway. It formed a crossroads, a portal between reality and the spirit world. They were trying to summon the spirits. The question is: *What did they want the spirits to do?*

American pop culture has misrepresented voodoo as a vengeful religion. In reality, it was associated with healing and protection. Enslaved Africans couldn't trust their white masters, so they turned to the spirits. They may have been asking for protection from certain members of the Brice family.

There are no journal entries or letters to prove that the Brice family mistreated their slaves, but there is one piece of evidence that remained hidden in the basement for centuries…

Archeologists unearthed the skeleton of a teenage girl hidden behind one of the basement walls. No white child would have been buried there. It had to have been one of the Brice family's slaves — and she may have been sealed into the wall alive. That would have been a horrible, traumatizing death. No one would have been able to hear her screaming for help, and she would have slowly starved or suffocated.

Locals think James's son Thomas had something to do with it. Why? Because he suffered a similar fate years later.

Thomas was a lifelong bachelor. By the late 1800s, he was the only member of the Brice family still living in the mansion. Slavery had long-been outlawed in Maryland, but wealthy families could still afford servants, so he had a staff that included a butler, a gardener, and a valet.

We don't know how he treated them. Maybe he was kind and generous. Maybe he was abusive. What we do know is that he was violently attacked, and it's rumored his servants plotted the whole thing.

One morning, Thomas was found bludgeoned in the library. He also suffered a slow, painful death… Gangrene infected his wounds, turning them black and necrotic, until the blood to his heart was cut off. When he finally succumbed to the infection, the city was shocked and terrified. The crime was never solved, but Thomas's valet was never seen again. Was he another victim… or was he wielding the club?

The Brice House remains shrouded in mystery. The only people who know what happened behind those walls are long gone — or so we thought. There are over a dozen spirits roaming the house, and some have been trying to reveal the secrets of the Brice House for a long time…

The most infamous spirit is the "crying girl." For decades, people have reported hearing screaming and crying coming from the basement. It's so realistic the police have been called out for wellness checks. Every time, they inspected every inch of the basement. There was no one down there — no one alive, anyway.

When the skeleton was discovered in 1998, the mystery of the crying girl was finally solved. Locals thought the noises would stop once her remains were given a proper burial, but nothing changed. Late at night, the sound of sobbing breaks through the silence of the house, echoing through centuries-old rooms. Why isn't her soul at rest? *What else is she trying to tell us?*

Thomas Brice has been spotted in the house too. They say his gruesome death plays out over and over in the library, where he was allegedly bludgeoned by his valet. Of course the most famous Brice to haunt the house is James Brice himself. After he died in 1801, his wife said she saw his ghostly form puttering around the house, checking on everything.

It's likely the haunted activity here has gotten worse since Historic Annapolis purchased the property in 2014, but they've stayed mum about it. They probably don't want to spread ghost stories, but they can't erase decades of reports. People have felt cold spots, they've seen items move on their own, and they've felt a cold, sinister energy emanating from certain rooms. Maybe it drove Thomas Brice's valet to pick up a club that night. If it did, who's to say it won't kill again?

The Little Brice House

There's another Brice House — nicknamed the "Little Brice House" by Annapolis residents. It belonged to James's father, Judge John Brice, and it's been haunted since 1741.

John was a wealthy planter and politician who owned land and enslaved workers in several counties. He's mostly listed as a footnote in the story of the James Brice House because he willed James the money and land to build it… but there's one other story about him that's a little more interesting: He experienced one of the earliest recorded hauntings in Annapolis.

John bought this house sometime around 1737. In 1741, his wife and young son were out of the house, and he was entertaining a young woman known only as "Miss Turner."

Turner left the bedroom and walked into the parlor to retrieve her locket, but something stopped her dead in her tracks. A violent chill overtook her and a shadow stretched across the room. The fire in the hearth crackled and hissed, and Turner realized there was someone sitting in the armchair in front of the fireplace. It was an elderly woman — her eyes unfocused as she stared down at the flames. She had a deathly pallor and her face and body were wrapped in oozing yellow bandages. In between the cloth, Turner could see blackened sores marking her skin.

She recognized this woman. It was Brice's mother-in-law, Ariana Jennings. But Mrs. Jennings had been in Britain visiting family, and she hadn't said she was coming back anytime soon.

Suddenly, the spirit's eyes snapped up. She glared directly at the younger woman with a snarled lip. The room grew even colder, and Turner felt the cold hand of death wrap around her heart.

Terrified, she ran out of the room and told Brice what she'd seen. The pair headed back to the parlor, but the figure was gone. The deathly chill had gone with her, and the couple held each other for a moment in the warmth of the fire.

Brice marked down the date and time that Turner had seen his mother-in-law. Sure enough, he received a letter in the mail a few weeks later: Ariana had died of smallpox at that exact date and time.

The house stayed in the Brice family until 1841. After that, it changed hands a few times before Katrina Loomis Halligan came along in 1917. The Halligans owned it from 1917 until May of 2023. As time went on, the tale of Ariana's ghost was passed down from owner to owner… but that wasn't the only ghost the Halligan family had to worry about.

Katrina's daughter says she experienced strange things in the house all throughout her childhood, but she didn't see a full-bodied apparition until she was an adult. In 2005, she woke up to a wispy figure standing over her bed. It looked like her grandmother, but her grandmother had been dead for years. She lifted her hand to touch the spirit and it disappeared.

Most people would bolt upright, screaming, if they woke up to their dead grandmother standing over their bed, but Kay was familiar with the house's history. She said goodnight to her grandmother and went back to sleep.

The Halligans never reported seeing Ariana Jennings, but she only appears at specific times.

It's said she shows up when someone in the house is lying or being unfaithful. Visitors have walked into the old parlor to find her sitting there, glaring at them. It's a gruesome sight. Her face and body are still covered in the oozing bandages she was wrapped in when she died.

Of course, some people choose to keep her appearance to themselves. They don't want to have to explain *why* she appeared to them.

The James Brice House, Annapolis, MD.

Galway Bay Irish Pub and Restaurant

Galway Bay Irish Pub and Restaurant, Annapolis, MD.

Galway Bay has been a fixture of Annapolis since 1998, when Michael Galway decided to bring a piece of his homeland to Crabtown. Warm woods and dim lighting give it a pub feel, and there isn't a single TV on any of the walls. Instead, people talk over genuine Irish dishes like potato leek soup, shepherd's pie, and reubens.

The building itself has historic charm. It was built between 1897 and 1903, and the property dates back to the 18th century. Before Michael stepped in, the restaurant was "Little Campus," a family-owned business that had been there since 1924. It hosted a mix of people over the years, including President Bill Clinton in 1997, but it was mostly known as a local haunt, where the same group would gather every night to blow off steam.

The staff stuck around too. Ethelda Kimbo — better known as "Peggy" — worked at Little Campus for 50 years. When new hires came in, she'd lean in and warn them: "There's a ghost in the basement."

Peggy had seen the misty apparition of a young woman walking from the bottom of the basement stairs to the corner of the room.

According to legend, the girl was a servant in the 19th century, when Galway Bay was a residential home. The man of the house took an interest in her and she was soon pregnant with his child, though he'd never admit it.
To make matters worse, she lost her baby not long after giving birth.

This was common in the 1800s, when disease ran rampant, but it was no less devastating.

The young mother couldn't bear her grief. She got a rope and walked down to the basement, where she hung herself in the back corner.

Now her ghost walks to that same corner over and over. At night, the sound of a haunting, grief-stricken lullaby will float up the stairs to the main floor. Peggy had heard it many nights. She had to comfort new employees when they heard it too: "Don't worry, she's harmless."

The other spirits aren't as docile.

In 1919, the 18th Amendment was ratified, ending the manufacture, sale, and transportation of alcohol in the United States. Well, the goal was to end it. Instead, the nationwide ban created a seedy, underground industry. Rumrunners moved alcohol from the Caribbean to the U.S. and delivered it to the mob for a fat stack of cash. If they came back short, they ended up *sleepin' with the fishes*.

Bootlegging was especially common in Maryland, where the alcohol never stopped flowing. Over 80% of the state opposed Prohibition. Even the governor, Albert Ritchie, refused to pass a state law enforcing the ban. He thought it was ridiculous the federal government was steamrolling the states.

Riots broke out in Baltimore. It was a violent time, and the Galway Bay building ended up scarred by it. Little Campus had just opened, and one of the employees was struggling with a gambling addiction. Like most gambling addicts, he was deep in debt and looking for that one big win that would solve all of his problems. He thought he'd found a way out when he overheard a hot tip one night.

Thinking he'd double his money on the bet, he gambled with the cash he was supposed to pay a bootlegger. The only problem was: He lost. Later that night, the bootlegger arrived with the goods. After they carried the crates of alcohol upstairs to the second floor, the employee explained what happened. With sweat beading on his brow, he threw his hands up and promised he'd get him the money he owed him. He just needed a little more time.

The bootlegger wasn't having it. A fight broke out. After a few punches, the employee pulled a knife and stabbed the bootlegger between the ribs, puncturing his lung. He watched in horror as the man gasped for air.

For a moment, he considered calling the police and trying to save him — but the guy would probably just come back and kill him.

He turned around and ran, leaving the bootlegger to bleed out on the floor.

Late at night, as Galway Bay employees are closing up, they'll hear the sounds of a scuffle on the second floor. It stops briefly, followed by the loud *thud* of a body hitting the hardwood, and panicked footsteps rushing away from the scene. The final sound is the most chilling. They'll hear the labored grunts and final breaths of a man dying, followed by silence. It replays over and over like a broken record. Time may pass, businesses may come and go, but the events of that night are eternal.

Galway Bay Irish Pub and Restaurant, Annapolis, MD.

Reynolds Tavern

In 1747, a hatter named William Reynolds leased 7 Church Circle and built a three-story building. He used it for his hattery, but he also opened a tavern called "The Beaver and Lac'd Hat" — one of the first taverns in the city.

Today, it stands as Reynolds Tavern, but William isn't the "Reynolds" it's known for… or the one who haunts it.

Eighteenth-century taverns were more than bars. They filled a variety of needs: Visitor centers, hotels, restaurants, concert halls, theaters, conference rooms… so the Beaver and Lac'd Hat was always packed.

Taverns also provided women the opportunity to break into the business world. There was no law preventing women from running a tavern, and they already had all of the skills needed to run one: cooking, cleaning, caretaking. If a woman's husband died, she could apply to turn her home into a tavern, and suddenly she had a stable source of income for performing her regular domestic duties.

Enter: Mary Reynolds, William's third wife.

Mary was a beautiful young woman, but she had no social status. She was working as a housekeeper when she met William. Their union caused quite a scandal in town, so she felt pressured to make a good impression on the people who dined at their tavern. She was incredibly finicky when it came to keeping house. The rooms were always spotless — not a flea or bedbug in sight. The food and alcohol were always high quality, and she expected the staff *and patrons* to behave themselves.

Mary was a sharp businesswoman with an astounding memory. She would remember minute details about her guests — what they liked and didn't like, where they lived, and what they did for a living. Many customers would come in just to enjoy her hospitality. Many fell for her charm. Of course, some of the men tried to make passes at her. She always refused them. She was a respectable woman who cared a lot about her reputation, and she wouldn't let one night ruin her hard work.

Legend has it one of her admirers was George Washington himself. He was often in Annapolis for business, and he'd always stop at the Beaver and Lac'd Hat to see Mary. She'd find herself trapped by his attention, only to be freed by her husband or — if George was being really persistent — her rolling pin.

Reynolds Tavern, Annapolis, MD.

In George's defense, these claims have never been proven, but the legend has been passed down for over 200 years. The image of George Washington being chased out of a tavern by a young lady with a rolling pin is too good.

When William Reynolds died in 1777, he left the tavern to his wife and daughter. Mary followed William in death less than 10 years later in 1785. Most of the town attended her funeral, congregating at the back of the tavern where Mary had dutifully served them all those years.

About an hour into the reception, a family member went up to one of the bedrooms on the third floor. What she saw when she opened the door frightened her so badly that she fainted on the spot. There was a woman sitting on the edge of the bed, smiling.

It was Mary.

Since that day, Mary has been spotted in every room of Reynolds Tavern. She stayed when her daughter lost the business in 1788. She stayed when it was transformed into a banking office. In 1935, the building was almost demolished by Standard Oil, but a group of citizens saved it by proposing it be used as a public library instead. Mary was there for that too — but her spirit was quiet and hidden.

It wasn't until the mid-80s, when Paul Pearson restored Reynolds Tavern, that Mary became active again. She was finally in charge of a tavern again — much to the dismay of the staff…

Mary proved to be just as strict in death as she was in life. If a table was set improperly, the cutlery would be moved by phantom hands. If a table needed to be cleaned, the vase or water pitcher would flip over. "Slacker" employees would have glasses and plates shattered near them to scare them into action. All of these antics continue today.

If you eat there, make sure you watch your language. Cursing is a surefire way to have a glass of water knocked in your lap, or a chair pushed in your way. Even when people stay the night and cuss in the privacy of their room, the lights flicker on and off… or burn out with a loud sizzle.

Rowdy guests are not tolerated. Mary's ghost will use every power she has to kick them out. She'll spill a drink in their lap, throw things at them, shake their chair, blow a cold draft in their face… If none of that works, she'll lock them in the bathroom. People have been locked in the bathroom for up to 30 minutes.

So be mindful of Mary's rules, or she'll give you a ghost story you won't soon forget.

Reynolds Tavern, Annapolis, MD.

The Maryland Inn

The Maryland Inn, Annapolis, MD.

The James Brice House may be the most haunted house in Annapolis, but the Maryland Inn is the most haunted hotel. It's arguably the most haunted hotel in the entire state of Maryland. There are spirits from every period of Maryland history — from 1772, when the hotel was built — to now.

Even if the place wasn't haunted, its mysterious doors and secret rooms are enough to creep anyone out. There's a secret tunnel in the old wine cellar. No one knows where it leads, but the prevailing theory is that it goes to the Maryland State House. Historians think it was used as an emergency escape route during times of war and strife. It could also be part of a larger network of underground tunnels. Many port cities — like Portland and Salem — used tunnels during the 18th and 19th centuries. They allowed people to move goods from ships to the basements of businesses.

Of course, the tunnels were also used for nefarious purposes. Bootleggers used them to transport liquor. Gambling rings used them as a hideout. And crimps used them to kidnap drunken sailors and sell them into a life of slavery on the sea.

Aside from the tunnel, there's a small room under the stairs that employees have lovingly nicknamed the "scary closet." Faded, 19th-century wallpaper shows mermaids sunbathing on rocks beside a poem that reads: "Pray that you may never meet women who have tails for feet. A golden harp has a bonny sound, but will you care when you are drowned?"

As for the spirits, the most famous ghost of the Maryland Inn is simply called "The Bride." Her story begins in 1817, when her longtime fiance, U.S. Navy Captain Charles Campbell, received word he would be returning to port.

Skilled sailors were in high demand in the 19th century, and they spent months — sometimes years — away from home. The separation had been excruciating for both of them.

Charles wrote her a letter asking her to meet him at the Maryland Inn so they could be married the moment he set foot on dry land. The woman eagerly headed to the hotel and booked Room 405, where she changed into a flowing white dress and paced back and forth, waiting for her love. She would stop every so often to glance out the window, searching for Charles.

After hours of waiting, she finally saw her dashing fiance standing across the road. She waved to get his attention and a giddy smile split across his face. He was finally going to marry the love of his life… but Charles was so excited to get to the hotel that he didn't look both ways before crossing. A horse and carriage came barreling toward him as he stepped into the road. The driver was unable to stop, and the carriage collided with the sailor, the horse trampling his body on the pavement… right in front of his would-be bride.

Distraught, the woman rushed down the stairs and ran across the road, where her lover's body lay broken and dying. She gathered him in her arms and whispered to him. *Please don't go. Please hang on.* But no amount of hoping and praying could save him. He died in her arms.

The bride returned to Room 405. Hours earlier, the room had glowed with her excitement. Now it felt like a cold, dark jail cell. The depression grew worse and worse as she sat alone, sobbing. By sunset, she couldn't take it anymore. She opened the window and jumped — dying on the same street her lover had died on earlier in the day.

Since then, dozens of people have spotted a ghostly woman wearing a white wedding dress. Guests in Room 405 will hear her pacing the floor at night, when the TV's been turned off and the streets are quiet. Sometimes they'll feel a dip on the bed, like someone just sat on it.
But they always tell the hotel staff the same thing: "She wasn't there to hurt

me. She's friendly and quiet."

In the taproom, a 19th-century naval captain smokes a pipe by the fireplace. He's usually there after a busy shift, and he'll raise a beer to the staff as if to say, "Well done." Though the two spirits haunt the same hotel, they're never seen together. The bride is trapped upstairs while the captain is tied to the lower floors. Even in death, they're still tragically separated.

But the bride has a lot of company on the fourth floor — it's the most haunted floor at the inn.

Legislators and military personnel stayed there for months at a time. Some of the rooms were turned into long-term apartments. At some point during the hotel's long history, a fight broke out between husband and wife.
No one knows the details… but their spirits play out the violent event over and over…

Guests have reported hearing an argument between two people, followed by the sound of a muffled shriek and a body tumbling down the stairwell, with no body to be found at the bottom. The staff has received so many frantic phone calls that they don't even bother checking anymore. They just assure the guest everything is fine.

The stairwell seems to be a common hangout for ghosts. Drunken Revolutionary War soldiers like to stumble around in their heavy boots, slurring out-of-tune sea shanties they learned from sailors. And there's a woman in black who lingers at the bottom. Is she the victim of the murder? Or someone else entirely?

The majority of the ghosts at the inn never reveal themselves. If you book a room, you might feel a sudden chill, a cold breeze. You may hear strange noises or find your suitcase moved to the other side of the room. The smell of vintage perfume wafts through the hallways and distant voices float up from the empty ballroom, where centuries of people have laughed and sipped champagne.

The average guest ignores or explains away all of these things. But if you pay close attention, you'll feel the spirits all around you, and they may reveal themselves to you…

The Maryland Inn, Annapolis, MD.

The Brooksby-Shaw House

The Brooksby-Shaw House, Annapolis, MD.

Built between 1720 and 1725, the Brooksby-Shaw House was the dream home of Cornelius Brooksby, the town butcher — but he didn't live to see it completed. He died one year before it was finished.

His wife Mary didn't waste any time finding a new husband. Months after his death, she married Thomas Gough, allowing him to move into her late husband's dream house.

The ghost of Cornelius Brooksby didn't like that very much.

The newlyweds were kept awake by pacing footsteps, shattered glass, and loud bangs. Mary was sure her late husband was haunting the house, and her suspicions were confirmed when his misty figure appeared in the middle of the night, hovering over Thomas. The angry scowl on his face said it all: He wanted revenge.

The activity escalated after that night. Thomas was poked and prodded in his sleep. He was pushed down the stairs by phantom hands. He had glasses thrown at him and furniture pushed in his path. Eventually, Mary and Thomas couldn't take the torment anymore. They fled the house and left it to Cornelius's granddaughter, Mary Brooksby-Long.

But her grandfather didn't give her a pass either. The younger Mary and her new husband were tormented night after night until they moved out too. The house sat empty until John Shaw came along in 1784.

Shaw was a humble cabinetmaker who took care of the Maryland State House from 1770 until his death in 1829. He built furniture, made repairs, looked after the grounds, and strung up lights for celebrations. Whatever the State House needed, he did. The work didn't make him rich, but he was one of the most well-respected men in the city.

Maybe that's why Cornelius never tortured him. Aside from the occasional bump in the night, Shaw's years in this house were quiet and peaceful.

In the early 1900s, the building was sold to the Annapolis Elks and used as a lodge until 1960. The State of Maryland purchased it in 1961 to use for legislative offices, given its convenient location near the State House.

Cornelius behaved himself during the day, when the politicians were working, but he would give the security guards hell at night. During one Christmas season, workers erected a beautiful, ornate Christmas tree with glass ornaments and sparkling lights. Late one evening, a night guard heard the unmistakable sound of glass shattering on a tile floor. It was followed by the sound of heavy boots stomping on glass shards, as if someone was angrily destroying the tree.

Thinking there was an intruder, the guard drew his weapon and ran to the foyer. The tree was lying on its side — the beautiful ornaments shattered all over the floor — but there was no intruder to be found. The doors were locked and the windows were intact. No one could have broken in to destroy the tree.

What's even stranger is that when the guard returned to the foyer, the tree was standing upright again. Every ornament was in its rightful place, glimmering like nothing had happened.

The guard shook it off and mumbled something about needing a cup of coffee… but that wouldn't be the last time he encountered strange activity at the Shaw House.

The Ghosts of Annapolis, MD.

The following August, he was making his final rounds. It was around 2 a.m. — hot and humid — and he was looking forward to getting home and changing out of his sweaty uniform. Just as he was about to leave, he saw a light burning in one of the upstairs windows. He figured one of the workers had left their office light on, so he climbed the stairs to turn it off. When he reached the second floor, however, all of the lights were off.

Now he was sweating even more. He sat down at one of the desks and basked in the air conditioning, telling himself he would only stay for a few minutes. He must have nodded off, though, because he woke up thirty minutes later to the feeling of someone standing over him.

Frozen in fear, the guard peeked one eye open and saw that, yes, someone was looming over him like they were about to attack. The guard tried to jump to his feet. He was stuck to the chair, immobile. The figure leaned in. It was dark, so he couldn't see the person's face. All he could see was a dark silhouette backlit by the lights outside the building.

Just as he began praying for his life, the figure vanished.

The guard was able to free himself from the chair, and he didn't spend another second inspecting the building. He ran as fast as he could — down the stairs, down the street, back to his car. He didn't even spare a glance over his shoulder to see if that pesky light had come back on. Someone else could deal with that.

The Brooksby-Shaw House, Annapolis, MD.

The Brooksby-Shaw House, Annapolis, MD.

The Shiplap House

The Shiplap House, Annapolis, MD.

The infamous, blood-red Shiplap House dates back to 1715. It was one of the earliest taverns in Annapolis — run by Edward Smith and his wife, Mary. After they passed, it was taken over by John Humprey, who changed the name to "Harp and Crown."

Just like the Beaver and Lac'd Hat, the Harp and Crown depended on a beautiful young woman to run the place, but her story isn't nearly as charming as Mary Reynolds's.

Adrienne began working there as a server in the taproom. Legend has it she turned down dozens of marriage proposals a day. Every man who entered the place wanted to wed, or bed, her. Eventually, she realized she could triple her salary if she offered certain services on the side, and it didn't take long for the men to come calling.

One evening, Adrienne abandoned her post. She was found outside, bludgeoned to death by an unknown assailant. Some say a disgruntled suitor murdered her when she refused to sleep with him. Others say she was involved with bad people. She may have owed someone money and ended up paying with her life.

The murder was never solved... and Adrienne's spirit still lingers at 18 Pinkney Street.

People have seen a young woman in 18th-century garb moving around the garden, while others see her entering and leaving the back of the house.

In 1877, the famous painter Frank Blackwell Mayer moved in. He would see Adrienne wandering through the backyard — always passive and quiet. He paid her no mind, and she left him alone. That changed when he married Ellen Benton Brewer.

One night, after Mayer laid down to go to sleep, he heard footsteps on the stairs. He figured Ellen was coming up to bed, so he sat up to greet her. He thought it was odd she wasn't carrying a lantern. The room was almost pitch-black, but she moved straight to the bed and pulled back the covers.

As she nestled into bed, Frank noticed the thick scent of floral perfume. Thinking his wife was putting the moves on him, he complimented the smell. She didn't respond. She just laid there. Maybe he had said or done something wrong? He moved closer to her and tried to cuddle into her side. That's when he noticed her entire body was freezing cold — especially her feet.

"Honey, your feet are freezing!" he said. She still didn't respond. Now he was getting angry. He shouted, "Are you going to talk to me or just lie there?" That's when he heard his wife's voice travel up the stairs. She was downstairs in the kitchen, and she wanted to know what he was yelling about.

The figure next to him shifted and let out a soft sigh. Mayer screamed. He jumped out of bed as his wife rushed up the stairs with her lamp. He grabbed it from her and searched all around the room, trying to find the intruder. No one was there. He began patting the bed, the thick smell of perfume hanging in the air. There was still a dip in the bed where the strange woman had been... but she was gone. After that, Adrienne couldn't keep her hands off Frank.

He would feel fingers on his back and neck as he lay in bed. Turning over, he'd find his sleeping wife facing the other direction. One morning, Ellen found the name "Adrienne" written in red lipstick on the mattress when she changed the linens. This continued until Frank's death in 1899. Ellen sold the house two years later. Whether she lived there alone for those two years, we don't know. Maybe she gave Adrienne what she wanted and moved out. The house gradually deteriorated until it was scooped up by Historic Annapolis in 1958. It served as their headquarters until 1981, when a couple purchased it. For the first time in decades, the house was a private residence again.

Having heard rumors the house was haunted, the couple — whom we'll call Debbie and John — decided to host a ghost-themed dinner party. They hid tape recorders in different rooms and played spooky noises to get a rise out of guests. It was all fun and games until the party guests went home and the pair got ready for bed. Debbie climbed into bed first as John got ready in the bathroom. As she lay there, she heard the wood floor creaking. It sounded like someone was walking toward the bed. But it was an old house. At that point, it was almost 300 years old. Old houses creak and groan, and Debbie wasn't worried about it… until she felt the bed dip behind her.

She knew her husband was still in the bathroom. She lay there, frozen in fear, with her back to the mysterious figure. The temperature in the room had plummeted in a matter of seconds. It felt like the dead of winter. Just as she was about to scream, she felt a pair of freezing cold feet hit her back and push — *hard*. She tumbled onto the floor and scrambled over to the wall, straining to see who had kicked her out of bed.

All she could see was a menacing shadow sitting on the bed, staring her down… and then it was gone. A second later, John walked in and switched on the light. He asked her why she was sitting on the floor. All she could do was sputter out a few words — something about "ghost" and "We need to move."

It should come as no shock that Historic Annapolis ended up buying back the property. It's been an office space ever since, so Adrienne hasn't been able to torment any other couples at night. These days, the most famous ghosts at the Shiplap House are two other girls named Mary and Audrey.

Audrey is a sweet, five-year-old girl with long golden ringlets and a blue dress. Mary is her nursemaid. She's often seen wearing a long, dark dress and an apron. Historians believe they died in a 19th-century epidemic. Audrey's soul was trapped here, and Mary stayed to continue taking care of her in the afterlife.

Audrey only appears to children who visit, but adults have heard her giggling when they drop something or stub a toe. Her nursemaid lingers in the old nursery, where she's been known to give kids a phantom swat on the butt if they aren't listening to their parents.

It's too bad she can't keep Adrienne in line.

Dock Street Bar & Grill

Dock Street Bar & Grill, Annapolis, MD.

Dock Street Bar & Grill set up shop in the early 2000s, and they've gained a reputation for serving no-filler crab cakes packed with hearty lumps of fresh crab meat. They also have an Instagram-worthy blue facade that complements the shimmering harbor.

The ironic thing is that 300 years ago, it was the last place you'd ever want to end up: It was the city jail. Every criminal in Annapolis was held there, regardless of the severity of their crime. Petty thieves were thrown in with violent murderers. It didn't matter, because in the 18th century, jail time wasn't a punishment; jail was where you *waited to be punished*.

The facility wasn't secured, so criminals were shackled and chained to walls. If they died, their bodies were left to rot — the stench of death lingering like a fog over the cells. The floors were covered in urine and feces, and inmates would have to fend off rats as they gobbled down their meager food rations.

An official report from 1766 described the conditions as "so filthy and nasty that it is excessively nauseous."

For lesser offenses, prisoners were whipped or locked into the stocks and pillory. It wasn't enough to punish people behind closed doors. It had to be done publicly, so that other citizens would see what would happen to them if they stepped out of line… and it was very easy to "step out of line" in the thirteen colonies.

The justice system was deeply flawed. Forensic evidence didn't exist back then, so they often relied on witness testimony, which can be skewed by false memories, biases, anger, and greed. In Salem, Massachusetts, twenty innocent people were executed over false accusations of witchcraft and dozens more were imprisoned.

While Maryland never had its own "Salem," Calvert County executed a woman named Rebecca Fowler as a witch in 1685. All other witches were acquitted.

By the 18th century, the long list of offenses punishable by death had been whittled down to eleven — arson, piracy, treason, murder, sodomy, burglary, robbery, rape, horse-stealing, slave rebellion, and often counterfeiting — but the system was still harsh and unforgiving, and innocent people were still put to death. Even children were killed. Age didn't become a factor in sentencing until the early 20th century.

Hanging was the preferred method of execution up until the 1950s. It was believed to be the most humane way of killing someone.

If done correctly, hanging is a quick and painless death. The noose is tied, a platform moves out from under you, and the force of the fall snaps your neck, killing you instantly. But a lot of things can — and did — go wrong. If the rope was too long, the fall could decapitate the prisoner. If it was too short, they could struggle and suffocate for upwards of ten minutes before dying.

In one case, a man had to be hanged *twice*.

Just after midnight on January 30, 1930, a 56-year-old man named Jack Johnson was led to the gallows at the Maryland State Penitentiary. When the trap door opened, Jack's weight broke the rope. His severely-injured body lay on the floor. The staff loaded him onto a stretcher and hoisted him back up to the top, where a fresh noose was placed around his neck. The second time the door opened, Jack died instantly.

The local newspaper reported on the incident — much to the horror of the public — but the gallows weren't officially retired until 1955. After that, criminals were executed in a gas chamber. By the 90s, lethal injection had been approved, but there was a growing movement to end capital punishment altogether.

Maryland executed its last criminal in 2005 and outlawed the practice completely in 2013, but the ghosts of those days linger…

The Ghosts of Annapolis, MD.

The jail was demolished in the early 19th century and replaced by the multi-use building that currently houses Dock Street. Several businesses have occupied the spot over the last 200 years. They've all been plagued by disembodied footsteps, hoarse whispers, and ragged coughing.

One evening, a chef was working alone in the kitchen when he heard a noise behind him. He turned around to find a disheveled man begging for a glass of water. His clothes were tattered and filthy and his lips were so dry and cracked he could barely speak. Shaken, the chef nodded and moved to get a glass from the cabinet. As he did, the man vanished.

The streets aren't safe either… Locals have seen ghostly figures entering the building or standing in front of it. Chained prisoners walk toward the bottom of Main Street, where the stocks and pillory were located. But the most chilling story doesn't involve a ghost at all… it involves a feeling.

Tourists who pass by the bar have been struck by an overwhelming sense of dread and fear. They say it's so intense it makes your stomach churn, and you can't focus on anything else. It's the spirits of innocent prisoners. They're reaching out and projecting their feelings onto the living. Maybe they're trying to get someone's attention. Maybe they're asking for help. Maybe they just want someone else to feel what they feel.

For some, death brings freedom. For others, the afterlife is just another prison sentence.

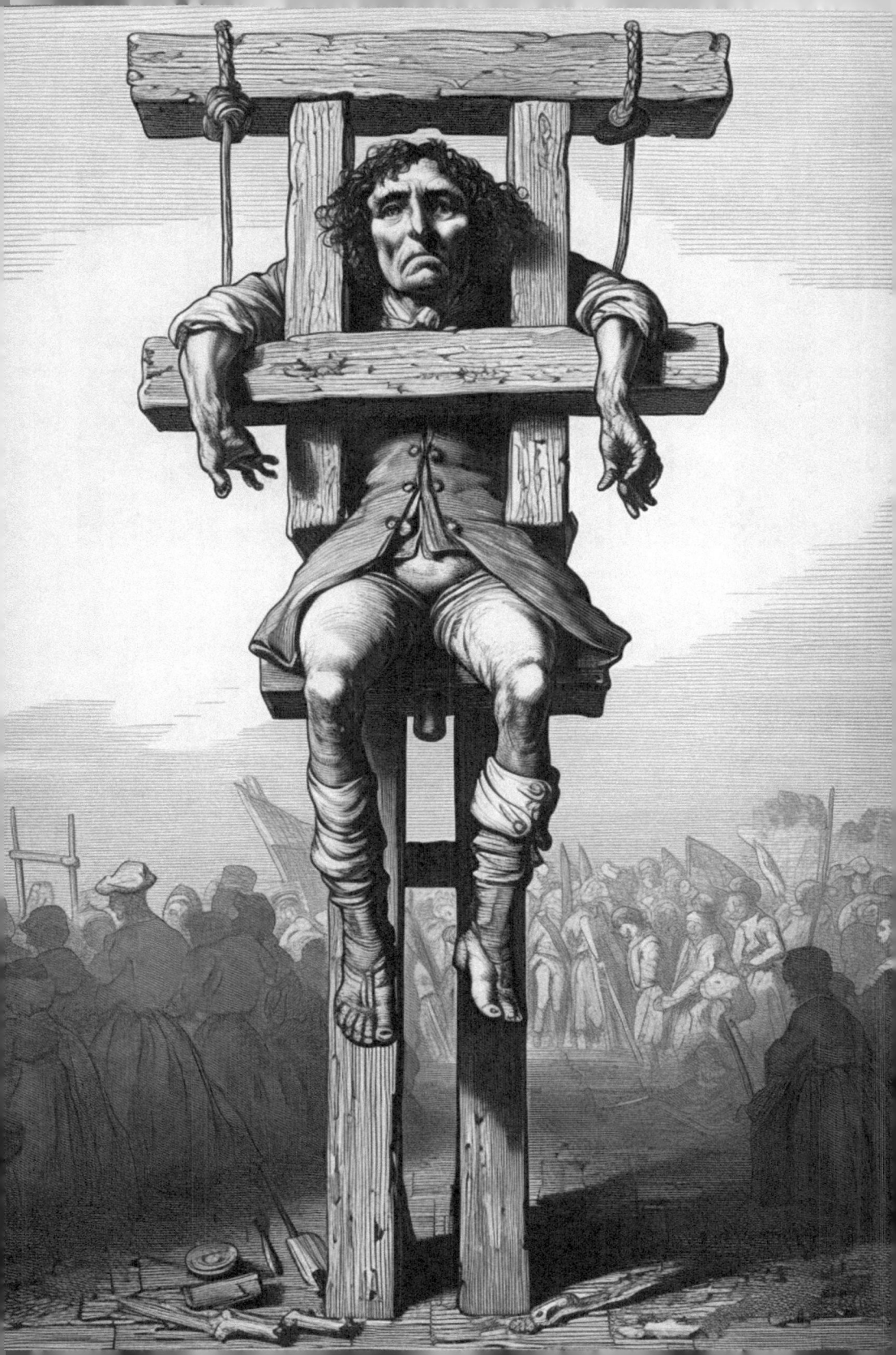

The U.S. Naval Academy

The U.S. Naval Academy, Annapolis, MD.

Founded in 1845, the United States Naval Academy has a long and dramatic history — and where there's history, there are ghosts. The first story takes us back to the Civil War.

After Fort Sumter was captured by the Confederates in 1861, the Naval Academy was moved to Rhode Island, where it was less likely to fall into enemy hands. The Annapolis campus served as a hospital for the remainder of the war. Soon, hundreds of wounded men poured into the city. Rows and rows of tents were erected to deal with the overflow.

The Civil War produced the most traumatic injuries the world had ever seen. The minié ball bullet expanded on impact, shredding tissue and shattering bone. A single shot would leave a soldier writhing on the ground, begging for mercy.

At the same time, the medical field was struggling to catch up to this new style of warfare. Lax medical laws meant the majority of surgeons had little to no surgical experience. They were learning on the job, faced with thousands of gruesome injuries. Surviving the initial wound was only step one. Soldiers also had to battle deadly diseases spread by improper care.

Most of the patients at the USNA were diseased and beyond help. It was basically a hospice center, where nurses would pace up and down rows of dying men, offering them words of comfort and soothing their nightmares.

The soldiers called them "sunbeams." But their sweet voices could only do so much to ease the pain. The entire campus was scarred by death and suffering, and those scars never healed…

Late at night, you can still hear the pained moans of dying men. Students have spotted ghostly soldiers moving through campus — their amputated limbs covered in bandages. But you're far more likely to feel a sudden cold spot. People have walked the grounds on 80-degree nights and felt a sudden, icy chill. Is it a Union soldier passing through, or is it someone else?

Wounded soldiers aren't the only men who have died on campus. It was also the site of a violent murder…

On October 12, 1907, the Academy was hosting a dance at Carvel Hall. It was all lit up. There was music playing. Couples were swinging each other around and sneaking kisses in the shadows. As the night wound down, a couple of marines left the building and began walking back to their quarters. That's when gunshots rang out.

The marines rushed down the hill to find Lt. James Sutton lying on Worden Field. He'd been shot in the head. There were three other lieutenants surrounding him — all distraught and wild-eyed. They claimed James had "gone crazy" and shot himself, but the marines noted that his face was bloody and covered in gravel, like he'd been beaten. They took him to Beach Hall, but it was too late to save him. He died around 1 a.m.

Now investigators had to piece together what really happened that night and determine whether it was a tragic suicide — or a cold-blooded murder.

Sutton was known as a charming, high-spirited young man. He liked to be social, and he especially liked the ladies, so it was no surprise he had gone out with three other officers that night. But when the group piled into a taxi hours later, the driver could tell they were tense. One of the men ordered the driver to stop. They forced James out of the cab, and they snapped at the man to drive off. As he did, he heard a gunshot.

The lieutenants stuck to their story. They said James had lost his mind and shot himself. But there was another witness who stumbled upon a completely different scene.

Sergeant James De Hart was sneaking down a back alley that night, trying to avoid a lecture about staying out late. As he rounded the corner, he heard men fighting followed by a shot. *That* got his attention. De Hart approached the men and asked what happened. They answered by thrusting a military-issued revolver into his hands and ordering him to "dispose of it." De Hart immediately threw the gun away and rushed back to his quarters. The next morning, he went back to the scene to get the gun and turn it in... but it was long gone.

The Navy wasn't convinced. The prosecution needed another witness — someone who could prove the lieutenants had murdered James Sutton. They turned to Sutton's mother.

Rosa Sutton was a known psychic. She had predicted the deaths of two family members, and she swore she'd seen her son that night. He came to her and said he'd been shot, and that the police needed to "look at the watch." The wristwatch he'd been wearing that night was broken and bloody — clear evidence that he'd been beaten before the shooting.

The prosecution pushed for murder charges. Clearly, the three officers had ganged up on Sutton, beat him, and shot him. They also had evidence the fight had broken out over a woman named Margaret Stewart. She had dated all four men and chosen Sutton in the end.

The case seemed cut and dry, but no one could prove James hadn't pulled the trigger. The lieutenants were set free, and James Sutton's mother never got the closure she needed.

Folks still see James Sutton's spirit wandering through campus — especially around Worden Field. Sometimes he'll appear as a glowing orb floating through the air. Sometimes his shadowy figure will walk through walls or close doors. Sometimes people hear him.

In 2007, an employee we'll call Leah was working late at Beach Hall. She'd been staring at paperwork so long she could barely keep her eyes open, so she told her boss she was leaving to get a breath of fresh air. The rest of the building was dark and quiet. All of the employees had cleared out at 4:30. Even the cleaning staff was gone for the night.

As Leah walked down the stairs, she heard a door slam above her. It echoed loudly against the concrete walls. Thinking her boss had followed her, she called out... but no one answered. Seconds later, a man's voice yelled something indiscernible, like he was fighting with another person. Leah was spooked now, and she yelled back, "Excuse me?"

That's when she heard her name, clear as a bell, whispered into her ear...

and then the stairwell went dead silent. All she could hear was the faint buzzing of the fluorescent lights. She abandoned her plan to get fresh air and rushed back to her office, where her boss was reading paperwork under a lamp.

"Did you hear that?" she asked. Her boss hadn't heard or seen anything. The pair searched the building. There were no other lights on. All of the suites were locked. Leah had just encountered a ghost — and he knew her name.

She never worked late in that building again.

The U.S. Naval Academy, Annapolis, MD.

GHOST TOURS HELD NIGHTLY YEAR-ROUND!

EMBARK ON A GHOST TOUR IN 85+ CITIES OR SPEND THE NIGHT IN ONE OF AMERICA'S MOST HAUNTED HOUSES.

- Albuquerque, NM
- Alexandria, VA
- Annapolis, MD
- Asheville, NC
- Atlanta, GA
- Atlantic City, NJ
- Austin, TX
- Baltimore, MD
- Birmingham, AL
- Boston, MA
- Charleston, SC
- Charlotte, NC
- Charlottesville, VA
- Chattanooga, TN
- Cheyenne, WY
- Chicago, IL
- Cincinnati, OH
- Cleveland, OH
- Dallas, TX
- Deadwood, SD
- Denver, CO
- Detroit, MI
- El Paso, TX
- Fall River, MA
- Flagstaff, AZ
- Fort Lauderdale, FL
- Fort Worth, TX
- Galveston, TX
- Gatlinburg, TN
- Gettysburg, PA
- Grand Rapids, MI
- Honolulu, HI
- Houston, TX
- Indianapolis, IN
- Jacksonville, FL
- Kansas City, MO
- Key West, FL
- Knoxville, TN
- Las Vegas, NV
- Los Angeles, CA
- Louisville, KY
- Lynchburg, VA
- Madison, WI
- Memphis, TN
- Miami, FL
- Milwaukee, WI
- Mobile, AL
- Monterey, CA
- Myrtle Beach, SC
- Nashville, TN
- New Orleans, LA
- New York, NY
- Newport, RI
- Orlando, FL
- Omaha, NE
- Outer Banks, NC
- Philadelphia, PA
- Phoenix, AZ
- Pittsburgh, PA
- Portland, OR
- Providence, RI
- Raleigh, NC
- Reno, NV
- Richmond, VA
- Sacramento, CA
- Salem, MA
- Salt Lake City, UT
- San Antonio, TX
- San Diego, CA
- San Francisco, CA
- San Jose, CA
- San Juan, PR
- Santa Monica, CA
- Savannah, GA
- Seattle, WA
- St Paul, MN
- St. Augustine, FL
- St. Louis, MO
- Tampa, FL
- Tombstone, AZ
- Virginia Beach, VA
- Washington, DC
- Williamsburg, VA
- Wilmington, NC

CHOOSE YOUR
GHOST ADVENTURE
ON-SITE OR ONLINE

SELECT A PRIVATE GROUP TOUR IN A CITY NEAR YOU OR JOIN ONE OF OUR EXPERIENCED TOUR GUIDES LIVE-STREAM FROM ANYWHERE.

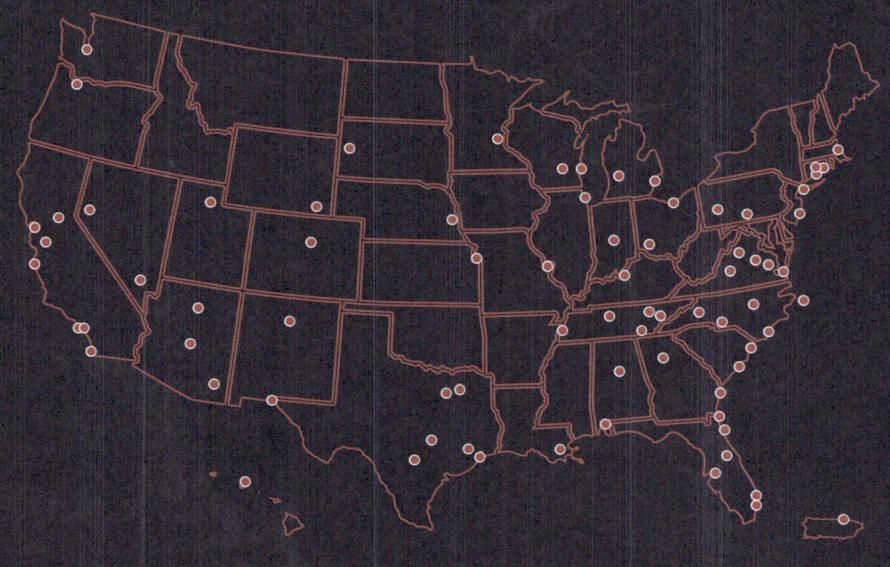

FEATURED IN

US GHOST ADVENTURES

USGHOSTADVENTURES.COM

BALTIMORE GHOSTS

BALTIMORE GHOSTS

CHAPTER II

The Ghosts of Baltimore

The streets of Baltimore thrum with three hundred years of history — from the days of cobblestones and shipbuilding to the rise of skyscrapers and stadiums. Its stunning blue harbor and diverse neighborhoods have earned it the nickname "Charm City," but beneath that charm, there's a dark and disturbing underworld.

Violent crime, drug abuse, and natural disasters have plagued Baltimore since its founding. Pirates poured into the local bars and brothels, knocking back drinks and leering at young prostitutes. The women can still be heard searching for their next lonely customer, their disembodied voices floating down deserted alleyways to tickle the ears of unsuspecting men.

At the Rye, a bludgeoned sailor wreaks havoc in the storeroom. His ghost is a chilling reminder of just how far captains would go to find a crew. Down the street, the spirit of William Fell stumbles out of an old brothel to return to his grave at the Fell Family Cemetery, where the Fells — and their secrets — lay six feet under.

When the sun dips below the water, the ghosts of Baltimore's past mingle with its present. Yellow fever victims, patriots, and factory workers emerge to terrorize the living. You may even run into Edgar Allan Poe, still searching for an explanation for his mysterious death.

The following chapters detail bone-chilling, firsthand accounts of Baltimore's most active spirits… and their grisly deaths. Should you venture into this historic city after dark, "charm" may be the last thing you find.

tourbaltimoreghosts.com

Max's Taphouse

Max's Taphouse, Baltimore, MD.

Nestled in the heart of the Fells Point historic district, Max's Taphouse has been a staple of Baltimore since 1986. Locals praise their massive selection of draft beers and house-made BBQ, but you'll find an entirely different set of fans hanging out at the bar around Halloween.

Max's is one of the most haunted bars in Baltimore, and the story begins with headless chickens.

Not long ago, a bartender had a terrifying experience on the evening shift. The bar was empty and dark, and he was alone with his thoughts as he changed out the kegs for the next round of customers. Suddenly, he noticed a faint but persistent sound emanating from the basement. The sound grew louder and louder as the minutes ticked on. It couldn't be, but he was almost certain it sounded like a dozen chickens, frantically clucking. As the sound came closer, the bartender whirled toward the basement door just in time to see a bunch of headless chickens rush up, surrounding him in a frenzy.

Overcome with terror, he fled from the room and didn't stop running until he was outside. Panting, he called the owner, relaying the horrible incident. All the hairs on his arms stood on end when the owner said that the basement had been one of the city's largest chicken slaughterhouses in the 19th century.

The chickens aren't the only spirits left over from that time. In the early 1800s, Max's was a tavern and brothel for sailors with money in their pockets and time on their hands. That money often went to two things — booze and women — and there were plenty of bars and brothels for them to choose from.

The women had to get creative.

As the sailors sauntered down the cobblestone streets of Baltimore's red-light district, young prostitutes would lean out the windows of the surrounding buildings, luring men into the warmth of their beds. They must have looked like angels, clad in sheer nightgowns with long, flowing hair. Many a weary sailor fell for their seduction, so they repeated it night after night.

It's said you can still see them today, especially on clear nights, when the moon is full. Their misty spirits call to young men who pass by. Employees at Max's who try to keep the window shut insist it will not stay closed, even when boarded up with nails.

These are likely residual hauntings — actions or images that become embedded in the fabric of a place itself. The spirits aren't really there. It's just a recording of them, and it's playing over and over like a broken record.

The ghost downstairs is far more sinister.

Both employees and regulars have seen a shadow person lurking in the back corner, staring at visitors with dark, dead eyes. The second someone manages to lock eyes with it, it vanishes. Sometimes it disappears through the wall, as if walking down an old hallway that no longer exists. Sometimes it's just… gone.

Who is this shadow person and what does he or she want? A boarded-up business across the street may hold a clue.

The Ghosts of Baltimore, MD.

807 S. Broadway

The Whistling Oyster, Rye Craft Cocktails, Green Cilantro… 807 S. Broadway has been a revolving door of bars over the last 20 years. One couple owned the property for less than a year. Another owner stated they'd had "some issues" with the building and set up shop in another area of Fells Point. Another said there were "evil forces" at work when they were forced to close.

The turnover could be chalked up to the fact that the building is old, but a former employee says that isn't the whole story. They believe it's plagued by a violent poltergeist.

In the 19th century — decades before the red brick building cropped up in 1920 — Baltimore was a thriving port city. Goods flowed in and out of the harbor, lining the pockets of merchants and captains… but not their crews.

Sailors were underpaid and abused. They spent long periods at sea doing backbreaking work, sleeping in dirty quarters, and shoveling down bad food. It was a life of misery with little reward… so it was common for sailors to abandon ship once they docked. A captain could lose his entire crew in one night.

This led to a wretched practice known as "press-ganging" or "crimping."

Crimps would wander the streets late at night in search of vulnerable young men. When they found one, they would buy him drink after drink until he reached delirious belligerence. Then, in the shadows of an alleyway or tunnel, they'd bash him over the head, rendering him unconscious. Hours later, the man would find himself aboard a ship, out at sea. By then it was too late to escape. Victims were held captive for months. They'd be forced below deck when the ship docked, ensuring they couldn't make a run for it.

Every once in a while, press-ganging went awry. Men lost their lives after being fatally bashed over the head. Most crimps would simply toss the dead man into a dark alley or throw him into the bay. Others would try to pass him off as "dead drunk," collect their payment, and move on before the captain realized he'd purchased a corpse.

This heinous practice went on until the early 20th century, when the federal government cracked down on crimps and labor unions fought for better working conditions for seamen. No one knows how many men were beaten, kidnapped, or killed before that time, but their spirits roam port cities on both U.S. coasts. And that isn't the only evidence.

Years ago, a Fells Point construction crew unearthed human bones and a damaged skull. Medical examiners determined he had died as a result of blunt force trauma to the head — very likely a victim of press-ganging. Before then, the stories of these violent interactions had been just that: Stories. Now the city had solid evidence.

It seemed to explain the odd happenings at 807 S. Broadway.

In 2007, two employees were chatting at the bar hours after last call. The building was deserted, dark, and quiet, so the loud *crash* of a pint glass shattering on the floor scared them both. The glass had rolled off the shelf at the end of the bar. It was followed by a second, then a third. There was no logical explanation for the accident — no explanation at all except "ghosts."

They had both heard rumors that 807 was the most haunted building on the street. A seedy bar had stood there during the district's red light phase, and multiple owners had passed down stories of "a presence." They could feel it the second they walked through the door. It was dark and possessive, as if it was guarding the place. Some locals believed it was a crimp warning people away from his territory. Others believed it was a murdered sailor seeking revenge. Whatever it was, it was angry.

A few years after the pint glass incident, a retired couple moved in and opened up a new bar. Being from out of town, they were unfamiliar with the legends surrounding the building — but it didn't take long for the spirit of 807 to fill them in.

Glasses were thrown off the shelves at random, as if some unseen force had picked them up and chucked them across the room. Upstairs, there was a constant feeling of being watched. Phantom footsteps snuck up behind them. Unexplained bangs echoed off the walls.

They sold the bar within a year. It was replaced by a Tex-Mex joint, which also closed.

These days, the narrow building sits empty and boarded-up. Perhaps the poltergeist is at peace all alone. Or maybe it's just waiting for its next victim.

Eat Bertha's Mussels

Eat Bertha's Mussels, Baltimore, MD.

Across from Max's Taphouse, you'll find a vibrant green building with a silly name.

When the restaurant opened in 1972, it was just known as "Bertha's." The current name came about when the business started serving seafood and the owners printed bumper stickers urging folks to "EAT BERTHA'S MUSSELS." The stickers became a city-wide meme, and the name stuck.

But before 734 S Broadway was known for its seafood and lively jazz music, the building was associated with illness and death.

In 1794, yellow fever swept through Baltimore. It had devastated Philadelphia one year earlier (a story you'll find later in this book), killing 10% of the city's population. Though Baltimore was a smaller city — with only 15,000 residents versus 50,000 — the disease was just as aggressive. It killed 25 people a day until the winter frost squashed the mosquito population and stopped the spread.

Many of those people ended up in the rooming house where Bertha's currently sits. Some had it easy. They came down with a mild fever and a headache before making a full recovery. Others grew delirious, developed severe jaundice, and vomited blood. In some cases, patients died within 12 hours of displaying symptoms.

Outside, the streets were eerily quiet. Anyone who had the means to flee the city did. The only proven way to avoid the illness was to get as far away from the outbreak as possible — usually out in the country, where people were more spread out. But fleeing posed a moral dilemma, especially if one family member was already sick.

Husbands and wives abandoned each other. Children neglected their dying parents, and vice versa. Sick orphans wandered the streets looking for their families. Neighbors refused to open their doors to them. They became lepers overnight. Often, the only places that would accept them were rooming houses and orphanages.

The staff at Eat Bertha's Mussels know that all too well.

Almost two centuries after the horrific outbreak, a couple from Washington, DC, purchased the historic building on S. Broadway, hoping to convert it into a hip Fells Point restaurant. From the first moment they stepped foot inside, they knew something was off. They weren't alone. Their suspicion was soon confirmed.

One evening, an employee walked up to the second floor to get a bottle of ketchup. As he reached the top of the stairs, a flash of light near the window caught his attention. A small girl, clad in a flowing 18th-century dress, stared back at him, stunned… As quickly as she had appeared, she was gone.

Investigators believe the girl is a yellow fever victim who was brought to the rooming house when her family skipped town. She's been seen several times over the last 50 years — both inside and outside of the restaurant. In 2019, a couple snapped a photo of a glowing blue figure reaching out of a window on the Lancaster St. side of the building. It looks like she's calling out to someone.

Though the girl can cause quite a fright, she's never threatened or hurt anyone. She's a peaceful entity who's just as spooked by the living as they are of her. The employees of Bertha's have started making announcements as they walk up the stairs: "If there are any ghosts up there, I'm coming up to get something out of the storage closet. Please don't scare me."

Fell Family Cemetery

Fell Family Cemetery, Baltimore, MD.

Journey down Shakespeare Street and you'll find cozy brick row houses with colorful doors, American flags, and lush planter boxes. You'll also find a very out-of-place cemetery.

Squished in between two homes, the Fell Family plot is guarded by a brick wall and a gothic, wrought iron fence. It's small and set back from the road. The average passerby could easily miss it, but few people miss the ghost who floats back to it night after night.

In the early 1700s, brothers Edward and William Fell moved to Baltimore from England, desiring a fresh start. Devout Quakers, they founded Fell's Point in 1763, and it quickly became one of the busiest waterfront cities in the country. The trading town eventually merged with two others to become Baltimore and grew from its ability to provide work for those who sought seafaring occupations.

As the city grew, so did the red-light district. Bars, brothels, and gambling dens catered to sailors looking to blow off steam — but they also caught the eye of Edward's son, William (named for his uncle). William shamelessly sauntered from bar to bar, getting roaring drunk, before finding a pretty young woman to spend the night with. Had he been more subtle, or limited his wild nights to once a month, his family might have let it slide. But William was seen in the red-light district every night.

Several family members pulled William aside, begging him to cease his debauchery. But whether William had little regard for his family's wishes, or simply couldn't part with his old ways, he refused to stop.

One morning, William was found dead. There was no discernible cause of death. He had no health issues, and he was only 27 years old.

Due to the strange circumstances surrounding his death, some community members heavily scrutinized the Fell family. Had they killed William off to save their good name? As rumors mixed with the truth, the townspeople whispered about how the family was not only capable but also desperate enough to perform the dastardly deed.

Regardless of his reputation, William Fell was laid to rest at Fell Family Cemetery. But if you walk past the plot where only three headstones lay, you'll quickly notice that none of the female members of the Fell family are buried on the property.

Why is this? Locals say all of the female Fells were carefully exhumed and relocated to an undisclosed location days after William Fell's body was placed in the ground. Perhaps the remaining Fells didn't want their female ancestors associated with William's tainted reputation… or his ambiguous death.

Now, on a dark, lonely night, if you happen to be on Shakespeare Street with an appetite for more than drink, you may be able to see the spirit of William Fell, dressed in colonial-era clothing, stumbling his way out of the local bars.

As he slowly makes his way back to the Fell Family Cemetery, politely let him pass, and remember how his past, one of sorrow and enigma, may prevent him from sleeping at peace and force his feet to endlessly return to his old haunts.

The Horse You Came in On Saloon

The Horse You Came in On Saloon, Baltimore, MD.

The Horse You Came in On Saloon dates back to 1775, making it one of the oldest taverns still in operation today. Its prominent location, mouth-watering food, and hit-the-spot drinks have made regulars out of many Baltimore residents — including Edgar Allan Poe.

Poe was a brilliant, 19th-century writer who became famous for haunting poems, passionate prose, and scary stories like "The Tell-Tale Heart." He drew inspiration from his own tragic life. He lost both of his parents and gambled away his education at the University of Virginia.

After his wife succumbed to tuberculosis in 1847, Poe remet his longtime love, Sarah Elmira Royster Shelton, and proposed to her. In 1849, when the two were ready to marry, ill fortune found Poe once more.

On October 3 of that year, Poe was found battered and semi-conscious in a gutter on Baltimore's East Lombard St. Over the next four days, he drifted in and out, fighting hallucinations and a fever. No one knew what had happened to him and no one could get a straight answer out of Poe. He was too far gone. On October 7, he uttered his last word: "Reynolds." The name — like all other circumstances surrounding his death — is still a mystery.

However, there's a popular theory as to what happened: When Sarah's three older brothers heard of the couple's impending union, they reacted with abhorrent disgust. Many years ago, their parents had prohibited Sarah from marrying Poe, and they had both married other suitors. Now, Sarah had a promising inheritance after she became a widow, and Poe was well known not only for his writing but also for his love of alcohol.

That fall, as Poe made his way to Philadelphia to complete an editing job, Sarah's brothers ambushed him. Pulling him into a nearby alley, they warned him not to return to Baltimore or their beloved sister. They made it very clear to the writer that if he were to step foot back in the city, he would be met with a bad end.

Utterly terrified, Poe remained in Philadelphia and kept well out of sight. He was certain Sarah's brothers had meant every word of their threat. But he soon ran out of money, as well as options. He returned to Baltimore on October 3, clad in secondhand clothes, hoping the disguise would fool his enemies. But he couldn't refuse a drink. He ventured into The Horse You Came in On Saloon, where he immediately ran into Sarah's three brothers, who recognized him on the spot.

There is much speculation as to what befell the prolific writer after that.

Some believe he drank himself into a permanent stupor, while others think he succumbed to some form of disease. But some are convinced to this day that he was savagely murdered by Sarah's angry brothers, making good on their violent threat.

The story says that, after finding Poe in the saloon, the brothers grabbed him by the collar and took him out into the alley. There, they forced a lethal amount of whiskey down his throat and tossed him into the nearest gutter, where he was found a short time later.

Today, Poe returns to haunt the bar many consider to be his last stop. Sometimes, people say they can see him thrust open the door and stumble toward the counter. His ghostly appearance is always accompanied by an overwhelming rush of frigid air, even in the peak of summer. Customers and staff have also noted swinging chandeliers, loud sounds, and cash registers they swear are haunted as they open and close by themselves.

Certain that it's Poe back from the dead for a visit, staff always leave a glass of cognac at the far end of the bar for him, should he choose to come wandering in. If you ever want to talk with Poe or offer him some respite from his tortured history, maybe you'll wait to have a drink with him and see if he will share the tale of his own heart with you.

Admiral Fell Inn

Admiral Fell Inn, Baltimore, MD.

Fells Point may be a classy, historic neighborhood today, but a century ago, it was a violent, seedy slum. Brawls spilled onto the streets. Sailors were robbed blind, beaten, and left for dead. Crimps stalked the streets, searching for their next paycheck.

In the midst of the chaos, a Christian organization opened a safe haven called "The Anchorage." Today, it's the Admiral Fell Inn — one of Maryland's most haunted hotels.

When disease swept through the city, nurses established hospital wards there, sacrificing their own health to comfort dying men; however, there was only so much they could do. An untold number of young men succumbed to their illnesses in the makeshift hospital rooms.

It's estimated that 50,000 sailors a year found a home at the sanctuary before it was sold in 1955. Though the name and purpose have changed, the spirits of battered sailors still roam the property — and they aren't afraid of a good time.

Guests often awaken in the middle of the night to the sound of a raucous party in the room next door. When they call the front desk to complain, they always learn the adjacent room is empty. Within seconds of this phone call, all noise from the room next door ceases.

One terrible night in 2003, when all the guests at the Admiral Fell Inn were forced to evacuate with the threat of Hurricane Isabel, a few employees were left to guard the inn. As the rain and wind howled outside the windows, sounds of a loud, vivacious party could be heard echoing from inside the empty hotel. The singing and laughter could have only been ghosts, for the entire inn had been evacuated, save for the ghostly guests.

Guests have also reported seeing ghostly butlers or nurses wander the halls late at night, knocking on doors and checking in on the patients and sailors of the past. These insistent ghosts are never mean and always vanish the moment someone answers the door to see who is there.

The basement bar is another magnet for paranormal activity. Employees are constantly barraged by strange-looking orbs that hover around the room. Often, when bartenders arrive for a late-night shift, they find that a ghost has moved numerous items around, as though they still want to fulfill their prior earthly duties.

But not all ghosts of the Admiral Fell are so innocuous. Something otherworldly lives in Room 413, and it isn't tied to yellow fever, or crimps, or fun-loving sailors. In 1999 — long after the current hotel had been established — a gruesome murder took place there.

On June 29, 1999, 25-year-old Gary William Mick followed 37-year-old Christopher Jones back to his hotel room. Jones was in town for a pharmaceutical convention, and the two had hit it off, or so it seemed. Once inside, Mick bludgeoned Jones to death with a claw hammer before robbing him. He later admitted he had killed Jones because the man was gay and he believed homosexuality was "evil."

Now 49, Mick is serving two life sentences at North Branch Correctional Institution — almost 150 miles away from the hotel where he ended a man's life — but Jones remains in the room where he died.

Guests who have no prior knowledge of the murder have called the front desk to tell them there's something "wrong" about their room. There's an immediate feeling of dread and panic. A shadowy figure darts from corner to corner. It's accompanied by bursts of cold air, like a strong breeze from an open door. Staff members have felt a hand resting on their shoulder as they clean. Some refuse to go into the room at all.

It seems, with hotels, ghosts are almost unavoidable. Thousands of people have passed through the doors of 888 S. Broadway, and even more have passed through the next hotel…

Waterfront Hotel

Waterfront Hotel, Baltimore, MD.

Considered to be the second oldest brick building in the city, the Waterfront Hotel passed through a few hands before being transformed into a hotel in the 1800s. But hotel living was far more dangerous in the 19th century than today. Disease spread quickly in close quarters, and the guests of the Waterfront were powerless to stop it.

Some reports claim those who were ill would be left on the street in certain places, for fear that if they came inside, they would spread the infection. Today, while the first and second floors of the building are dedicated to the bar and restaurant, the third floor remains closed to the public. Why, you ask?

Customers and guests have begun to provide strange accounts of shocking interactions with those whom they suspect to occupy the land of the dead. People have reported the sounds of ghosts walking back and forth on the floor above them, audibly talking amongst themselves. However, recently, the owner of the tavern reports the strangest story of all.

One morning, as he prepared for the busy day ahead at the bar, the owner saw someone breeze past his shoulder. Bidding the figure hello, he froze when he realized he was the only one there — he hadn't opened the bar yet.

Running into the room to see whom he had bid good morning, he realized there was no one there.

Curious and sure he had seen a ghost, the owner asked his co-workers to set up an electronic voice phenomena (EVP) reader. They spent hours listening to whispers of silence, but then, they swore they heard someone tell them their name was Samuel. When they shared their story with some of the other staff members, they were aghast to find that a ghost had occupied the tavern when it was a hotel — and his name? Samuel.

Waterfront Hotel, Baltimore, MD.

Cat's Eye Pub

Cat's Eye Pub, Baltimore, MD.

Much like Max's Taphouse, the Cat's Eye got its start as a popular brothel in the 18th century. Not far from the deep water ports, liquor and merriment lured in lonely sailors — even pirates — offering them enticing company after they had been tossed on the stormy seas.

But the women at the Cat's Eye were a bit more cunning than the window callers at Max's. They quickly learned to nick their clients' wallets at the end of the evening, ensuring these unfortunate men had no choice but to accept the jobs onboard ships that were forced upon them if they fell victim to press-ganging. Many of these women earned money by working with crimps to target specific victims.

Women who worked as prostitutes led a wretched and lonely existence in the 1700s. Shunned by any semblance of good society, they would make a living spending the night with winsome sailors until time eventually robbed them of their beauty. When clients stopped calling, the women often rented a small room on the top floor of the Cat's Eye, where they lived out the rest of their days in poverty and obscurity.

That suffering imprinted on the building, and it's said the spirits of these women linger on the upper floors. Bartenders hear the sounds of the girls' high heels clicking against the floor as they wander throughout the building — never seen but always heard.

The red light switches used by the women to signal wayward sailors to the brothel have started to turn themselves on and off ever since they were rediscovered, as if the ghostly girls are still hungry for clientele. Buckets, bottles, and even haunted harmonicas have been known to reappear after going missing, supposedly disturbed by the dead. When a ghost hunter was called in one day in 2007, he caught signs of a spirit haunting a table where a staff member had sworn she had felt the brush of a hand on her arm as she passed.

However, prostitutes are not the only spirits to haunt the Cat's Eye. One former owner enjoys hanging out behind the bar, still carrying out tasks as though he were alive. Many customers have reported having conversations with him, completely unaware that he has been dead since the 1990s.

In 2003, a woman entered the pub to buy a t-shirt and had a lovely interaction with the man behind the bar. A few months later, she went back and asked another employee where the man had gone. Had he gotten another job or been fired? She hadn't seen him around. The employee stared at her like she had two heads. The man she was describing had been dead for years.

The bar has created what they lovingly call the "Wall of Death," a shrine dedicated to owners and customers who have crossed over to the other side. It isn't until these customers see Jeff's portrait on the wall that they realize their mistake — that they were talking to Jeff's ghost, and not the past owner himself.

A similar story focuses on another owner of the Cat's Eye Pub. After his death, a memorial meal was held at the pub. A group drank and reminisced around a table, taking turns sharing memories and compliments about the past owner.

However, when one of the ladies at the table began loudly disparaging the deceased man, his portrait flew off the Wall of Death and struck the woman in the back of the head. Dozens of people witnessed this supernatural event and refuse to speak ill of the man while visiting the Cat's Eye Pub, in fear of what may happen to them in turn.

Alexander Thompson House

Alexander Thompson House, Baltimore, MD.

The story of how this row home became haunted begins in 1810 when it was purchased by Alexander Thompson. A wealthy and well-respected merchant, Mr. Thompson enjoyed his home, built in 1780, and led a life free from strife and drama. But everything changed in 1814.

One morning, Baltimore residents awoke to hear that British troops had infiltrated Washington, DC, and set it ablaze. Outraged at the news, many horrified locals demanded quick retaliation.

But when word spread that the British navy was headed to Baltimore, the country's third largest city, Thompson couldn't sit by. He hastily put together his own navy and led an attack on the Bahamas, which was under British governance. The crew of his ship, *Midas*, set numerous homes ablaze and, without mercy, desecrated the gravesites of prominent British citizens.

Word of the attack spread, and when President Madison caught wind of it, he was infuriated. Revoking the commission of Thompson's private vessels, he forced Thompson to pay the British colony for all the damages he had caused.

When Baltimore residents heard of the punishments bestowed upon

Thompson by the president himself, they were collectively embarrassed for the man. They noticed that he spent the rest of his life hidden away from his peers, dying alone in his house at 1729 Aliceanna Street.

Today, Thompson still haunts his historic home. Many locals have witnessed him hovering slightly above the ground as he ventures from Broadway Street to his door — often between the hours of 11 p.m. and 2 a.m. As he drifts past, the streetlights tend to flicker. Be careful if you catch sight of him. He's been known to turn sharply and stare back at anyone staring at him. After giving you a good fright, he'll disappear behind the walls of his former home.

Alexander Thompson House, Baltimore, MD.

Sticky Rice

Sticky Rice, Baltimore, MD.

Though permanently closed, Sticky Rice was once a beloved Baltimore restaurant that became popular due to its tantalizing sushi and gourmet noodle bowls. It was also notoriously haunted. Sailors, prostitutes, and even Billie Holiday were rumored to roam the halls — echoes of the restaurant's former life.

1634 Aliceanna Street was known as the Dix Hotel in the 1930s. On the bottom floor, patrons shot back whiskey at an Irish bar. On the upper floors, red-light women entertained eager customers. It seems those interactions replayed over and over for the folks at Sticky Rice.

Customers would sit down to enjoy a nice meal, only to have their evening interrupted by the sounds of disembodied moans and a squeaky bed frame in motion above their heads. Staff members had to make up excuses, knowing all too well the second floor was completely devoid of beds and the sounds were snapshots of long-dead affairs…

But it's lucky the customers were only confronted by squeaking and not the apparition who haunts the upstairs. One day, when the owner's sister was all alone in the second-floor office, she got the impulse to take some selfies. When she pulled the camera back to look at the picture, her mouth fell open in terror. The last photograph showed a gaunt, dead face hovering just behind her shoulder.

Downstairs, a much less sinister female ghost took up residence.

During Billie Holiday's rise to fame, she came back to the Dix several times, and some believe she loved the place so much she decided to stay forever.

In the late 90s, a group of young women visited the bar and were the only customers left by the time the last call was announced. The bartender was closing up when suddenly the girls grew silent and deathly pale. Trembling in their chairs, they told him that Billie Holiday had materialized right beside them, singing and dancing her way around the room before quickly fading from sight.

The bartender found the testimony all the more credible when he discovered the group had no previous knowledge of the singer's history with the bar. Several bartenders had also heard Billie singing on occasion from an adjacent room but found it empty every time they looked inside.

But Sticky Rice was rumored to be haunted by more than just women. During World War II, the hotel operated as an unofficial landing spot for sailors on the brink of shipping out. These sailors slept in shabby, inhospitable beds as they contemplated war and the probable horror that awaited them. For some, the fear was all-consuming. At least one man hung himself on the second floor before deployment day.

The room where he perished was immediately haunted by his restless ghost. It was always deathly cold, no matter how many times the heat was adjusted, and several guests had terrifying encounters with a violent entity. One night, a man was startled awake by phantom hands wrapping around his throat. As he struggled against the specter, he felt its hands tighten their grip for several moments before vanishing altogether. Fighting for air, the man fled from the hotel and refused to ever return.

The building has transformed several times throughout the years, but the myriad of ghosts remain, ready to entertain, surprise, or terrify…

Bar Vasquez

Bar Vasquez, Baltimore, MD.

On the edge of Baltimore's affluent Harbor East neighborhood, there's a long brick building boasting the name "E.J. Codd." The story behind those large, white letters is the story of the Industrial Revolution — a time when cities boomed, money flowed, and workers suffered.

Though the Codd building has hosted a variety of upscale restaurants and stores over the last 20 years, the daily toil of 19th century factory workers lingers...

Edward Codd founded his company in the 1850s, when Baltimore was a mecca for shipbuilding. His Aliceanna St. factory pumped out boilers, propellers, and engines — all essential for the steamships of the 19th century — and Codd soon became one of the best-known businessmen in the city. But the industrial boom went hand-in-hand with the abuse of factory workers.

Though there isn't specific evidence of abuse in Codd's factory, it was widespread across the United States.

The workday stretched on for ten to twelve hours in hot, cramped, unsafe conditions. Diseases like yellow fever and tuberculosis spread rapidly, yet employees were not given health insurance or paid time off. This only furthered the spread of disease, as sick workers continued coming to work.

Safety equipment was more or less nonexistent. Burns and other injuries were common, especially among children. Child labor laws weren't passed until 1938. The tragic truth is some children preferred their factory jobs to being at home. Employers were restricted in how harshly they could punish young employees. Their parents weren't…

Still, there was a rising tide of support for workers' rights. Unions formed after the Civil War, and Codd yielded to an 1899 strike fighting for a nine-hour workday. It was a victory, but the life of a factory worker was still painful and dangerous.

Fast forward to 2004, when Tony Foreman and Cindy Wolf opened a Spanish restaurant in the old Codd building. It later served Southern Italian cuisine before the pair turned it into an Aregentinian bar and lounge called "Bar Vasquez," which closed in 2021.

Employees of all three restaurants reported strange occurrences. They'd hear phantom footsteps and see the lights flicker. A former manager admitted she hated being there alone. She would come in on Sundays to handle paperwork and find herself immediately spooked by the energy of the empty building. One noise and she would bolt.

The manager never saw a ghost, but her employees weren't so fortunate.

A few years ago, a waiter was hustling back and forth serving a private party on the second floor, delighted at the prospect of a hefty tip. As he carried a tray up the stairs, he almost ran into a figure that had stopped directly in front of him. Just as the words "I'm sorry" were about the leave his lips, he looked up and saw that this figure was translucent.

Riddled with fear, he immediately shut his eyes and began to count to ten, resisting every urge he had to run. When someone called to him, wondering what was wrong, he finally dared to open his eyes again — but the ghost had vanished.

A few months after this harrowing incident, the apparition appeared again at the top of the same stairs, scaring a waitress half to death. Locals believe it's one of the factory managers still lording over employees from his perch on the second floor. Whoever the spirit is, it's abundantly clear they believe they're still in charge… 150 years later.

Blue Moon Cafe

Blue Moon Cafe, Baltimore, MD.

Baltimore's final haunted hotspot is a critically acclaimed restaurant with a brunch menu so good it was featured on *Diners, Drive-Ins, and Dives*. The only things more famous than the cafe's Captain Crunch French Toast are its resident ghosts.

Built in the 1700s, the Blue Moon building served many purposes before it was converted into a restaurant. Locals believe it's haunted by spirits from several different time periods. Though they've never properly introduced themselves, they like to get attention.

It began with the lights.

Every time the owners stepped into the basement, the lights would flicker, as if spirits were waiting on the other side. Not long after, employees and patrons heard disembodied voices.

Staff members began to notice incessant whispers emanating from one particular corner of the room, especially late at night. Anyone who heard these hair-raising whispers was immediately overcome with a sense of dread. It got so bad that employees assigned to tasks in the basement would beg for other duties, claiming the area was "supernaturally cold" and "extremely creepy."

One fateful day, the owner's mother visited the restaurant to assist her daughter with some paperwork. She ventured down into the basement in the hopes of finding a particular document. When she came back up, a disembodied voice called out her name from the darkness.

Utterly terrified, she ran screaming up the steps in search of her daughter. Reunited, the two mustered up the courage to investigate the basement together but could find no evidence of the entity, save for a chill in the air.

Ever since that bizarre incident, the activity has ramped up. Orbs float through the air. Angry voices travel through the cafe as if they're emanating from the walls. One evening, the manager heard a faint, robotic noise coming from another room. Puzzled, she slowly followed the source of the noise until she discovered a children's toy cat rhythmically moving back and forth on the ground.

She laughed with relief and thought the toy was adorable…until she discovered it was missing the batteries necessary for it to operate.

Blue Moon Cafe, Baltimore, MD.

BONUS CHAPTER

Maryland's Most Haunted Continued

Looking for more Maryland haunts? Don't worry. There are plenty of spooks outside of Annapolis and Baltimore.

Head west, to where Maryland meets West Virginia at the Potomac River, and you'll find one of America's most haunted battlefields: Antietam. More than 3,600 men lay dead after the smoke cleared on September 17, 1862. Since then, visitors have heard gunfire and pained moans echoing through the fields. But none of that compares what they've witnessed in the farmhouse at the edge of the battlefield…

Farther south, you may run into the fearsome "Goat Man" of Fletchertown Road — a government experiment that spiraled out of control. Locals believe the cryptid has claimed dozens of lives, and how he does it will keep you awake for many nights to come.

Take a trip down Route 5, and you may come face to face with the ghost of John Wilkes Booth. After shooting and killing President Lincoln, Booth fled to Charles County, where Dr. Samuel Mudd mended his broken leg. Now a museum, the Mudd House is plagued by the spirits of that fateful April night.

The following stories will take you off the beaten path, to the isolated places where Maryland's most terrifying spirits and creatures hide in the shadows. If you go, don't go alone…

The Witch's Grave at Truxton Park | Annapolis, MD

The Witch's Grave at Truxton Park, MD.

In the middle of Annapolis, perched at the end of Spa Creek, you'll find a quaint little park with a hidden secret. If you visit the park on your own, you might miss it. But if you follow directions from the locals — just past the third baseball field, go into the woods and look for the slanted tree — then you may find yourself face to face with a witch.

Sometime in the 1800s, a woman lived alone on the land that is now called Truxtun Park. Some say she was just a recluse, but others accused her of being a witch. There were rumors that at the witching hour, strange noises and peculiar smells would emanate from her small house, as if someone were chanting wicked spells and burning cursed ingredients for a magickal brew.

This was colonial America, and witch hunts were common at that time, especially in the settlements that were religious in their origin. Before the capital of Maryland was called Annapolis, its name was "Providence." It was given this moniker by the Puritans, who were the original Europeans to settle the area. It is therefore no surprise that the hysteria of witch hunts may have tainted the early years of the city, with persecutions and executions of those accused of witchcraft, often innocent people.

As for the aforementioned recluse, many locals were utterly convinced that she was indeed a witch. Though she was barely seen by anyone, her mere presence frightened children and the superstitious. In one of the few documented cases of her interacting with others, she spoke with a group of sailors who were heading out to sail down Spa Creek.

"Don't go," the women told the sailors. "You'll never make it out of Spa Creek. Your ships will go down!" The sailors dismissed her warnings and instead told others that she was putting a curse on them. We don't know the fate of those sailors, so no one knows whether or not the so-called curse came true. Unfortunately for the woman, it didn't matter. Her fate was sealed by the townspeople who believed what the sailors had said.

Eventually, the terrified people decided to rid themselves of the witch once and for all. The woman was hanged from a tree on her own property, then buried in a shallow, unmarked grave in the woods that surrounded her house.

But what came after… was even more gruesome.

The story goes that the witch rose from the grave to get revenge on her executioners. In the woods past the third baseball field, right under a fallen tree and behind a section of an old, rusty iron fence, there it lies — a hollow in the ground that looks much like a shallow grave from which someone (or something) has escaped.

Despite killing her killers, the witch's spirit was never laid to rest, and she is said to haunt the area to this day. Anyone walking around the park after midnight might catch a glimpse of her shadowy apparition lurking at the treeline, perpetually in search of those who put the noose around her neck all those years ago. Several witnesses have testified that on Halloween night, you can see the witch's victims hanging from the trees, the phantoms of her vengeance.

Amateur ghost hunters have captured frightening evidence at the site: shuffling noises, high EMF readings, and a temperature recording that read "666." During one group's search for paranormal activity, they decided to call out to the witch and summon her from the grave. Shortly thereafter, one of them was pulled down toward the grave by an unseen hand. When he got up and was examined by the others, they saw scratches down his back that were too uniform to have been caused by a tree branch or natural means — it distinctly looked like four evenly spaced claw marks.

The group made a rapid departure from the location, but it seemed that they did not escape the witch so easily. Later in their apartment, two members of the group claimed that they heard weird noises like something scratching at the walls. They took a picture of themselves, and between their heads was something that made their blood run cold — a ghostly face with a sinister grin. The two were convinced that the witch had followed them home and made a pact never to return to that accursed site again.

Thanks to these and other tales from personal experience, the legend of the witch's grave in Annapolis lives on today. The site remains in the woods around Truxtun Park like an open mouth telling dark secrets. It appears to have been largely undisturbed since colonial days… yet many who have visited the grave have been extremely disturbed.

Terrors of Maryland.

Fletchertown Road | Bowie, MD

The Goat Man.

Although Bowie has boomed in the last century and a half, parts of it still look like they did when it was first settled. Fletchertown Road is one such area.

This stretch of rural road cuts through a wooded residential area in which the houses are mostly hidden by dense patches of forest. There's a sense of isolation as you drive down the road. Between the narrow lanes and the flanking vegetation, sometimes taller than any vehicle, it also gives you a feeling of claustrophobia.

At night, the eerie atmosphere is only increased. Headlights barely penetrate the trees lining either side of the winding road. Whatever lies around each dark corner cannot be seen until you are right there, forcing you to slow down when all you really want to do is quickly get to the end of the sinister-looking street.

Fletchertown Road looks like the setting of a horror movie. So it comes as no surprise that one of Maryland's biggest urban legends revolves around this stretch of old road — the Goat Man. It is a cryptid story so terrifying that it has become famous across the country. The question is: Is it real?

The legend begins in the 1950s at Beltsville Agricultural Center, a research facility for the U.S. Agriculture Department located about nine miles west of Bowie. Rumors circulated that secret government experiments were taking place in Beltsville. It was believed that doctors and bioengineers were attempting to merge human and animal DNA.

In one such experiment, a doctor decided to include his assistant, William Latsford. The name of the doctor is unknown, possibly because he was working under a pseudonym to conceal his true identity. Some versions of the story say that the doctor forced Latsford at gunpoint to participate in the experiment. The assistant's DNA was combined with that of a goat's.

The result was a hybrid creature — half man and half goat — that was impossible to control.

Perhaps it was Latford's side of the beast's brain that was lashing out, feeling betrayed that the doctor forced him to become a guinea pig for his demented experiment. Whether or not the creature killed the doctor depends on who tells the story, but all accounts agree on one thing — the Goat Man escaped the facility.

In the late 1950s, the Bowie area was plagued by a series of strange incidents involving dogs. People's pet canines went mysteriously missing, and some were later found dead in fields and on the side of the road. It didn't take long for people to attribute these animal deaths to the Goat Man. This theory was given further credibility when people began spotting the creature.

Many of the sightings have occurred on Fletchertown Road. Witnesses say that as they drive down the creepy road, they see red eyes peering out from the trees and vegetation. Some have seen him standing at the treeline in a frozen stance as if hunting his prey. What they describe is truly terrifying: a horned and hoofed creature, covered in fur, at least six feet tall, with the torso and arms of a man and the lower body of a goat's hindquarters.
His face is a twisted mixture of man and goat, with eyes that glow red like hot coals.

Some have claimed to have an even closer encounter with the abominable creature. Imagine driving down Fletchertown Road, wary of the sharp turns, when suddenly the Goat Man leaps out of the woods, bounding straight for your car. You put the pedal to the metal, risking a crash around snake-like bends, as the Goat Man's flailing claws scratch and scrape at the trunk of the car. And amidst all the other chaotic noise, you hear a consistent, demonic growl emanating from his throat.

No one knows why the Goat Man seems to be tethered to Fletchertown Road. It is assumed that he makes the surrounding woods his home. Some believe that he lives in a cave-like hollow beneath Governor's Bridge, though there are no documented sightings of the Goat Man at that specific location. However, when a group of hikers in that area went missing in 1962, the Goat Man was blamed for their disappearance. People said that the group got too close to the creature's cave, and they were never seen again.

Certain details of the Goat Man stories may vary depending on who's doing the telling. Many believe that the Goat Man attacks like an animal, using his talon-like claws and sharp fangs to tear into his victim's flesh. Other versions, however, paint the Goat Man as a more cold-blooded killer who hacks his victims into bits with an ax. Perhaps the truth is somewhere in the middle, and the Goat Man uses both methods of attack, depending on which side of his dual-DNA brain is in control at any particular moment.

By the mid-1970s, there were dozens of Goat Man sightings and exponentially more stories related to the hybrid monster. The frequency of sightings seemed to lessen substantially after that time, although interest in the cryptid did not. Curious seekers of urban legends still go out to Fletchertown Road looking for a glimpse of the Goat Man, and people still occasionally see him out there in those woods.

It's likely that the Goat Man simply became better at hiding — a sign of intelligence that makes this half-human creature all the more terrifying. Any fiend that can track you down as a man and take you out like an animal is worthy of our fear and the enduring legacy that the Goat Man legend enjoys even to this day.

Terrors of Maryland.

U.S. Coast Guard Ship Taney | Baltimore, MD

U.S. Coast Guard Ship Taney, Baltimore, MD.

Docked on Pier 5 of Baltimore's Inner Harbor is a historical behemoth, the U.S. Coast Guard Cutter 37, also known as USCGC Taney. This 327-foot-long vessel is the last warship still floating that was present during the 1941 attack on Pearl Harbor and is sometimes referred to as "The Last Survivor of Pearl Harbor."

It was built in 1936, originally designed for maritime patrol, law enforcement, and search and rescue missions. After more than fifty years of service, it was decommissioned in 1986.

Today, the USCGC Taney is a public museum, famous for its detailed Pearl Harbor exhibit. It's also become famous for being extremely haunted. Even the Coast Guard says the ship carries the souls of the deceased aboard — a harrowing reminder of December 7, 1941.

"Air raid, Pearl Harbor! This is not a drill!" Chaos erupted as the alarms sounded. It was an attack that the U.S. did not expect but had prepared for anyway.

The Taney was docked at Pearl Harbor when the Japanese bombed the U.S. naval base. In preparation for the war, the ship had received a substantial upgrade in its armaments. During the battle at Pearl Harbor, the Taney engaged enemy planes that flew overhead and went on anti-submarine patrols following the attack. It is said that the Taney was targeted by kamikaze pilots 119 times but shot them all down, valiantly staying afloat and assisting in defending Pearl Harbor to victory.

In one capacity or another, the Taney served in every other major war the U.S. was involved in until its decommissioning. After World War II, the Taney carried out "peacetime duties," including Ocean Weather Patrol and numerous search and rescue efforts.

During the Korean War, it was again equipped with anti-submarine and anti-aircraft weapons. These were also employed during the Vietnam War, as the Taney participated in Operation Market Time, intercepting illegal arms and supplies before they made it to the North Vietnamese forces. Following Vietnam, the Taney returned to peacetime duties and drug patrols until it was gracefully taken out of service exactly fifty years after being built.

Much of the Taney has been restored for the museum, but it still displays some of the battle scars of its time as a Coast Guard cutter. Peeling paint on the inner walls tells tales of past events; scratches along the gun mounts speak of the many battles this ship has seen. But some say that the Taney's scars go even deeper than the knicks and dents in the ship's hull.

Footsteps seem to travel down sections of the ship where nobody is walking. During a tour, everyone present heard the sound of a man's voice coming over the ship's old PA system, even though it hadn't been in operation for years. In the boiler room — another area that has long been inoperative — mechanical sounds rise up, as if the Taney is still setting out to sea.

People have also heard indistinct voices of unknown origins. Specifically near the galley, some have claimed to hear a male voice speaking Japanese. Some say this is the spirit of a wounded Japanese pilot who was brought aboard during the battle at Pearl Harbor. The fact that the galley once doubled as a medical ward gives merit to the theory.

Much of the ghostly activity occurs after dark and often in the front part of the ship, especially near the damage control office and the Chief's Mess, the lounge where commanders would eat and have meetings. Museum employees working the graveyard shift have noticed something weird while making their nightly rounds. On several occasions, they've seen someone inside the Chief's Mess, though the display room remains locked at all times. Whenever they unlock and enter the room to investigate, the person is gone.

Spectral figures have been spotted on the main deck too, quickly gliding past and sometimes sliding down the hatches. In the ship's berthing area, shadowy forms have been seen moving through, followed by locker doors opening and closing by themselves. It's as if the ship's crew is still on board, carrying out their daily duties.

World War II-era ships were built like small cities, capable of fulfilling the needs of a large crew for months — if not years. Crewmen often repeated the same schedule day after day during that time, and those actions imprinted on the ship itself. Now they're replaying over and over in front of employees, tour groups, veterans…

The echo of frantic boot-steps on a ladder tells the story of the Taney better than any display ever could.

Terrors of Maryland.

Antietam National Battlefield | Sharpsburg, MD

Antietam National Battlefield, Sharpsburg, MD.

Today, Antietam Battlefield is a national park and a community center. On September 17, 1862, it was the site of the bloodiest single-day battle in all of U.S. history. Though more than 160 years have passed, the events of that day linger like a scar that will never fade, making Antietam one of the most haunted places on earth…

By 1862, the Civil War had already gone on for about a year and a half, and the outcome was still uncertain. The Union Army had suffered recent losses, and at that point, things were looking to be in favor of the Confederacy. Confederate General Robert E. Lee decided it was time to lead his troops into northern soil. His soldiers collided with Union troops, led by Commander George McClellan, at Antietam Creek near Sharpsburg, Maryland.

The Battle of Antietam began at dawn, just as the fog was lifting. Union soldiers fired first, taking shots at the Confederate troops flanking them by hiding in the surrounding cornfield that spread in either direction. Retaliation was swift and furious. Massive amounts of fallen soldiers sprayed the stalks red, converting the cornfield into a killing field. It is believed that in the first eight hours of the battle, there were more than 15,000 casualties.

Another four hours of intense slaughter occurred near the center of the battlefield, on a dirt road between two hills that separated two farms. Aptly named Sunken Road, it was here where Confederate troops, outnumbered two to one, piled fence posts along the embankment of the road in order to fortify their position. Fighting in this narrow stretch of land was brutal, with bodies falling on top of bodies in piles akin to the makeshift fortifications. Someone later described the deathtrap like "shooting animals in a pen." So much blood flowed down that road that it became known under a new name: Bloody Lane.

Before the sun set that evening, the battle that began at dawn was over. Technically, Lee withdrew from the battlefield first, for which some historians give McClellan the victory.

However, in a battle with such great loss on both sides — 12,410 Union soldiers and 10,317 Confederate soldiers — the concept of victory is debatable. Despite this truth, the Battle of Antietam is still considered a turning point of the Civil War. It effectively ended the Confederacy's push into the north and prompted President Abraham Lincoln to issue the Emancipation Proclamation.

There has yet to be another battle in any war that has resulted in so many dead American troops. Antietam National Battlefield is still stained with many memories that linger, the incredible amount of trauma that occurred there, and some even say the fallen soldiers that still haunt the land.

Several visitors have reported hearing gunfire in the distance — the phantom crack of muskets like violent thunder. Sometimes the sounds are accompanied by the smell of gunpowder, though no smoking gun has ever been found. Others have heard the marching dirge of war drums and even shouts as of a man writhing in pain.

Not surprisingly, Bloody Lane seems to be a hotspot of ghostly activity. Men in Confederate uniforms have been spotted walking up and down the Sunken Road. People assume they are reenactors, as can be seen in certain parts of the national park today, until the troops completely vanish before their eyes.

One story involves a group of Baltimore schoolboys who were walking down Bloody Lane when they heard the faint sound of singing coming from the fields. It was almost a chant, a fa-la-la in unison similar to the Christmas carol "Deck the Halls." They were near an observation tower when they heard the singing, the same spot where Confederate soldiers were charged by the Irish Brigade and their battle cries of "Faugh-a-ballagh," which is Gaelic for "Clear the way!"

On the edge of Antietam Battlefield stands an old farmhouse: the Pry House, believed to be haunted. This building was commandeered by General McClellan during the battle and used as his headquarters. It quickly became a place to bring the wounded soldiers. With so many wounded, however, medics were overwhelmed, and many of the troops died there.

Though the building is not open to the public today, workers who have been hired to renovate the building have reported unexplainable phenomena. The ghost of a woman in a long dress sometimes appears in one of the upper windows, longingly looking out as if wishing to escape some painful prison. People say she may be the wife of General Richardson, who died in the house. One contractor got so spooked at the sight that he immediately abandoned the project and never returned to the job site.

The bloodiest day on U.S. soil has created one of the most haunted places in Maryland. Visiting Antietam National Battlefield is like taking a trip back in time to one of the darkest periods in our nation's history. The many entities that still dwell on the battlefield are eternal reminders of America's violent past and the terrible state of division that we must be careful never to find ourselves in again.

Antietam National Battlefield, Sharpsburg, MD.

Terrors of Maryland.

Dr. Samuel Mudd's House | Waldorf, MD

Dr. Samuel Mudd's House, Waldorf, MD.

Down in southern Maryland, in a little community called Waldorf, you'll find the Dr. Samuel A. Mudd House Museum. The house looks as quaint and unassuming as Mudd himself. Before the morning of April 15, 1865, he was a quiet, country doctor. But all of that changed when he heard a knock at his door. On the other side of it was John Wilkes Booth, the man who had just murdered the president of the United States.

That moment would alter the course of Mudd's life — and afterlife — forever.

On Good Friday, April 14, 1865, Samuel Mudd was at his home. He was 31 years old, a father of four, and a respected doctor in the area. It's likely he went to sleep that night completely unaware that, earlier that evening, President Abraham Lincoln had been assassinated at Ford's Theatre.

Around 4 a.m., there was a knock on his door. A man on horseback calling himself Mr. Tyler was in need of emergency medical attention. He had a leg injury and told the doctor that he sustained it from falling off the horse. Dr. Mudd graciously invited the distraught man in and took a look at his injured limb, determining that his leg was broken. The doctor splinted Mr. Tyler's broken limb and gave him an orthopedic shoe to wear.

He let the traveler rest in an upstairs bedroom, telling him that he would arrange for a local carpenter to make him a pair of crutches.

The next morning, Mr. Tyler paid Dr. Mudd $25 in greenbacks before heading out on his horse. He never returned for the crutches or a follow-up appointment. Instead, Mr. Tyler took the nearly two-week trip to ride into Virginia, making his way to the Garrett farm near Bowling Green. While he slept in a tobacco shed, Union calvary surrounded the structure. The soldiers set fire to the shed. Mr. Tyler woke up to the flames and smoke. He tried to escape out of a window when he was shot dead by a Union troop.

The Union soldiers knew that he was really John Wilkes Booth, the man who had assassinated President Lincoln two weeks prior. Booth sustained his leg injury when he jumped from the Ford Theatre presidential box after shooting Lincoln.

Though Dr. Mudd had strong sympathies with the Confederate cause, he claimed to have no idea that he was treating Booth. Nor did he know that the president had been assassinated until long after "Mr. Tyler" had left. The authorities were not so sure about Dr. Mudd's story. When they found Booth's personal belongings at Mudd's house, the doctor was arrested and tried for conspiracy. He was found guilty and sentenced to life in prison.

When a yellow fever epidemic broke out in the prison, Dr. Mudd provided medical assistance for both guards and prisoners. After four years of imprisonment, he was pardoned by President Andrew Johnson in 1869. He returned home, but life was never the same for the doctor. He was constantly sick, his immune system taking a toll from exposure to yellow fever. On top of that, reporters constantly hounded him and neighbors judged him. Mudd died of pneumonia in his home at the young age of 49.

Today, his home is a museum where you can find 19th-century medical instruments, items Mudd crafted in prison, and his original tombstone. You may even find Mudd himself. Several visitors have heard phantom footsteps creeping up behind them when they're alone. Others claim to see artificial candles flickering on by themselves.

If it is Mudd, he isn't alone. Up in the "Booth Room," where the assassin spent the night, employees have found a dip in the bed in the morning… when no one stayed there the night before. No matter how tightly the sheets get tucked in, there seems to be the human-shaped indentation in the bed, as if someone recently slept upon it. Paranormal investigators believe that this is the ghost of John Wilkes Booth, returning to his place of healing after committing his horrible crime.

Members of the Mudd family agree there's something off about their relative's home. His granddaughter, Louise Mudd-Arehart, remembers her dad showing them the "light," a bouncing orb that travels around the property. As a kid, she watched it in awe — an eerie chill taking over. It moved like a lost soul looking for somewhere to anchor itself.

Louise is now the owner of the Mudd House Museum, and she is convinced that her grandfather is still around to oversee things at his house.

She tells of an apparition she began seeing in the 70s, a "man wearing a long brown topcoat and cap." One night, the spirit visited her in the kitchen, so close that she felt its spectral breath like a cold breeze upon her cheek. She could see clearly now that it was the ghost of Dr. Mudd, and she instinctively knew that he was telling her something: "to save the Dr. Mudd home for the next generation." So that is what she has done to this day, and the museum continues to shed "light" upon the days of old and her grandfather's place in American history.

Dr. Samuel Mudd's House, Waldorf, MD.

HOST A GHOST

LILY

LILY - A Halloween Season Tradition

Handmade Halloween dolls like Lily were left out to frighten off pagan spirits and new world ghosts, an archaic custom dating back to the Vikings and the Romans. The tradition of protection from ghosts during October returns with LILY - HOST A GHOST

Use Lily to ward off other ghosts and ghouls around Halloween. Put Lily on a porch, hang her on a door, put her on a shelf, or use her to scare friends, family, and children. Don't put Lily in a room where you sleep! Make Lily move around and appear in a different place for others to find each morning.

WHO IS LILY? READ HER STORY HERE

Historians have tracked Lily's background to the early 1600s, unearthing reports of occult practices, pagan rituals, and warding rights imported from Europe by the Dutch Colonists of Lower Manhattan. Handmade figurines like Lily were left out to frighten off local spirits and new world ghosts, an archaic custom dating back to the Vikings and the Romans. The conquers of foreign lands brought with them a piece of their folklore as protection. The original Lily was delivered to a paranormal research group from its owner, who stated: "I found her outside my door one morning, with a note that said to not put her by mirrors or in the same room I sleep in. I gave her a flashlight so she could drain the batteries, but instead she made my lights flicker at night. My cat would not go near her, and my dog would just stare. At times I would be woken up from a dead sleep smelling burnt toast, or sometimes a sweet fruity smell. Her favorite color is red. That is all I know."

Upon further research, the doll was crafted to mimic the infamous Elizabeth Bàthory de Eased, and in doing so, the tradition stated she contains part of the Countess' menace. Báthory was a noblewoman condemned in the 1600s for killing over 650 people, and is referred to as the 'Blood Countess' and 'Countess Dracula'.

LILY is a **limited-edition** doll reproduced alongside the original Lilly. She's the best option to spice up the spirit of Halloween season in your home, and the perfect gift for any person or family, as she can both protect, and haunt! Bring Lily home and experience the supernatural first hand... **If you dare!**

usghostadventures.com/lily

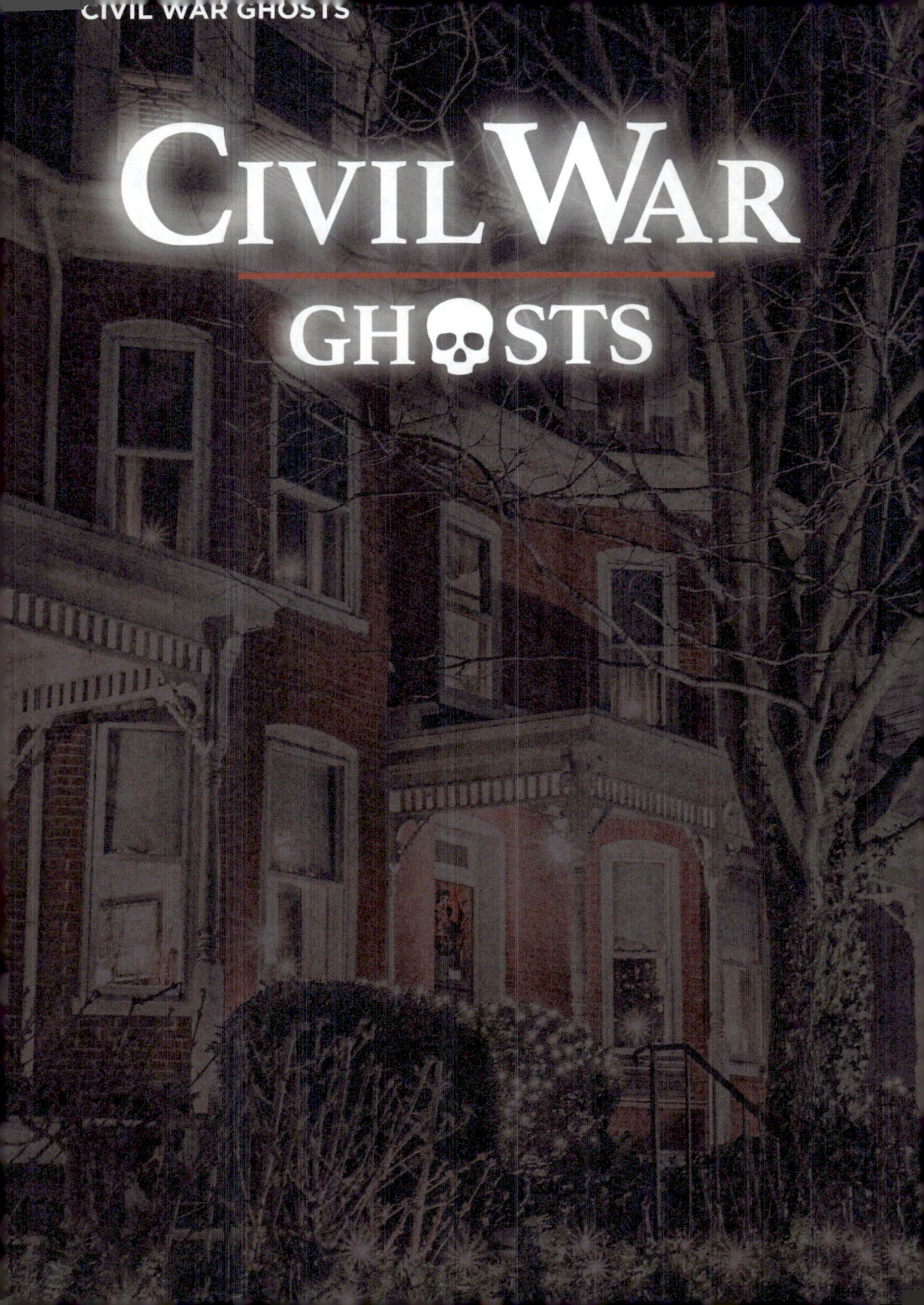

CHAPTER III

The Ghosts of Gettysburg

On July 1, 1863, the Civil War came to Gettysburg, Pennsylvania. If the hundreds of ghost stories are anything to go by, it never left.

For three days, there was nothing but chaos — the flash of gunpowder, the boom of cannons, the relentless rhythm of horses galloping toward the enemy. Bullets flew through the streets as screaming, wounded men were carried into houses. And then there was silence, and the silence was worse.

By the end of the bloody, three-day battle, over 7,000 bodies blanketed the fields outside of town. More than 33,000 others lay wounded in makeshift hospitals, their amputated limbs piled in the corners of bedrooms and churches. Every inch of Gettysburg had been touched by death, but they wouldn't realize its lasting impact until much later.

Today, the town is a cherished historic site that welcomes a million visitors a year. Sites like Soldiers' National Cemetery and the Jennie Wade House cover all sides of the battle — but the real stories unfold in the shadows, when there's no one else around. Hotel guests are jolted awake by phantom voices. Drivers spot hazy apparitions through their windshields. The battle plays out, all over again, when the sun sets behind those vast fields.

The following chapters contain spine-tingling descriptions of Gettysburg's most haunted locations, from a Confederate hideout to a museum that locks you in a room with Lincoln's ghost. The town may do their best to teach the history of the war, but there's no better historian than the dead.

usghostadventures.com/gettysburg

Rupp House

Rupp House, Gettysburg, PA.

As the battle raged on Baltimore Pike, John Rupp watched the fighting from his basement hideout. His account of the violent, three-day battle is now a treasured artifact at the Adams County Historical Society. It seems his house recorded the battle too.

The Rupp House at 451 Baltimore St. was in a unique position during the fighting. It became its own separate battlefield. Union soldiers on the porch exchanged fire with Confederate soldiers in the rear, littering the floor with spent bullets, and forcing Rupp to remain in the basement for over 48 hours.

"I gathered up a double [handful] of Minie Balls in my [dwelling] after the battle that [were] shot into it from [both] armies," Rupp wrote. "If you could have heard the shells fly over our house from [both] sides. It was awful… [General] Steinweir told me we had 330 [cannons] in play, and you may know the rebs had as many more. It was awful thunder."

Across the street, he could see the Welty House, where confederate sharpshooters were aiming at the Union men on Cemetery Hill. Between those two positions was the McClellan House, where Virginia Wade was baking bread for the soldiers. Today, she's known as "Jennie Wade," the only civilian casualty of the battle. Rupp likely saw the bullet that shot and killed her — though he didn't realize it until the battle ended.

"Virginia Wade was killed while [kneading] up her bread for her sister up in the house that Ellen Frieberger used to live," Rupp wrote. "Several others were hit on the shin with spent balls, [where] if [they] had stayed in [their] houses, [it] would not have happened [to] them."

Rupp didn't dare move until the last shot had been fired. When the dust finally settled on July 4th, he gingerly removed the furniture he had used to barricade the basement door and climbed the stairs. What he found was a complete mess. His house had been ransacked — every morsel of food stolen. The walls were riddled with bullet holes and the floors were covered in minie balls.

Rather than try to rebuild the house, John decided to tear it down and erect a new one on the property. It would be called the "grandest house on Baltimore Hill" when it was finished. After the horrors of 1863, the Rupps were getting a fresh start — or so they thought. As soon as the house was completed, the Rupps began experiencing tragedy after tragedy. Their one-year-old daughter died in 1868. Months later, their eldest daughter fell into a pile of hot ashes and sustained debilitating burns. A few years after that, two of their sons succumbed to encephalitis.

By the time John Rupp fell ill with dysentery in 1871, the family had grown used to constant heartache. He died at the age of 46.

Today, the Rupp House is a children's museum designed for elementary school kids and their families. But no matter how family-friendly the programming is, the house continues to terrify visitors.

Guests at the Brickhouse Inn have photographed a ghostly face peering through the museum window late at night. A disembodied male voice is said to float through empty rooms. Random cold spots send a chill down the spines of visitors.

Many believe it's John Rupp lingering in the house that was supposed to be his "fresh start." His death was so tragic and abrupt that his spirit is eternally tied to the property, even though his family ended up moving away.

Rupp may be the museum's only spirit, but he isn't the only *haunting*.

It's said the house replays the sounds of war — the gunfire, the cannon blasts. Dozens of people have reported hearing metallic, clinking noises as they're walking through the exhibits. No one could figure out why for months, until someone pointed out this fact:

Springfield Model 1861 rifles were loaded via ramrod, which made a distinct "clink" against the barrel of the gun. The soldiers fighting at the Rupp House would have had to reload their weapons over and over again, since each bullet was loaded individually. It's possible those repeated actions created a residual haunting.

Residual hauntings are recordings of past events. These are especially common when something traumatic has happened, like a murder, or — in this case — a violent battle. Certain actions become imprinted on the place and they start to replay, like a broken record.

While Rupp was taking in the sights and sounds of the battle raging around him, so was his home. The two ended up eternally linked, and their ghostly activity does more to educate visitors than any document or exhibit ever could.

———

Below are excerpts from John Rupp's 1863 letter to his sister-in-law, Anne. The letter was donated to the Adams County Historical Society in 1966, where it was transcribed by Timothy H. Smith. These excerpts are taken from Smith's version.

Our house was under fire of boath armies from Thursday morning until Saturday morning. An I hardly know whare to begin to tell of you about our trials… The Rebs had my Tannery in thair possession for four days thay used the shop for a fort. It was full of Rebs firing on our pickets up at Welty's fence…

The Rebs occupied the whole of town out as far as the back end of my house. Our men ocupied my porch, and the Rebels the rear of the house, and I the cellar… Our men knew I was in the cellar, but the Rebs did not. I could hear the Rebs load thair guns, and fire. Thair was one of our men killed under my big oak tree in the lot, and one in Snyders meadow close to our house…

I sustained no loss in Stock, but the Rebs broke all the glass and sash in the shop. I gathered up a double hand full of Minie Balls in my dwelling after the battle that ware shot into it from boath armies. If you could have heard the shells fly over our house from boath sides. It was awful. I cannot describe it to you …

Virginia Wade was killed while neading up her bread for her sister up in the house that Ellen Frieberger used to live… Our house is pretty well riddled, thay balls passing through our bed steads…I think we have given the Rebs a sample of Penn life in wich thay will remember Gettysburg.

Jennie Wade House

Jennie Wade House, Gettysburg, PA.

As John Rupp watched the battle unfold from his basement, Virginia "Jennie" Wade was baking bread in her sister's kitchen down the street. She refused to let the Union troops go hungry. Her fiance, Jack, was a Union corporal, and she carried his photo in her apron pocket as she baked.

She had no idea Jack had died in a hospital outside of Winchester, Virginia, two weeks earlier… or that she was about to join him.

Around 8:30 a.m. on July 3, 1863, Jennie was standing in the kitchen when a stray bullet shot through two doors, striking her in the shoulder and piercing her heart before coming to a stop in her corset. She fell to the floor with a loud crash, causing her mother to come running into the room. When she saw her daughter, she screamed. Jennie was dead.

The house had been under heavy fire all morning. Jennie's sister, Georgia, had been jolted awake by a bullet crashing through the window and landing on her pillow — right beside her newborn baby. Jennie had remarked that if anyone were to die in the house, she hoped it was her.

Now the Wades were shocked and numb, staring down at Jennie's body.

Two Union soldiers heard the commotion and ran into the house to check on the family. That was the worst thing they could have done. Confederate sharpshooters opened fire on the house, blocking all of the exits. The terrified family was trapped.

After some creative maneuvering, they managed to move Jennie's body down to the basement, where the cool air would stave off decay. They laid her on a table, covered in a sheet, and prayed for the fighting to end. It would take 17 hours, but the gunfire finally ceased.

They buried Jennie's body on the property on July 4, 1863. There were no other options at that point. Thousands of dead soldiers had overwhelmed the town cemeteries and they couldn't delay her burial any longer. She was eventually reinterred at Evergreen Cemetery, close to her fiance, Jack. Her burial site is the most-visited grave at the cemetery. It's also one of only two graves of American females that has a flag flying over it 24/7. The other grave is Betsy Ross's in Philadelphia.

Though her body was laid to rest almost half a mile away, her spirit remains at the McClellan House — now known as the Jennie Wade House Museum. People have seen her misty figure baking bread in the kitchen. They've smelled a mix of freshly baked bread and floral perfume wafting through the ground floor.

The house looks the same as it did in 1863, bullet hole and all, so Jennie may not know she's dead. The prevailing theory is that she's still waiting for her fiancé to return home. They say if you place your left ring finger in the bullet hole in the door, your significant other will propose — a little gift from Jennie Wade herself.

In the basement, paranormal investigators have captured floating orbs and snippets of conversations with the spirits of the house. The name "Jennie" has been recorded several times, by several different teams. They believe the Wades linger there, still guarding the space where Jennie's body was placed.

But the Wades aren't the only spirits in the house. There are at least two children there. One afternoon, a school group was touring the second floor when they saw a little boy wearing a white shirt and suspenders sitting at the bottom of the stairs. The boy turned and looked at them, made eye contact with the tour guide, and then vanished. The kids were so scared that a few of them refused to come down the stairs.

Some folks can't stand being on the second floor for more than a few seconds. It's associated with dread, panic, sadness, and bouts of nausea. Soldiers had

The Ghosts of Gettysburg, PA.

to carry Jennie's body up the stairs and break through a brick wall to get her to safety — all while fleeing from Confederate gunfire. Jennie's mother and sister were probably terrified as they watched the soldiers slam their guns into the brick over and over, and those emotions may have imprinted on the house.

It's said the Jennie Wade Museum is the most emotional site in Gettysburg. It's a moment of terror frozen in time — one that reminds us that war isn't contained to neat, bordered battlefields.

Jennie Wade Museum, Gettysburg, PA.

Who Killed Jennie Wade?

Since the morning of July 3, 1863, Gettysburg has been asking, "Who killed Jennie?"

The McClellan House was a sitting duck between the confederate sharpshooters on Baltimore Pike and the union soldiers on Cemetery Hill. The townspeople believed the fatal bullet could have come from either side.

Years later, historians proposed the "Farnsworth House Theory" — that the bullet had originated from the Farnsworth House attic, where rebel sharpshooters were holed up behind a small window. But recent studies have shown the bullet may have come from the Welty House, which was closer.

At the time of the battle, lush, large trees and fencing surrounded the McClellan House. With the addition of the foliage by the window, the only direct shot into the home was through a break in the trees directly in front of and to the left of the side door.

The Welty House (now part of the Brickhouse Inn Bed and Breakfast) is just across Baltimore Street, roughly 423 feet up the hill from the Farnsworth House. This location also served as a sharpshooter's hideout, and this house is 0.1 miles from the Wade House, a mere 528 feet. That short distance would have made all the difference.

If the fatal shot came from the upstairs of the Welty House, it would have been nearly horizontal with the Wade House, allowing it to smash through two doors and enter the kitchen.

Either way, it's likely the soldier who killed Jennie Wade was also killed during the battle. Both the Welty House and the Farnsworth House are haunted by confederate soldiers whose final moments were exactly like hers: the flash of gunpowder, the sting of a minie ball. In the end, they were all victims of war, and regardless of what side they were on, they're united in death.

Farnsworth House

Farnsworth House, Gettysburg, PA.

As the Wades dodged bullets, Union soldiers were preparing to storm Harvey Sweeney's attic, where Confederate sharpshooters had been wreaking havoc for two days. Today, the house is one of Gettysburg's most famous, and most haunted, landmarks: The Farnsworth House Inn.

You'll often see people standing outside, staring up at the roof. A long brick wall on the left side leads up to a tiny attic window. That's where rebel snipers were holed up between July 2nd and July 3rd, taking turns shooting their rifles at the Union men on Cemetery Hill. The Union's response is still visible on the wall, in the form of dozens of white pockmarks. By the third day of battle, they realized shooting at bricks wasn't working. The only way to take out the sharpshooters was to storm the house — so they did. It was violent and bloody. There's no death count or detailed record of the attack, but we know the attic was stained with blood, and there was more death to come.

After the battle, the house served as a small hospital, healing wounded soldiers who had been trapped in the harried gunfire. Amputations were common, and infection and disease were almost guaranteed. Many of the soldiers who ended up in makeshift hospitals would die there, and the Farnsworth House was no exception.

In the years after the war, the house changed hands several times before Loring and Jean Schultz took over in 1972. That's when it became the "Farnsworth House," named for Brigadier General Elon J. Farnsworth, a little-known Union martyr.

But the ghosts of the house have since overshadowed him.

The bed and breakfast is said to house *at least* 16 spirits. The moment the Schultzes opened for business, those spirits made themselves known.

The property manager became a quick and easy target as she made her way through the halls at night. Unseen eyes seemed to watch her every move at every single moment. She recounts voices whispering from shadowed corners of rooms and sightings of what can only be ghosts flickering at the corner of her vision.

One evening, she arrived at work just in time to hear footsteps anxiously pacing the attic above her. Ever so slowly, she worked up the courage to investigate the noise, but the only thing she could find was strange, red-colored dirt scattered all over the floor. That night, when no one was around, footsteps crossed the attic above her head, moved down the noisy stairs, and slowly crept into her room. That was her breaking point.

The woman hired a psychic to visit the property in the hopes that they could provide some much-needed answers. The moment the psychic entered the Farnsworth House, she was bombarded with a heavy wave of emotions: sadness, loneliness, and rage echoed back to her from the floors and walls.

As she ventured deeper into the house, the psychic picked up on three distinct entities roaming the property. Two male spirits came forward and identified themselves as Walter and George Sutton III, but the final ghost had a quiet presence and shunned all attempts at communication.

Later that night, the property manager did some research on the names the psychic had given her. What she found sent a chill up her spine. George Sutton III had been part of a regiment of rebel soldiers from Savannah, Georgia. He was one of the soldiers holed up in the Sweeney House attic on July 3rd, and he was known to have boots caked in Georgia red clay.

Encounters with spirits at the house have only increased throughout the years — especially when guests and employees least expect it. The property manager remembers one night when she had just arrived at work when the forms of three Confederate soldiers suddenly emerged from the basement, carrying a large, coffin-sized box between them. Her mouth dropped open as the nearest soldier slowly turned to acknowledge her through the darkness. She is convinced it was none other than George Sutton, III, ceaselessly continuing his tragic duties.

While George roams the attic and grounds, the spirit of Walter slips throughout the house in search of humans to torment — especially women. One night, there was a report of hands clamped tightly around someone's throat, choking them awake. A ghostly presence can sometimes be felt, and guests still swear they can hear voices that make them question if they really are spirits, whispering unintelligibly to them from the darkness.

Women in the kitchen have been shocked when their apron strings are pulled, there is a severe chill in the air in certain rooms, and no one has any explanation for the sounds of unnerving, ethereal music permeating from the attic.

Today, the Farnsworth House remains so active with ghosts that the property manager offers ghost tours for brave and curious souls. Many people have reported feeling unseen hands incessantly tap them on their shoulders while on tour. One can only hope the spirit is George, because if it's Walter, you better cross your heart and hope not to die.

Gettysburg Battlefield

East Cemetery Hill, Gettysburg Battlefield, Gettysburg, PA.

East Cemetery Hill

On the outskirts of town — just past the "Welcome to Historic Gettysburg" sign — you'll find a quiet stretch of grass dotted with trees and statues. This is East Cemetery Hill, the beginning of the Gettysburg battlefield.

During the day, it's a peaceful, solemn space. Tour groups meander around the field and cars crawl past. At night, it's a completely different scene. The sounds of Union artillery fire break the silence — echoes of the night Oliver Howard's Eleventh Corps defended the hill from advancing rebs.

Howard's choice to establish a Union base on Cemetery Hill would earn him the Medal of Honor, but he would go through hell to get it. The Confederates quickly took control of the town, climbing into the upper floors and attics of every house and business. From there, they could fire their rifles through the windows and shield themselves behind brick walls. Between Howard and the snipers stood rows of greybacks: Harry Hays's Louisiana Tigers and Isaac "Ike" Avery's North Carolinians.

On the night of July 2nd, they launched their attack.

Shooting blindly through darkness and smoke, the two armies clashed for hours, littering the field with minie balls and fallen soldiers. As soon as one man fell, another would appear — like a ghost — running through the thick, gray smoke. They stabbed each other with muskets and swords. They whipped each other with pistols. The Union's cannons mowed down rows of enemy soldiers with a single blast. A wounded private watching from a window recorded that he saw "heads, arms, and legs flying amid the dust and smoke…"

In the chaos, the Yanks managed to knock Ike Avery off his famous white horse with a fatal shot to the neck. Bleeding and partially paralyzed, the Confederate leader removed a scrap of paper and a pencil from his pocket and scribbled the words: "Major, tell my father I died with my face to the enemy." The blood-stained note is preserved at the North Carolina State Archives.

Hays's Louisiana Tigers didn't fare any better.

The major carrying the Tigers' colors was killed by a member of the 75th Ohio, causing the flag to fall limp onto the grass. A group of Union men ripped it to shreds and kept pieces of it as souvenirs.

In the end, the hill was littered with dead soldiers from both sides, but the Union had held their position. They would deliver the final blow to Lee's army the next day, a mile south of where Avery and the Tigers fell. Today the site is known as the High Water Mark of the Confederacy.

The Union's victory was bittersweet, however.

Some 23,000 northern soldiers lay wounded or dead across Gettysburg. Every home, business, and church was filled with suffering men — their amputated limbs piled as high as the picket fences outside — and every field was blanketed by corpses. The carnage was captured by an unnamed New Jersey soldier:

"Upon the open fields… lay the dead. Some with faces bloated and blackened beyond recognition, lay with glassy eyes staring up at the blazing summer sun; others, with faces downward and clenched hands filled with grass or earth, which told of the agony of the last moments. Here a headless trunk, there a severed limb; in all the grotesque positions that unbearable pain and intense suffering contorts the human form, they lay."

The Ghosts of Gettysburg, PA.

Gettysburg alone had claimed the lives of over 7,000 soldiers — and the war wouldn't end for another 21 months.

Today, Cemetery Hill is blanketed by memorials and markers instead of bodies. On one side, you'll find Evergreen Cemetery. On the other: Soldiers' National Cemetery. The latter was established in November of 1863 in an effort to properly bury and honor the Union dead — but no amount of statues could erase the pain and suffering of war, and the dead were never truly laid to rest.

In the last few decades, hundreds of tourists have experienced spectral activity on the battlefield. Orbs and foggy outlines appear in photographs. Music floats over the empty fields. After Pickett's Charge ended in disaster, the Confederate Army Band welcomed back survivors with a solemn rendition of "Nearer my God to Thee." Their bugles and woodwinds still echo in the night, accompanied by the *clomp* of horses' hooves.

In September of 2020, a tourist captured spine-chilling video evidence of an apparition running in front of two cannons. Though internet sleuths have since debunked the footage, the man says he knows what he saw. He's backed by dozens of others.

Much of the activity reported at East Cemetery Hill comes from the guests at the Inn at Cemetery Hill. They've been jolted awake by phantom cannon fire. They've heard footsteps following them through the halls. They've felt eyes on them as they're lying in bed.

One guest heard a man wheezing in the darkness of his room. After switching on the lamp, he found a hazy apparition of a Confederate soldier hovering at the end of his bed. The ghost was missing both legs, and it was gripping the bedpost as it gasped for air. Too stunned to speak, the man watched as the apparition took one last, heaving breath and faded from view.

It's possible the soldier died where the hotel now sits — his legs taken by a Union cannon blast. Now his restless spirit is forced to relive his final moments over and over in front of horrified guests. And that isn't even the most shocking ghost story from the battlefield.

East Cemetery Hill, Gettysburg Battlefield, Gettysburg, PA.

Gettysburg Battlefield

Devil's Den, Gettysburg Battlefield, Gettysburg, PA.

Devil's Den

Four miles south of East Cemetery Hill, there's a rocky formation known as "Devil's Den." How it got that name, no one knows. There's a longstanding legend that early Gettysburg settlers saw a giant snake-like creature lurking between the boulders, and they dubbed the entire formation "Devil's Den" — but that's never been proven.

Regardless, it's earned the name since then.

On the second day of the battle, Devil's Den became a Confederate stronghold. Rebels filled every groove and crevice, using the bullet-proof rock as a natural shield against Union gunfire from Little Round Top, but the high ground proved to be the better position. One soldier wrote, "We whipped the Devil in his Den, but Round Top ran up too much toward the heavens."

Union canon fire rained down on the rocky fort, killing over 1,800 Confederate soldiers. Another 800 were lost on the Union side. In the grisly aftermath, their bodies lay in mangled positions where they fell over the rocks — some slung over a ledge, others in crevices. The dramatic scene attracted photographers Alexander Gardner and Timothy O'Sullivan, who traveled to Gettysburg to capture the carnage.

But it seems reality wasn't quite "picture perfect." By the time the men reached Devil's Den on July 6, many of the bodies had been buried, and the battlefield didn't look like a "harvest of death" anymore. Gardner may have been feeling desperate. He was running out of time, and he needed at least one more dramatic shot.

So, Gardner's famous photo, "Home of a Rebel Sharpshooter," was *staged*.

He dragged a Confederate soldier's body over 40 yards to a stone wall at Devil's Den, and leaned a prop gun against the stones. When the photo was published, it was accompanied by a theatrical caption describing the sharpshooter's final moments. The visual had its intended effect: Americans were shocked by the violence of Gettysburg. Even today, many people defend Gardner's "creative license," saying he was only recreating what had been erased by burial parties.

But the spirits of Devil's Den have a very different take.

Thousands of people visit Devil's Den each year, and many of them bring cameras, hoping to snap an Insta-worthy photo on the infamous rocks. But cameras and smartphones tend to die, shut off, or malfunction as soon as they get near the area. Perhaps the Confederate soldier is angry he was used as a prop?

It's also worth noting that the Gettysburg Battlefield wasn't always a solemn, protected site. From 1888 to 1902, there was an amusement park at Devil's Den. People would host parties there and have a photographer take their photo posing in front of the rocks. Photography was a new invention at that time, so this was a huge novelty for tourists. There was very little respect for the dead… so it seems the dead are demanding respect now.

It's said the Gettysburg battlefield will make a believer of a skeptic. Many people have admitted to feeling a strange, "heavy presence" as they walked the battlefield — like nothing they'd ever felt before. They were walking in the footsteps of 160,000 soldiers. And, whether those soldiers lived or died, each one left a piece of their soul in the fields of Gettysburg.

Sachs Covered Bridge

Sachs Covered Bridge, Gettysburg, PA.

On the outskirts of the battlefield, there's a red wooden bridge with a bloody history.

By day, Sachs Covered Bridge is one of Gettysburg's most picturesque landmarks. Couples pose in front of its latticed woodwork, and history buffs breathe in the ambiance of Pennsylvania's "most historic bridge." But at night, this pedestrian walkway becomes a ghost hunter's paradise. Legend has it three Confederate soldiers were hung there, and they weren't hung by the Union. They were executed by their own men.

Though the famous faces of Gettysburg are all older men (Robert E. Lee was 56 and George Meade was 47), the majority of soldiers were in their teens and twenties. Brothers, friends, and schoolmates enlisted together, spurred on by a sense of adventure and duty. But they quickly found that fighting a war was not as glorious as they had pictured.

Soldiers deserted, on both sides, for a variety of reasons. Some were worried about their families back home. Some were physically unable to go on. Some disagreed with three-year enlistment and left after two years. Regardless of their reasoning, desertion was punishable by death. But the fields of Gettysburg were a death sentence too, and the Confederacy was outnumbered 72,000 to 94,000. Shell-shocked by the blood and screaming all around them, three soldiers slipped away from the battlefield and headed for safety. They made it as far as Sachs Covered Bridge before they were caught.

Built in 1854, the criss-cross beams on the roof were still thick and strong. Ropes were slung over the trusses, and the men were strung up to die — their lifeless bodies left hanging over the center of the bridge. Later, when the battle was lost and Lee's army retreated into Virginia, the troops likely cut them down and threw the bodies into the creek below. They would remain there until nature took its course.

As time passed, the tourism industry grew around the town, the cemetery, and the surrounding battlefield, but the bridge was largely forgotten. In 1938, it was declared Pennsylvania's "most historic bridge," but it didn't become a popular destination until 1968, when it was closed to vehicular traffic and turned into a pedestrian walkway.

People began lingering there… and the spirits didn't like that.

At night, the 100-foot-long bridge transforms into a pitch-black tunnel, its red paint reflecting like blood in the beam of a flashlight. It's exactly the kind of place that attracts ghost hunters, but some of them get more than they bargained for. Several of them have reported seeing disembodied heads floating over the center of the bridge. Sometimes they appear in the moment. Sometimes they only appear in photos. Either way, their slack jaws and cold, lifeless eyes are downright bone-chilling.

The other spirits are more subtle but no less terrifying. Many people smell the overwhelming scent of cigar smoke when they cross the bridge. Some have even felt an unmistakable *tap-tap* on their shoulder, only to find there's no one behind them. And of course, there's the distant sound of gunfire. It could be from hunters in the nearby woods… but it's often mixed in with the sound of artillery weapons.

The battle left scars on every inch of Gettysburg. Who knows what other spirits linger at the edges of town? For every famous Gettysburg ghost story, there could be hundreds left untold.

Evergreen Cemetery

Evergreen Cemetery, Gettysburg, PA.

After the last shot was fired on July 3rd, a massive thunderstorm blew through Gettysburg.

The torrential downpour washed away the blood and soot that blanketed the fields, but it also exposed the bodies that had been hastily buried in shallow graves. By the morning of the 4th, the thick stench of death had invaded the town, and citizens were faced with burying 7,000 dead soldiers. All eyes turned to Elizabeth Thorn.

Elizabeth's husband, Peter, was the superintendent of Evergreen Cemetery, the graveyard that gave "Cemetery Hill" its name. But Peter had enlisted in the 138th Pennsylvania Regiment in 1862, making Elizabeth the de facto caretaker. She had fled with her parents and three young sons when the fighting began. When she returned on July 7th, the cemetery was a trampled mess, and bodies were piled at her doorstep.

Because Evergreen was the town's largest cemetery, the townspeople expected Elizabeth to get to work burying the bodies — even though she was six months pregnant at the time. Two soldiers stayed behind to help her, but the stench of decay was so overwhelming they abandoned their shovels and left her to do the work alone. She eventually enlisted the help of her elderly father.

For six weeks, they dug grave after grave in the relentless summer heat, breathing in the putrid stink of death. As she dug, Elizabeth tried to remember that each soldier was someone's son, brother, or husband. They were more than bodies. They were people.

When her daughter was born on November 1, she named her Rose Meade Thorn after General Meade, the commander of the Union Army of the Potomac. Like Meade, Rose would suffer the high cost of war. She was sick from the time she was born until she died in 1877, at the young age of 14. Historians believe Elizabeth's constant stress during the summer of 1863 contributed to the girl's health issues.

Her sacrifices earned her the nickname "Angel of Gettysburg." She's also honored with a bronze statue at the entrance to Evergreen. It depicts a pregnant woman wiping her brow with one hand and holding a shovel with the other — a reminder of the hellish mess the townspeople were left with when the armies moved on.

But that isn't the only reminder.

As visitors drive into Gettysburg via 97 North, the sprawling, 30-acre cemetery appears on the left side of the road and the seemingly endless battlefield stretches out on the right. Peering through the car windows, passengers have spotted a ghostly figure moving from headstone to headstone with a 19th-century lantern. Its movements are accompanied by the sound of a baby crying in the distance — a sound that normally wouldn't be heard from the road.

Locals believe it's Elizabeth, still standing watch over the cemetery 160 years later.

She was interred at Evergreen in 1907, joining 66 of the 91 soldiers she buried during that miserable summer. The other 25 were moved to Soldiers' National Cemetery. Her husband and daughter are also buried there. With so many visitors passing by each day, she may be guarding their tombstones, afraid that if she lets her guard down she'll return to find the graveyard trampled and wrecked like it was in July of 1863.

When Elizabeth's spirit isn't visible, people have spotted orbs hovering over the grave markers. Orbs are believed to be little balls of spectral energy — a representation of a ghost who isn't powerful enough to manifest as a full-bodied apparition. Some are faint specks. Others are so bright they appear to make the entire headstone glow in the dark.

They could be soldiers, or they could be one of the countless Gettysburg residents buried there. James Gettys, the town's founder, is interred at Evergreen. It's also the final resting place of Jennie Wade and her fiance, Jack.

The most common report associated with Evergreen, however, has nothing to do with misty figures or orbs. It's a smell — the strong, unmistakable scent of peppermint, like a field of candy canes. It wafts through the cemetery day and night. Visitors often ask where it's coming from. Is it coming from a candy store on Baltimore St.?

No. The truth is a lot darker.

In the weeks after the battle, the stench of death was so overpowering that it spread to other towns. It was thick and sickening and inescapable. Gettysburg's only respite was peppermint oil, which residents wiped under their noses and poured onto handkerchiefs. The burial parties used it in the fields. Elizabeth likely used it at Evergreen.

So there were two starkly different smells in the aftermath of the battle: death and peppermint. One represented the violence of war, and the other represented the compassion of a town caught in the crossfire. We're lucky it's the latter that lingers in the air today.

Evergreen Cemetery, Gettysburg, PA.

Evergreen Cemetery, Gettysburg, PA.

Gettysburg College

Gettysburg College, Gettysburg, PA.

As the two armies clashed on July 1, Gettysburg College Professor Michael Jacobs was still attempting to teach math. Students' eyes drifted over to the windows, where the battle was unfolding in the fields outside — the booms of cannons interrupting Michael's lecture every few minutes.

Finally, with a begrudged sigh, he said, "We will close… You know nothing about the lesson anyhow."

The students were ushered into town, where they took shelter with the other residents, and the school — then named Pennsylvania College — became a field hospital. Though the wounded were cleared out by July 29, those few weeks in July scarred the school for all eternity. Today, it's one of the top 5 most haunted colleges in the U.S.

Pennsylvania Hall saw the brunt of the action. More than 600 confederate casualties were dragged down to the basement, where crude surgeon's tables were set up for amputations — by far the most common surgery on the field. Minie balls shattered bones and shredded muscle. If a soldier was struck in the head, chest, or torso, they were a dead man. If they were struck in the arm or leg, they had a chance at surviving, but they were going to lose the limb.

Surgeons were called "sawbones" and "butchers" because of the overwhelming amount of amputations that took place in field hospitals. It didn't help that soldiers screamed and thrashed during the procedure. Doctors used chloroform to induce twilight sleep, but it didn't knock the wounded men out completely. They were awake during the procedure; they just didn't remember it later.

The real suffering came after the amputation, when the chloroform wore off. Wounded soldiers endured phantom limb pain, horrific infections, and disease. Surgeons didn't wash their hands or their equipment. The bloodied blade that sawed off one soldier's leg would be used on the next, and the next, and the next. Twice as many Civil War soldiers died from disease as from battle wounds.

In the midst of all this, two students — Michael Colver and Horatio Watkins — stayed behind to care for the injured Confederates. The boys recorded that the pained moans of the dying echoed through the halls night and day.

Modern-day students hear the same thing.

Today, "Penn Hall" is touted as the most haunted building on campus. It's plagued by phantom moans, footsteps, and hushed whispers — all thought to be residual hauntings from its days as a hospital and morgue. But the most terrifying stories involve a time portal.

In the 1980s, two administrators were working late. The building was deserted. They got onto the elevator to head down to the basement and made idle chit-chat as they waited for the doors to open. Nothing could have prepared them for what they were about to see. The doors opened to reveal a fully functional field hospital, where doctors were preparing their saws and nurses were tending to suffering soldiers.

The pair slammed the "close door" button and headed back up to the main level — their hearts beating rapidly. They rushed to the night guard and told him what they'd just witnessed. Skeptical, he followed them back down to the basement... but this time they took the stairs. When they opened the basement door, they found a dark, empty room. No doctors. No soldiers.

For years, people believed the administrators were crazy — and then it happened again. In 2003, a student took the elevator down to the basement. When the doors opened, he saw the same scene: a chaotic field hospital. Investigators believe the elevator may be a time portal that transports the living back to 1863. Thankfully, the journey is only temporary.

The college's other famous ghost isn't associated with the Civil War. Stevens Hall is haunted by the "blue boy," a freezing cold spirit who presses his face against the windows of the dormitory. Legend has it he's an orphan who snuck into the dorm to get warm. When the house-mother discovered him, she shoved him onto the third-story window ledge to teach him a lesson. However, when she opened the window to let him back in, he was nowhere to be found.

Now he terrifies current residents by pressing his frozen blue face against the glass, begging to be let in again.

These are only *some* of the ghost stories connected to Gettysburg College. The campus is so haunted that prospective students have thrown out their acceptance letters, too terrified to even visit. Who could blame them? Would you be willing to share your dorm room with a ghost?

Gettysburg College, Gettysburg, PA.

The Ghosts of Gettysburg, PA.

Tillie Pierce House

Tillie Pierce House, Gettysburg, PA.

The Battle of Gettysburg is one of the most well-recorded events in history. Letters, journal entries, photos, and reports have been stitched together to provide a detailed account of every charge and retreat. But one of the most gripping accounts of the battle was published 26 years after the last shot was fired: "At Gettysburg, or What a Girl Saw and Heard of the Battle: A True Narrative."

It's a perfect explanation as to why 301 Baltimore St. is haunted.

Tillie Pierce was 15 when war spilled into the streets of her hometown. Like many civilians, she tried to flee to safety when the fighting started, but she ended up in the middle of the fray — holed up at a farm between Big Round Top and Little Round Top. Soon, miserable, wounded men filled the house — some begging to have their limbs amputated just to escape the pain of the bullet.

Tillie could have hid or run away. Instead, she launched into action. She retrieved water, applied wound dressings, and comforted dying soldiers. By the end of the battle, she was so disheveled her mother hardly recognized her.

In 1871, Tillie married Horace Alleman and moved to Selinsgrove, but the traumatic memories of 1863 followed her. She began sharing her battle stories with friends and neighbors, and — as friends often do — they encouraged her to publish a book. Her shocking, first-hand account of the battle was published in 1889, and the timeless narrative is still in circulation today.

Considered one of the heroines of the battle, Tillie is honored by her former hometown. The James Pierce House on Baltimore Street is now the Tillie Pierce House Inn. It's the house she returned to after tending to the soldiers at Weikert Farm. If she expected to find a better scene, she was sorely disappointed. Wounded soldiers filled every room of her childhood home… and many guests believe they never left.

The Hettie Shriver Room, also known as the "blue room," is said to be the most haunted bedroom in Gettysburg. Guests walk in to find an elegant wooden bed, a dresser with vintage mirrors, a sunny window, and a brick fireplace — all accented by the powder blue walls. It looks like a peaceful retreat, but some guests have had downright nightmarish experiences there.

Imagine peeling back the blue and white quilt and settling in for the night. The inn is dark and quiet. Shadows are dancing on the walls from the window. Suddenly, you feel a presence enter the room. You think it's your imagination until the bed dips next to your leg, like someone is sitting there. You can feel them staring at you. It takes all of your courage to switch on the lamp. When you do, the room is empty. The presence lifts. Whatever came into your room is gone.

Later that night, you hear footsteps outside your door. It could be another guest. That doesn't explain the footsteps you hear above your room, though. That's the attic. No one should be up there — especially at 2 a.m.

The next morning, you decide to check out a day early. You don't think you can spend another night in that room. As you round the corner, something catches your eye on the stairs. It's a misty figure. You think it could be a smudge on your glasses, but no — it's clearly a soldier. You can make out the faint details of his uniform. He looks your way, but you don't think he sees you. It's like he's looking straight through you at the person who was standing in your spot in 1863.

As the soldier vanishes, you think, "I'm definitely checking out early."

National Soldiers' Orphans' Homestead

National Soldiers' Orphans' Homestead, Gettysburg, PA.

When Union Sgt. Amos Humiston was found dead at the intersection of Stratton and York St., no one knew who he was. Civil War soldiers didn't wear dog tags. The only clue to his identity was a photo of his three young children, clutched tightly in his hand.

Dr. J. Francis Bourns, a surgeon from Philadelphia, knew something had to be done. By circulating the image in the papers, the surgeon finally found the family of the sergeant, and the four moved to Pennsylvania to open the National Soldiers' Orphans' Homestead in 1866.

The orphanage was well managed during the first few years of operation, but everything changed when a new matron was placed in charge of the property during the 1870s. It didn't take long for the matron's sadistic nature to emerge. Children at the orphanage endured round after round of physical abuse at her hands, withering behind closed doors until finally, they never could leave.

Rumors spread of the matron's wretchedness, of the horrible treatment of the children and the chains she had in the basement for them, and she was eventually exiled from town… but the damage had been done. Her thirst for violence and dominance had soaked into the walls, forever tainting the orphanage.

Today, it's believed children still roam the halls of the last place they called home.

Some attest they still seek refuge in the basement and can be heard whimpering softly in the darkness. Children who have made contact with the living, desperate to get their attention, tug on the clothes of passing visitors. Some hear the dead children's whispers and cries and flee the orphanage, too afraid to stay.

Others have become convinced the matron herself haunts the orphanage and taunts the living any chance she gets. She slams doors in peoples' faces and moves objects whenever she's feeling vindictive — which is often.

A few less fortunate visitors have reported walking into a room to find the dead matron lying in wait for them in the shadows, ready to stare them down until they run from the room. Whether or not you believe the tales of the horrors she inflicted upon the orphans in the 1800s, it is abundantly clear this cruel woman plans to stay.

National Soldiers' Orphans' Homestead, Gettysburg, PA.

Lincoln Train Museum

Lincoln Train Museum, Gettysburg, PA.

If there's one ghost that's mysteriously absent from Gettysburg, it's Abraham Lincoln.

When he arrived at the train station on November 18, 1863, something in the air shifted. It was as if the ghost of every Union soldier who had died there was standing at attention. Eyes followed him down the street as he entered the David Wills House, where he'd spend the night finishing his short address for the Soldiers' National Cemetery dedication ceremony. It would become one of the most iconic speeches in American history.

Standing at a podium on Cemetery Hill, he told the crowd: "The world will little note, nor long remember, what we say here, but it can never forget what they did here."

Lincoln was, of course, being modest. The Gettysburg Address has been quoted, memorized, and etched into stone. It was a defining moment in American history — and one that produced intense emotions. But no one claims to see Lincoln's ghost lingering in the cemetery. No one hears his voice at the David Wills House or sees the sheets ruffled where he slept.

The 16th president's ghost exists elsewhere, which brings us to the Lincoln Train Museum.

Tucked away on Steinwehr Avenue, the museum is a replica of the town's Civil War-era train station — the one that would have delivered Lincoln on November 18th. But it doesn't focus on that train journey. Instead, it focuses on Lincoln's funeral train.

After the president was assassinated on April 15, 1865, his body was loaded into an ornate, black funeral car to be taken back to his hometown of Springfield, IL. The train passed through most major cities between DC and Springfield — purposely heading north so it would stop in Philadelphia and New York City.

Today, people all across Ohio, Indiana, Pennsylvania, and New York claim to see a ghostly version of the famous train. Sometimes it's a misty blur with steam rising from a faint smokestack. Other times, it's clear as day. People have reported seeing a crew of skeletons operating it, with some of them standing guard over Lincoln's casket.

The sightings started as early as 1879. That year, a newspaper published a story from the workers at the Hudson River Railroad, who claimed the ghost train rushed by them one April night. They said it looked like "the outline of a train," but every detail was visible. As it passed, the rush of wind felt "cold, clammy, grave-like," and it let out a terrifying shriek as the bell clanged mercilessly.

Since then, ghost enthusiasts have gathered at the tracks every April, trying to catch a glimpse of the spooky, black steam engine under the light of a full moon. Even 158 years after his death, Abraham Lincoln is still drawing crowds.

Though the ghost train doesn't pass through Gettysburg, its journey is immortalized at the Lincoln Train Museum, where visitors get to sit in a train car with the ghostly president himself. For years, he was played by James Gettys, a phenomenal impersonator who passed away in 2015. Now both Abe and James are honored by the museum. Ghosts or not, they live on in Gettysburg, in the hearts and memories of the people they impacted.

ADDITIONAL SCARES

Voice App. Ghost Stories

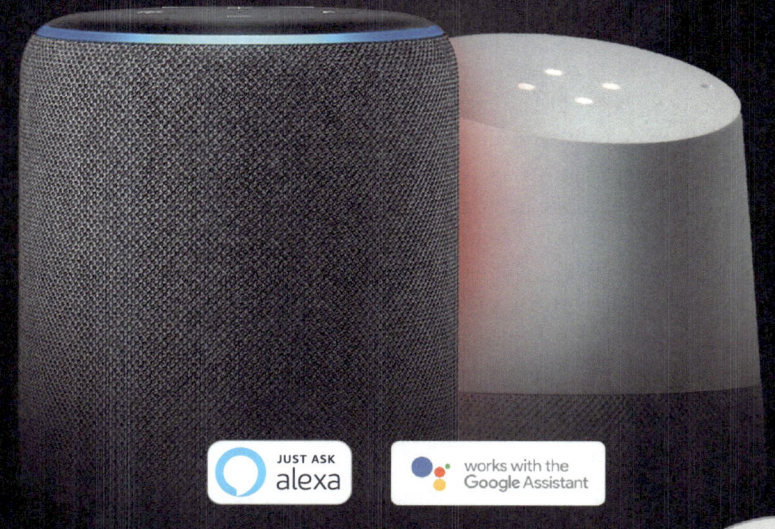

Listen to one of over 200 narrated ghost stories from home on Alexa or Google Assistant
Alexa: "Alexa, Open Ghost Adventures"
Google Home: "Hey Google, Talk to Ghost Adventures"

Who Doesn't Want To Hear a Ghost Story on Echo? ★★★★★

I love the idea of listening to a spooky story at night. The stories are all very interesting and entertaining and have been pulled from many different cities across the U.S. I would listen to them in a distraction free place so as that I can listen attentively. It's a great way to learn about US history in an engaging way. I highly recommend trying this skill, especially with a group. It is easily one of my top favorite Alexa skills for sure!
Sana - Amazon Prime Review

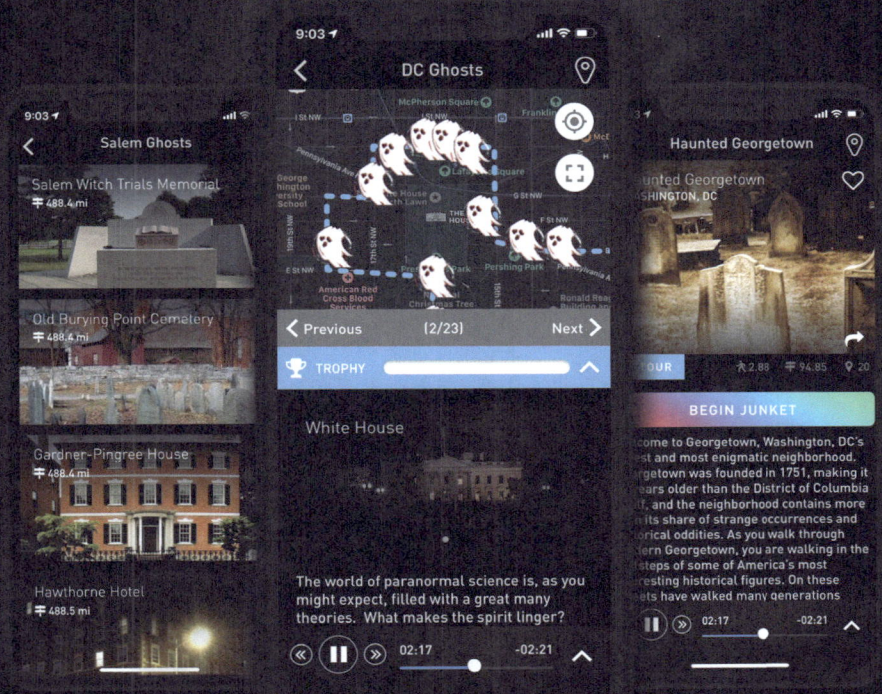

junket

Turn Your Phone Into A Ghost Tour!

Download the Junket app for GPS-based, audio guided Ghost Tours of over 25 cities across the U.S. Hear terrifying stories and see historical haunted places as the app delivers ghost tours at your fingertips!
Take a tour in person on location, or from home!

Visit wejunket.com/what-is-junket

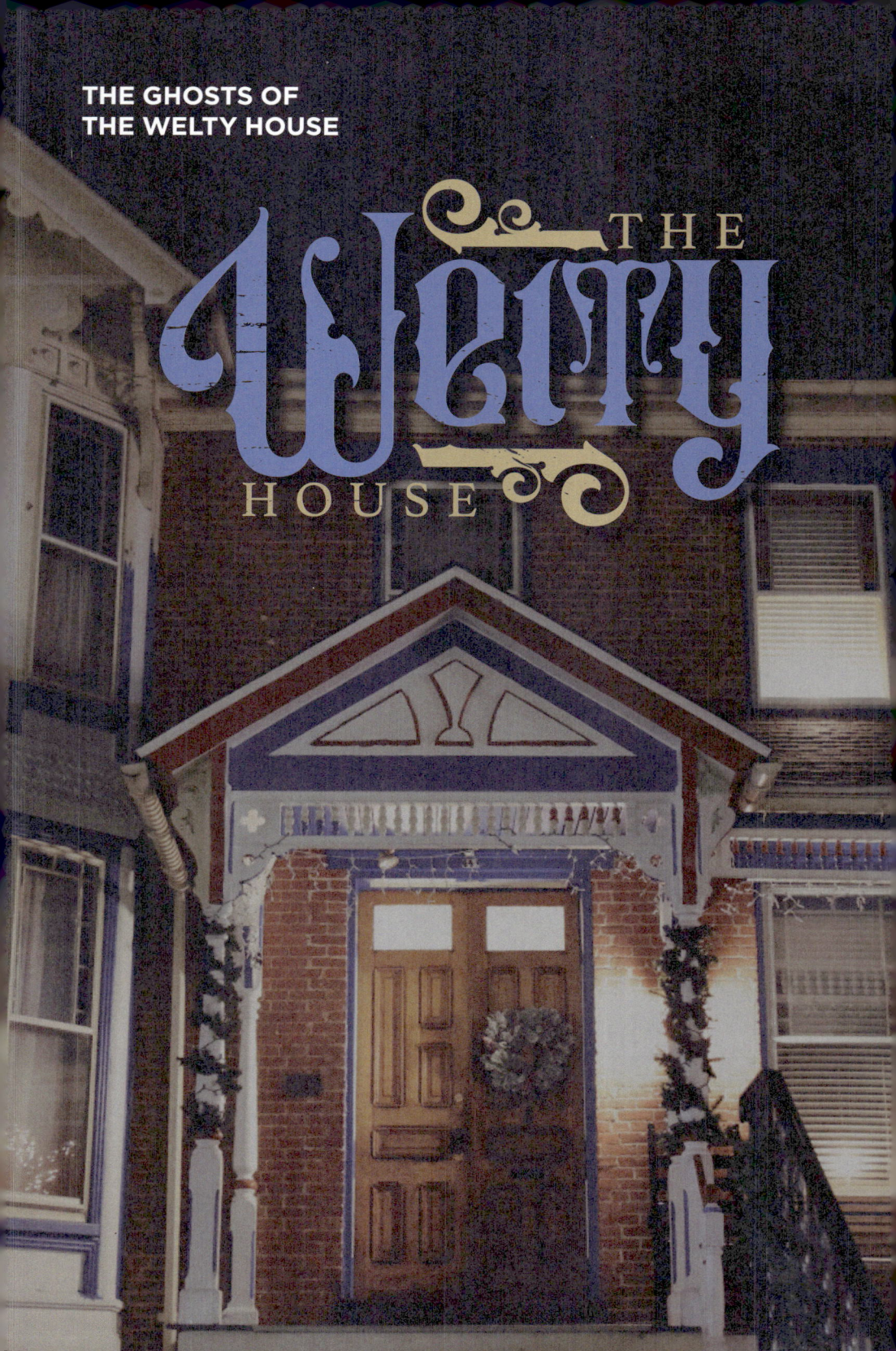

CHAPTER IV

The Ghosts of The Welty House

Solomon Welty built 452 Baltimore St. in the 1830s, when Gettysburg was still an up-and-coming town. Untouched by war, it was known for carriage manufacturing and education, and it was a fine place to build a farmhouse.

All of that changed in July of 1863.

As confederate troops poured into the streets — shouting and shooting their guns into the air — the townspeople locked their doors and shuttered their windows. Some would end up treating wounded soldiers. Others, like the Welty Family, fled to their basements to wait out the violent battle.

Finding an empty house, confederate sharpshooters quickly turned the upper floor into a sniper's nest, where they could pick off the union soldiers on Cemetery Hill. Many sharpshooters were young boys who were skilled at hunting. Now, instead of killing a rabbit for dinner, they were killing their brothers in arms. The union returned fire, striking the bricks of the farmhouse. The pockmarks are still visible 160 years later.

Across the street, John Rupp watched the violence from his cellar. In his July 19th letter to his sister-in-law, Anne, he reported, "The Rebs had my Tannery in thair possession for four days thay used the shop for a fort. It was full of Rebs firing on our pickets up at Welty's fence… "

usghostadventures.com/welty-house

At least nine union soldiers would be killed at that fence, as they tried and failed to take down the rebels spraying bullets over Cemetery Hill. In total, 36 men were buried on the property. The specifics of their deaths, however, are lost to history.

How many soldiers were holed up in the Welty House? Who were they? How did they die? Only the dead know… and it seems they may be trying to tell us.

Today, the house is part of the Brickhouse Inn Bed and Breakfast, one of the most haunted inns in historic Gettysburg. Guests are plagued by phantom footsteps, voices, and gunfire. The smell of cigar smoke wafts through the lobby. Doors open and slam on their own.

But the most nightmarish accounts come from guests who have seen the spirits of the house — ghostly Civil War soldiers, still clad in their uniforms. They stare out at the darkened streets of Gettysburg as if there's still a battle raging outside. For them, the battle never ended.

The following stories are taken from years of guest and staff reports, each one more bone-chilling than the last. If you ever book a room at 452 Baltimore St., be prepared for a history lesson you won't soon forget.

The Welty House, Gettysburg, PA.

The Welty House, Gettysburg, PA.

The Texas Room

The Texas Room, The Welty House, Gettysburg, PA.

The Protective Soldier

Located on the first floor of the Welty House, the Texas Room features a romantic canopy bed and fireplace — the perfect setting for a peaceful weekend away. That's exactly what one Pittsburgh woman was hoping for when she booked the room in May of 2022.

But her stay was anything but peaceful.

After a day of tours and window-shopping, she settled into bed next to her husband around midnight. It wasn't long before they both fell asleep. The room was warm and quiet, and they were both grateful to have a large, plush bed to snuggle into after hours of walking.

But around 2 a.m., something shifted.

The woman jerked awake. It felt like the air was vibrating around her, like she was surrounded by an electric current. Suddenly, there were cannons firing, there were bullets whizzing past her ears. She could hear horses galloping full-speed across a field. She could hear their terrified squeals as they fell to an enemy's bullet. There were shouts and screams and, under it all, there was a drum beat thumping in her chest:

Thump-thump-thump-thump. Thump-thump-thump-thump.

Frozen in bed, she was surrounded by the chaos of war. All she could do was squeeze her eyes shut and wait.

As the minutes ticked by, she felt the room shift again. A freezing cold breeze wafted over the bed. The chaos in her head began to lesson, but she was afraid to open her eyes. She knew there was something else in the room.

Sure enough, she saw a tall man looking down on her from the opposite side of the bed, where her husband was still sleeping. His gray uniform was accented by a wide-brim hat with a feather on one side, and his unkempt whiskers and wrinkles gave him a fatherly look. As she looked at the spirit, her fear was replaced with a sense of calm. He hadn't appeared to frighten her. He had come to make it go away.

She closed her eyes and took a deep breath. When she opened them again, the room was dark, quiet, and empty — save for the sound of her husband's light snores.

The ghostly soldier hasn't appeared since then, and no other guest has experienced the same paralyzing, chaotic feeling. But some guests — the ones who are more sensitive to the spirit world — say they feel a presence when they enter the room. It's strong and protective. Is the whiskered soldier protecting the living from more malicious spirits? If so, he isn't alone.

The Texas Room, The Welty House, Gettysburg, PA.

The Ghosts of the The Welty House, Gettysburg, PA.

The Illinois Room

The Illinois Room, The Welty House, Gettysburg, PA.

The Sharpshooter
One floor above the Texas Room, you'll find a large, sunlit bedroom with honey-gold hardwoods and a large bay window. The Illinois Room is one of the city's most popular stays — a historic haven with a sprawling view of Baltimore Street… But many of the guests who book it have no idea the floor under their feet was once drenched in blood and bullets.

Before Solomon Welty expanded the house, and Gettysburg developed around it, the Illinois Room faced East Cemetery Hill. The attic space above it is where sharpshooters shielded themselves from the enemy, and the poor souls who died would have been carried out through the room. What happened in that hot, cramped space? How many men were killed? And how many men did they kill in return?

One guest got a horrifying, behind the scenes look at exactly what they went through.

It was around 3 a.m. when she was jolted awake by a loud crack. She hurried to the window to see what had caused the noise, but the street was empty and quiet. In the corner of the room, she felt something strange — like someone else was in the room with her. As she turned toward the corner, she heard a rough male voice say, "Keep your head down, ma'am."

The woman gasped and ran to switch on a lamp. Golden light lit up the room… and there was no one there. She sat on the edge of the bed, her heart beating erratically, and tried to take steady, deep breaths. As she did, she could smell the thick scent of gunpowder. She stayed there with the light on for the rest of the night.

The Handsy Ghost

Months earlier, another woman had a very different experience. Kate had booked the Illinois Room for her best friend Becca's birthday. They were both self-proclaimed history nuts with a love of all things paranormal. The Welty House checked both boxes.

It was around 4 a.m. on their second night when Kate was startled awake by the thick smell of cigar smoke. It was so strong it made her cough, like someone was blowing it directly in her face.

"Do you smell that?" she rasped, but Becca was out cold.

How was she sleeping through this? Maybe someone was smoking outside and it had wafted over to her side of the room. Kate closed her eyes and waited for the air to clear, but the smell seemed to get stronger.

All of the sudden a freezing cold breeze passed over the bed and every button on Kate's silk pajama top came unbuttoned at once. She gasped and pulled her shirt closed. As she did, the cold breeze vanished and the cigar smoke dissipated… but they were replaced by something else: The sound of a woman whispering. It was muffled, like she was eavesdropping on a hushed conversation happening in another room.

Kate looked over at Becca, who was still sound asleep. Just as she was about to shake her awake, the noises stopped. Kate lay there in silence for a few moments, waiting for another sound, another breeze. Nothing happened. Whatever had been in the room with them was gone.

Who was this woman? And had she saved her from the handsy ghost who'd unbuttoned her shirt? No one knows. But one thing is certain: In the Illinois Room, the daylight hours are no safer.

Residual Hauntings

One morning, an employee was cleaning the first floor when she heard a dragging sound above her, like someone was pulling a heavy sack across the floor. When she went to investigate, the Illinois Room was empty and locked. Minutes later, it happened again. Each time she entered the Texas Room, she heard it: a distinct, loud dragging noise directly overhead.

When the manager came in later that evening, she asked her about it.

"I've heard it too," she said. "I think it's a ghost dragging a body."

It's estimated that 36 soldiers were buried on Welty's property — likely men killed in or around the house. Imagine a group of young soldiers are huddled around a small opening in the attic, sweat beading on their brows. One sidles up to the window. It's his turn to shoot. But a Union sharpshooter fires first, hitting him between the eyes. The rebels shift his body to the side and wait for some brief moment of peace, when they can drag his body through the room below, down to the yard, and bury him properly.

Now, 160 years later, the sound of that moment plays over and over like a broken record — an eternal reminder of everything they went through… and it isn't the only reminder the Illinois Room has in store.

The Officer

One April afternoon, a group walked by the room and saw a man standing at the window. Something about him caught their eye: He was wearing a pristine Civil War-era uniform. They assumed he was a reenactor getting ready to head to the battlefield, but he was standing placidly at the window, as if watching for enemy soldiers.

Suddenly, he turned to them, gave a short nod, and completely vanished.

Employees believe he's a soldier waiting for the last call that would dispel him from his spiritual active duty. His phantom harmonica can be heard emanating from the room at all hours — a jovial tune meant to provide a brief moment of joy in the midst of so much pain and suffering.

The Basement

The Illinois Room, The Welty House, Gettysburg, PA.

The Welty House basement draws paranormal investigators from around the country. Armed with EMF detectors, spirit boxes, REM-PODs, infrared cameras, thermometers, and flashlights, they venture down the dark stairwell — hopeful that a spirit will reach out to them.

They are usually rewarded with a slew of insults:

"Monster."

"Idiots."

"Danger."

The basement's resident ghost has been nicknamed "Sassy." She refuses to give up her real name, or share any personal info. Instead, she likes to hurl insults and curses at anyone who tries to talk to her. The employees are so familiar with her they treat her like a grumpy nextdoor neighbor, laughing off her scathing remarks. But Sassy isn't alone… and the other spirits are desperate to share their stories.

The Music Box

The first time someone connected with the ghostly children in the basement, it was an accident. A staff member was cleaning up after an investigation. It was late. Everyone had gone home or gone up to bed. She had just finished packing the equipment away when she heard it: The distinct sound of a music box.

Her eyes darted to the back corner, where one of the investigators had placed the small, baby blue box. She had completely forgotten about it. They didn't normally use a music box during investigations. Sassy certainly didn't interact with them.

But *something* had connected with it.

Setting the equipment crate on the floor, she walked over and picked it up. It had a golden key on the back — which had been turned slightly to the left, producing a few seconds of music. She placed it down gently and took a few steps back.

"Hi," she said. "Can you make it play music again?"

Silence.

She waited a few more minutes, but nothing happened. It was almost 3 a.m. by that point, and she was too tired to play around with ghosts. Maybe Sassy was pranking her. She turned around, picked up the equipment crate, and headed for the stairs.

There it was again. The first few notes of, "Twinkle, Twinkle Little Star" echoed through the room before stopping. It was like the ghost was asking her to stay. She stood there for a minute chewing her lip before announcing, "I'll come back tomorrow, okay? I have to go to bed."

When she came back the next evening, the little blue box had been knocked to the floor.

The Children

The second time someone connected with the ghost children, they did more than play music.

It was during an investigation. Two team members were using the Estes Method, which requires one person to wear noise canceling headphones connected to a spirit box while the other calls out questions. After thirty minutes of Sassy's usual insults, an odd question came through: "Where is my mother?"

Similar questions followed: Where are my parents? Where is my family? Where did my father go?

After a few minutes, a team member called out: "Who are you? What happened to you?"

The response was, "Let me show you."

Seconds later, the young woman wearing the noise-canceling headphones ripped them off. The sound pouring through the speakers was so loud the rest of the team could hear it. They eyed her with questioning looks.

"It just sounds like a little boy screaming," she said.

Employees believe the boy is from Rosa Carmichael's orphanage down the street, where children were locked and chained in a dungeon-like basement. Some went missing and were never found. While it's too late to save him, investigators have started leaving toys down there for the boy to play with.

No matter how neatly they're lined up, the toys are always scattered the following day.

The Illinois Room, The Welty House, Gettysburg, PA.

The Brickhouse

The Brickhouse, Gettysburg, PA.

Mysteries Abound

Though the Brickhouse Inn was constructed 35 years after the battle, the Victorian home is also plagued by the ghosts of the past. Doors often open on their own, as if a chivalrous soldier is holding it open for guests. One evening, the basement door began shaking so violently that the clipboard hanging from it swung like a pendulum.

Guests have reported seeing an odd apparition traveling through the halls. It looks like a pair of disembodied legs. There's no torso, head, or arms — just legs. The theory behind this bottom-half ghost offers a gruesome look at the aftermath of the battle.

By the fall of 1863, the union soldiers buried throughout Gettysburg had been moved to Soldiers' National Cemetery, where they were honored as heroes. The confederates were given no such honor. Instead, they were left in shallow, unmarked graves all across town. As Gettysburg developed into a tourist destination — with hotels, houses, and businesses cropping up — those remains may have been scattered.

Maybe a pile of leg bones ended up under the Brickhouse foundation, cursing the house with a pair of ghostly legs searching for their upper half. Who knows what else lurks under the centuries-old plot...

In between these stories are dozens of little mysteries — an odd sound, a smell no one can place, an object someone "swore they set down over there." There is constant activity. Most of it goes unnoticed. But the employees pay attention, and they're constantly adding new little clues to the puzzle.

But for all of the Brickhouse's mysteries, there is one ghost with an obvious backstory.

Charlie Toot
In 1891, the Weltys sold the house and surrounding lot to Harriet Toot. By then, the battle had turned Gettysburg into a tourist destination with several hotels and businesses. Each anniversary, dedication, and reunion brought crowds of people to Baltimore Street — their pockets lined with money to spend — and Harriet's son, Charlie, had found success as a banker and businessman.

In 1898, Charlie built the grand, Victorian mansion that's now the Brickhouse Inn. He dressed to match his new home — keeping his shoes shined and his lampshade mustache neatly trimmed. He lived in the house until his death in 1962, and the locals believe he's sticking around to make sure the house is kept in shape.

Numerous guests have reported seeing the "hazy image" of a man in pleated dress slacks with shiny brown shoes. Employees have heard him call their name. Some have even had a door slam behind them — a clear indication that "Charlie isn't happy."

The long-time plumber of the house has come in several times to find the hot water switch turned off. After his toolbox mysteriously moved on its own, he started bringing his wife with him if he had a late-night call. But then… the house gave her the creeps too.
Were they being pranked by an unknown soldier? Or scolded by the man of the house?

The property manager has learned to live with the unknown. Every unexplained bump, slam, and misty figure reminds her that the Brickhouse Inn Bed and Breakfast is only one chapter of 452 Baltimore St. There are hundreds of other stories etched into the walls. Some will remain a mystery forever. Others are being slowly revealed, piece by piece. Maybe the ghosts are waiting for the right person to listen to their stories… Will it be you?

JOIN OUR TEAM!

US Ghost Adventures is a great place to work, offering great pay and flexible schedules! We're always looking for skilled **storytellers** in each of our 85+ cities. If you have a passion for telling engaging stories or think you'd be great at it, please apply via the QR/website on the next page. We look forward to meeting you!

WE'RE LOOKING FOR STORYTELLERS IN EACH OF OUR 85+ CITIES.

 @usghostadventures   @usghostadv

THE GHOSTLY DETAILS

US Ghost Adventures is looking for energetic storytellers to lead walking tour groups downtown. Tours are held nightly at 8pm, last one hour to 90 minutes, and cover about one mile of ground. Candidates must be **great with people** and skilled in public speaking. This position is ideal for self-motivated candidates looking for a fun way to make extra income part-time in the evenings.

GREAT PAY
$50 – 60 per tour plus cash tips

TOUR DURATION
Approximately 90 min. and have anywhere from 2 to 35 guests.

SCHEDULE
Tours operate year-round, seven days a week.

COMMITMENT
Commit to an availability of 3 nights a week, for a period of 1 year.

RESIDENCE
Applicants must reside nearby, within 15 miles of downtown.

DARE TO JOIN OUR TEAM?

LEARN MORE & APPLY TODAY:
USGHOSTADVENTURES.COM/CAREERS

CHAPTER V

The Ghosts of Philadelphia

Every year, millions of history lovers flock to Philadelphia to bask in the hallowed halls of America's birthplace — from Independence Hall to the First Bank of the United States. These meticulously-preserved monuments have weathered every war, natural disaster, and tragedy in U.S. history, yet they still stand tall and proud, just as they did when Benjamin Franklin and George Washington roamed the streets.

But preserving history comes at a price… Three hundred years of spirits linger in the Cradle of Liberty.

Some are protectors, like the misty Revolutionary War soldier patrolling Washington Square. Some are American icons, still hard at work even in the afterlife. Others are casualties of the devastating epidemics that ripped through the city in its early years. They stand over their unmarked graves, angry and restless.

The following chapters delve into the enigmatic world of haunted Philadelphia, weaving together historical accounts, eyewitness testimonies, and extensive research to lay out the most bone-chilling stories the city has to offer. As we peel back the layers of time and peer into the shadows, one thing will become clear: The past is never truly laid to rest.

phillyghosts.com

The Ghosts of Philadelphia, PA.

Washington Square

Washington Square, Philadelphia, PA.

Philadelphia's haunted history begins with a burial ground.

In 1706, the city transformed Southeast Square — a public park designed by William Penn in 1692 — into a potter's field. They would bury any undesirables there: the poor, free and enslaved blacks, John Does, prisoners of war, suicide victims… anyone who couldn't afford, or didn't "deserve," a proper church burial.

The burials were hasty and cheap. Bodies were often interred without a coffin. They were simply wrapped in canvas and tossed into a hole.

This went on until 1783, when the Revolutionary War delivered 2,000 American and British casualties to Philadelphia's doorstep. At the time, the city had some of the best hospitals in the area. Thousands of men were transported there for treatment, and Southeast Square is where they ended up when treatment failed. Massive burial pits were dug along Walnut Street, where coffins were lined up, side by side, and covered with dirt.

Ten years later, another catastrophe would make the war look like child's play: Yellow fever.

In 1793, Philadelphia was the largest city in the U.S., with 50,000 residents packed into close quarters. It was also a major port that received ships from the Caribbean islands — ships that carried mosquitoes. One bite was all it took. The first cases of yellow fever appeared in the spring of 1793. By August, it was a full-blown epidemic.

The disease didn't discriminate. People of every age, race, sex, religion, and class fell ill. In serious cases, their skin would turn yellow with jaundice and they'd bleed from their noses, mouths, and urinary tracts. Black vomit would erupt from their throats in between fits of fevered delirium. Those patients were sure to die, while others made a quick recovery and became immune.

Unlike the Revolution, this war was impossible to win. No one knew what caused the disease or how to cure it, and it would take another century for doctors to realize the deadly illness was carried and spread by tropical mosquitoes.

The wealthy fled the city, leaving the poor to suffer. Within four months, 5,000 people had died — an estimated 10% of the population.

Believing the bodies might spread the disease, gravediggers were expected to work as quickly as possible. Southeast Square became the site of quick, sloppy burials. The smell of decay covered the square like a thick film. People died at a rate faster than they could be sufficiently buried, and graves were hastily, improperly dug. Eventually, the square was considered to be a disgusting, vile-smelling place.

By 1815, city residents were ready to end burials and transform the space into the park Penn had envisioned. Walkways were built and trees were planted, but none of the bodies were moved. The park was simply established on top of them.

Since then, a handful of people have reported feeling suddenly ill when they walk through the park. The symptoms are accompanied by feelings of dread, sadness, and abandonment — energy broadcasted by the spirits of the deceased. Only the select few can feel it, because it requires a fine-tuned sensitivity to the spirit world.

The other spirits of the park are a bit less subtle.

In the 1950s, a group of archaeologists began carefully excavating the square in search of unmarked remains. The team was shocked when they uncovered a 20-year-old soldier from the Revolutionary War with a gaping, musket ball-sized wound in his skull.

The discovery of this forgotten fallen soldier prompted the installation of a special tomb in his honor, located at the center of Washington Square. His headstone, now called the "Tomb of the Unknown Soldier," reads, "Beneath this stone rests a soldier of Washington's army who died to give you liberty."

Now, locals believe the dead soldier keeps watch over the cemetery. He is often seen on cloudy nights, slowly walking between the headstones. Some believe the poor man's apparition is doomed to wander the grounds until his identity is finally known — but at least he isn't alone.

For decades, people have seen the misty figure of a woman standing watch over the park. It's rumored she was tasked with guarding the graveyard after the Revolutionary War. She may have been the wife of a fallen soldier — someone who would have been dedicated to shooing away body snatchers and curious animals.

Whoever she is, she's fiercely protective of the dead... so it's best not to cross her.

Washington Square, Philadelphia, PA.

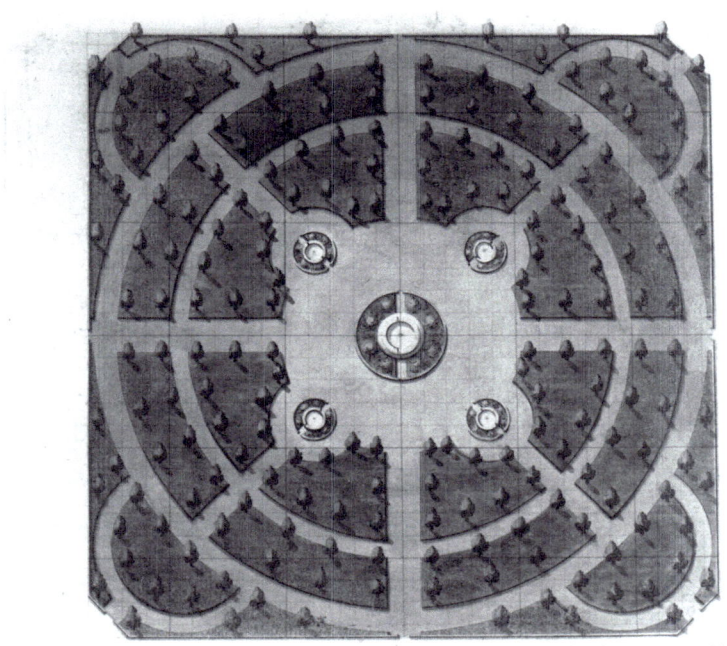

Washington Square, Philadelphia, PA.

The Ghosts of Philadelphia, PA.

Independence Hall

Independence Hall, Philadelphia, PA.

Marked by its iconic steeple, red brick, and white windows, Independence Hall transports visitors to 1776 before they even step inside. It's where the Second Continental Congress met and signed the Declaration of Independence; it's where George Washington was named Commander in Chief of the Continental Army; and it's where the U.S. Constitution was ratified when the war ended.

Dozens of men traveled to Philadelphia to help craft the nation's government, but Benjamin Franklin was on his home soil. It seems the Pennsylvania delegate never left…

Tourists and park rangers have witnessed his ghost on numerous occasions. He's typically hunched over the Declaration of Independence, put on display in the very room where it was signed. Some wonder if he routinely mulls over its contents as political turmoil continues in the country.

The founding father's appearance is always accompanied by an inexplicable mist and a pungent, musty odor. All five senses are assaulted by his presence, and that may have been how his peers felt about him when he was alive.

Franklin was originally from Boston, but he fell in love with Philly in 1723. He worked tirelessly to improve the city over the next 67 years, developing a fire brigade, an insurance company, a college, a hospital, and the Philosophical Society he's famous for. When he died of pleurisy in

1790, almost half the city attended his funeral — so you'll find his ghost all throughout Philadelphia.

While rare, a person can haunt multiple places at once, because each ghost represents a different piece of them. At Independence Hall, Franklin is in his political element, arguing and agonizing over the laws of a new nation. At the American Philosophical Society, he's younger and more playful, dancing and flirting with women.

That ghost has the library all to himself, but Independence Hall is a different story. There's another spirit there, haunting the building out of pure spite.

In 1780, Benedict Arnold was convinced he was on the brink of a promotion in the Continental Congress. When he was steadfastly overlooked for the position, he became bitter and angry at the new government. He betrayed his fellow patriots and joined forces with the British not long after.

After the Revolutionary War ended, Arnold was officially exiled from America and told never to attempt to return. He spent the rest of his life in England, still riddled with bitterness over everything that had occurred during the war.

Upon his death, Arnold's spirit traveled back to the U.S., where he set up shop in the very place that had started his lifelong pursuit of vengeance: Independence Hall. His ghostly figure has been seen in 18th-century attire, walking around by himself on the first floor. Witnesses suspect even in death Arnold doesn't dare to venture any higher within the building, for fear of running into Ben Franklin.

Both immortalized in American history in very distinct ways, these two spirits seem determined to haunt Independence Hall indefinitely.

Independence Hall, Philadelphia, PA.

American Philosophical Society Library

American Philosophical Society Library, Philadelphia, PA.

In 1743, Benjamin Franklin enlisted the help of George Washington, Alexander Hamilton, and Thomas Jefferson to fund and build the American Philosophical Society Library.

The library is a treasure trove of information about the Revolutionary War and houses 13 million manuscripts, 350,000 periodicals, and over 250,000 images. But this library contains more than just historic documents… It's also home to Franklin's ghost.

Some residents speculate Franklin has been haunting the library since 1790, but the first *official* account came from a cleaning lady who encountered his ghost in 1844. She had just turned down a row of bookshelves when she came upon his specter, clad in 18th-century clothing, muttering incessantly under his breath. Utterly shocked, the woman ran away but could still hear his voice trailing after her as she fled.

This was only the first in a series of encounters she would have with him. Franklin made an appearance a few days later…and a few days after that. As the founding father grew more comfortable around her, he also grew more troublesome. She frequently came to work to find books strewn all over the place in messy piles. Franklin's ghost appeared between the aisles, always eerily muttering to himself.

One day, she was hard at work cleaning the library when — out of nowhere

— the spirit appeared and knocked her to the ground as he rushed past. Shocked and hurt, the cleaning woman eventually mustered up the courage to seek him out and reprimanded him for his actions. He kept his distance after that, settling for staring at her from behind bookshelves.

But he could only behave himself for so long.

By the mid-twentieth century, he was back to his usual hijinks — only this time he was even bolder with the ladies. Several female visitors reported seeing his misty figure staring at them. Some even had their bums pinched.

Outside, Franklin is even more disruptive. There's a statue of him posing above the entrance to the library. Clad in a Romanesque toga, he's standing tall with his right arm leaning on a stack of books, and his right hand pointing a scepter down at the ground. It was meant to symbolize his belief that republics would replace monarchies.

But some claim the scepter is used as a dancing prop late at night. Legend says the statue comes to life and dances down the street. Multiple people have reported seeing it. They've even seen the statue enter a local pub called City Tavern.

Hearing the rumors about Benjamin Franklin's supernatural statue, one man flew to Philadelphia to put it to the test. With an electromagnetic field (EMF) meter in hand, he approached the statue. The moment he got close, the meter started going crazy. The man was shocked to see the reading was off the charts.

Another tourist was taking photographs of various buildings in the city when she came across the American Philosophical Society Library. She snapped a couple of photos and moved on without a thought. When she reviewed her photos later on, she was horrified to see an eerie figure staring at her from one of the library windows.

Franklin takes many shapes and forms to haunt the library, as well as the rest of Philadelphia. It's abundantly clear that our founding father has not let death keep him from pursuing life's pleasures, both good and bad.

First Bank of the United States

First Bank of the United States, Philadelphia, PA.

Established in 1791, the First Bank of the United States is tied to one of America's most famous murders: The duel between Vice President Aaron Burr and former Secretary of the Treasury Alexander Hamilton.

Incredibly keen in finance, Hamilton was generally well-liked and respected by everyone in New York, save for one man. Burr openly despised Hamilton with a fiery passion, because Hamilton saw him for what he was: Someone who simply wanted power. When Burr tied Thomas Jefferson in the 1800 election, Hamilton advocated for Jefferson to win, and he did, costing Burr the title he'd dreamed of for years.

But the final blow came four years later, when Burr ran for governor of New York. Hamilton was horrified at the idea of his political rival leading his state, so he threw his support behind the opposing candidate. To add insult to injury, he held a dinner party where he berated Burr behind his back… and word got out.

Desperate to save his reputation, Burr challenged Hamilton to a duel. Up until that point, duels were rarely fatal. The parties would usually sort out their differences before a single shot was fired. That didn't happen on July 11, 1804.

Dueling had been outlawed in New York, so the men rowed across the Hudson to New Jersey, where they met at the Weehawken dueling grounds. The weapon of choice? A .56 caliber pistol. Hamilton had privately admitted he planned to shoot wide, but Burr was out for blood. He aimed and hit Hamilton in the abdomen above his right hip, causing massive damage to his diaphragm, liver, and spine. Thirty-one hours later, Alexander Hamilton was pronounced dead.

Unfortunately, Hamilton had failed to make preparations for his death and his wife, Eliza, acquired a mountain of debt the moment he was buried. Now, some people believe Hamilton haunts the First Bank of the United States, perpetually trying to settle his debts on behalf of his wife.

When the First Bank closed, Philadelphia merchant Stephen Girard opened his own bank in the building. Several others followed after that, up until the National Park Service took ownership of it in 1955. Employees complained that Hamilton's ghost wrecked the place every night. They'd come in to find piles of paperwork knocked over and scattered. Files went missing. Others were moved.

At times, it seemed like the meticulous ghost was scrutinizing their work and trying to throw out anything that didn't meet his standards.

When renovation plans were announced in 1902, staff members successfully petitioned that a Catholic priest should exorcise the premises, in an attempt to release Hamilton's spirit once and for all. Unfortunately, the exorcism did not affect the founding father.

The bank has been closed to the public for decades, but there's some talk of renovating it and turning it into a museum. Will Hamilton begin making appearances again once the halls are filled with people? Only time will tell.

Bishop White House

Bishop White House, Philadelphia, PA.

Haunted by a yellow fever victim, a cat, a cook, and an elderly man, this unassuming row house on Walnut Street may be the creepiest building in all of Independence Park.

The Bishop White House is named for William White, the first bishop of the Diocese of Pennsylvania and the second United States Senate Chaplain. White was extraordinarily fond of his house. Kind and respected by his parishioners and the Philadelphia community, he lived on the premises for over fifty years before passing away in his bedroom in 1836.

Several people have spotted his ghostly form over the years. He stares out of one of the third-floor windows with a pensive expression, as if puzzled by the changing landscape of Philadelphia.

He isn't the only spirit — not by far.

When yellow fever wracked Philadelphia in 1793, many wealthy citizens fled in a desperate attempt to outrun the disease. Black nurses and members of the clergy were credited with staying behind to help care for the sick, and William White was one such clergyman. He bravely sat by victims' bedsides and delivered last rites, but he paid heavily for his decision to stay.

The disease eventually found its way to the Whites' House, infecting White's wife and five children. He buried them all. But how did the bishop avoid dying from the disease himself? Historians theorize that White's love of cigars saved his life. He was permanently shrouded in a cloud of smoke, which kept disease-carrying mosquitoes away.

Sadly, several of his servants, like his family, weren't so lucky.

When his coachman, John, contracted the fever, he arranged for Dr. Benjamin Rush to treat him. Looking back, Rush's treatments were barbaric and useless, but he was praised as one of the leading medical minds of the time, and his methods were used during future outbreaks of the disease.

Rush was a big proponent of bloodletting and forced vomiting. He believed patients needed to "purge" the disease from their body to get better, and many of his patients did recover. But we know now they recovered in spite of his treatments — not because of them. When John died, they assumed the disease had taken him, but it's just as likely that Rush's torturous treatments had hastened his death. They may have even caused it.

Now John's ghost lingers in the house alongside the cook, Mrs. Boggs, who also died of fever. Visitors have seen John's transparent figure walking from room to room, while Boggs continues her work in the kitchen. Phantom footsteps and clanging sounds emanate from the room, as if someone's preparing a meal.

Perhaps what's strangest of all is the house is now home to a ghost cat, seen crying softly by the library door. What makes this strange is the simple fact that nobody that lived on the property, including the servants, ever owned a cat.

The Bishop White House witnessed much death in its time, causing despair to permeate the walls of the house ever since. Many are convinced the house is cursed, and the onslaught of death that occurred here is unfortunate proof of that.

It also isn't the only structure associated with William White that's haunted…

The Ghosts of Philadelphia, PA.

St. Peter's Church

St. Peter's Church, Philadelphia, PA.

White presided over St. Peter's, a historic Episcopalian church where several founding fathers worshiped during the First and Second Continental Congress. Today, the church is home to many notable burials, including the 11th vice president of the United States, and Navy Commodore Stephen Decatur, who was killed in a famous duel.

Sadly, weather and time have worn away a majority of the markings on the headstones, now rendering them unreadable. Many visitors suspect these souls, now doomed to remain unknown, have come back to haunt the church indefinitely. But the hauntings at St. Peter's began long before the headstones faded.

In November of 1793, the yellow fever epidemic began to wane. Mosquitos died off as the weather turned cold, and terrified residents slowly returned to their homes and businesses — including the U.S. government.

With Washington back in town, chiefs from several indigenous tribes traveled to Philadelphia to meet with him. The war between natives and white settlers was being fought with both weapons and handshakes at the time, as the U.S. would sign over 350 treaties between 1778 and 1871. But each trip to Philadelphia (and eventually Washington, DC) posed a huge risk for indigenous delegates. These big cities were hotbeds for disease. Yellow fever was only *one* of a long list.

Eight of the chiefs who visited Philadelphia in 1793 would be killed by smallpox. Unlike yellow fever, which thrived in the summer months, smallpox was a winter disease. It began with fever, vomiting, and back pain, and developed into a painful rash. By the time they died, their bodies would have been covered in contagious pustules that even gravediggers recoiled from. So the chiefs were unceremoniously buried at St. Peter's Church in unmarked graves. This complete lack of regard rightfully infuriated the chiefs, who now haunt the cemetery.

Locals pass down tales of the "St. Peter's Phantom," a dark shadow that hovers over the chiefs' unmarked graves. Every night at 9 p.m. — like clockwork — the shadow materializes in the cemetery and lingers there until dawn. Why 9 p.m.? Disease victims were often buried at night. That's also when troublemakers and vandals sneak into cemeteries.

If the phantom doesn't scare them off, the other spirits of the graveyard usually do.

Late-night visitors have had to jump out of the way of a driverless horse and carriage. It appears out of thin air and dashes across the cemetery lawn, through the tombstones, as if fleeing from some unseen enemy. Some say the horse is from the shops at Market Street. It became tired of being driven by strangers and escaped to freedom. While nobody seems to know its origins, it's best to stay out of his way while he charges!

The final spirit is a man in 18th-century clothing who weaves and wanders through the cemetery all night long. This quiet spirit is so clear that some people mistake him for a reenactor and try to ask him questions. He never answers. In most cases, he never stops his aimless wandering. He's even walked right through people — much to their horror.

It's likely the man is not a spirit at all. Instead, he's a residual haunting — a recording of an action that was repeated over and over in life. Maybe the man had a loved one buried at St. Peter's, so he visited often. Maybe he came to the cemetery to think.

He, like so many of the ghosts in Philadelphia, remains a mystery.

The Ghosts of Philadelphia, PA.

Old St. Joseph's Church

Old St. Joseph's Church, Philadelphia, PA.

Built in 1733, Old St. Joseph's Church is the oldest Roman Catholic Church in the city. It's also the site of one of Philadelphia's most famous ghost stories: The story of Mary Barry (no, not the British baker).

The story begins with John Barry. Now considered the "Father of the American Navy," Barry had a humble Irish-Catholic upbringing, which is exactly why he chose Philadelphia as his new home port. Pennsylvania founder William Penn was a Quaker who embraced religious freedom. He wanted Philadelphia to be a place where people loved (phileo, the Greek word for love,) each other (adelphos, the Greek word for brother). That's how it earned its tagline, "The City of Brotherly Love."

Against war, inequality, and slavery, Quakers believed men and women were equal in the church, and shared this message with others. So the Pennsylvania Assembly allowed the Jesuits to establish St. Joseph's Church at a time when Catholic mass was strictly forbidden in the other 12 colonies.

Barry became a weekly worshiper at St. Joseph's Church. In 1767, he met and fell in love with a young woman named Mary Cleary, and they were wed at St. Joseph's on October 31st of that year.

For seven years, life was bliss for Mary and John. John happily divided his time between living with Mary in Philadelphia and setting impressive sailing records out at sea — but Mary was destined to live a short life. While John was away, she contracted a fatal illness. There was no way to reach John to tell him his beloved was about to die, and he wouldn't find out she had passed until he returned to Pennsylvania.

Mary knew this, but she found comfort in the fact that her husband would remain mournfully devoted to her. She imagined that he would never marry again. He would visit her gravesite each time he returned to the colonies, and launch into a teary monologue at her headstone, confessing that no other woman could fill the hole Mary had left in his heart.

But John remarried three years later… and Mary's spirit was livid.

John's new wife, Sarah Austin, was considered to be one of the most beautiful women in town — and John was clearly happy to have a pretty, young thing on his arm. Mary was overcome with jealousy, even in death. She loathed watching her husband dote on the younger, prettier woman so soon after her demise. Mary's hatred for Sarah only intensified once she discovered the woman had once been Episcopalian. Upon learning that John was a devout Catholic, Sarah converted so she, too, could attend services at St. Joseph's Church.

The pair sat together in the same pew where Mary and John had sat, in the same church where they'd been happily wed. It was too much for Mary's ghost to endure, so she began to haunt the happy new bride.

From that point forward, every time John and Sarah attended mass, Mary did everything in her power to slowly torment the young woman, causing the wind to whip the edges of her dress, calling to her quietly during the mass… These supernatural interactions grew so intense that Sarah and John began attending mass at a different church altogether.

But it's entirely possible Mary didn't stop there. For several long years, John and Sarah tried to conceive without success. Friends and family became convinced that Mary had cursed Sarah to remain forever barren, depriving the young woman of the one thing she wanted most. Each year that they remained childless took a substantial toll on Sarah's well-being.

Upon her death, Sarah was buried right beside Mary at St. Mary's Cemetery. They even share the same gravemaker. But the death didn't stop Mary's activity at St. Joseph's. She's often heard sobbing quietly in the otherwise empty hallways.

And the story doesn't end there…

The Ghosts of Philadelphia, PA.

St. Mary's Church and Cemetery

St. Mary's Church and Cemetery, Philadelphia, PA.

Head down S. 4th Street and you'll find Old St. Mary's Church and Cemetery, the second oldest Roman Catholic church in Philly. This is where Commodore Barry and his two wives — Mary and Sarah — are all buried. But they aren't the only Barrys to haunt the cemetery.

Four years after Mary's death in 1774, John also lost his brother, Patrick. Patrick had boarded a ship called the *Union* in August of 1778 and disappeared, never to be seen or heard from again. Sadly, that was a common occurrence in the 18th century, when storms and pirates could easily take down an entire crew.

Thanks to his mysterious death, Patrick now joins Mary's ghost on her nightly walks around the graveyard. They're often seen hovering over John's headstone, standing guard.

Visitors say Patrick always appears donned in 18th-century clothing and is friendly toward them… unless they overstay their welcome. Tourists who linger too long at John Barry's grave find themselves overcome with waves of inexplicable anxiety until they are forced to leave the premises. It's said these spirits are most active on nights when the moon is full.

One curious visitor risked Patrick's wrath and lingered by John's grave late one night. He had only been there for a few minutes when he was suddenly encased in darkness. Terrified, the man looked up to see a massive black cloud hanging low on the horizon, blocking out all light from the moon. The man suddenly found himself overcome with fear and the unwavering desire to run as far away as he could.

As the man swiftly made his way toward the exit, he noticed the strange black cloud had already begun to dissipate. He dared a quick look back at John's grave and was shocked to see that a faint halo had materialized right above the headstone.

Needless to say, he never went back.

St. Mary's Church and Cemetery, Philadelphia, PA.

The Ghosts of Philadelphia, PA.

Thaddeus Kosciuszko National Memorial

Thaddeus Kosciuszko National Memorial, Philadelphia, PA.

Most Americans have never heard of Thaddeus Kosciuszko. A Polish war hero, Kosciuszko fought alongside the colonists during the Revolutionary War. He's credited for using his engineering background to help fortify American strongholds.

He returned to Poland shortly thereafter to fight against oppressive Russian forces and survived 17 grievous battle scars as well as Russian imprisonment. When he was finally released, the Czar advised that he could only return to his homeland if he recognized Russia as the ruler of Poland. When Kosciuszko refused, he returned to America in 1797 — the place he felt was another home.

While Kosciuszko lived in Pennsylvania, he took to entertaining very notable figures, among them Thomas Jefferson and Chief Little Turtle of the Miami Indian Nation. It would seem he had such a good time socializing in his Philadelphia home that Kosciuszko has returned to it in the afterlife…

The second you step inside, you can feel his presence in the room that once served as his bedroom. Visitors routinely find themselves overcome with feelings of chivalry and hospitality they know are not their own.

But one young lady had a very different experience when she found herself alone in the bedroom. Cold air flooded the room, engulfing her. The woman could barely process what was happening when she found herself filled with passion seemingly out of nowhere. It felt as if Kosciusko was trying to make a romantic connection from beyond the grave.

But the ghost isn't always in the mood for such overtures. Two sisters visited the house together and began to explore when one of the sisters felt a phantom hand tap her shoulder. The sisters both turned around to see a handsome gentleman standing eerily close to them. The moment they made eye contact with him, he asked them, "Is the war over?"

The sisters noticed the man's tattered and dirty clothing and assumed he was a historical reenactor. They smiled and weren't sure how to respond. However, looking at him once more, they saw splotches of blood begin to burst and spread all over — as if there were more than a dozen scars seeping in deep crimson down his shirt.

On the cusp of screaming, they watched in horror as the man stumbled forward, fainted, and then vanished seconds before he collapsed upon the floor. Riddled with terror, the women fled from the room and didn't look back.

Thaddeus Kosciuszko National Memorial, Philadelphia, PA.

Todd House

Todd House, Philadelphia, PA.

Though it's named for John Todd, the story of the Todd House is all about James Madison, the fourth president of the United States... and the victim of a vengeful spirit.

On January 7, 1790, Madison's future wife Dolley married a successful lawyer named John Todd. Todd was well-liked within the Quaker community, and their marriage was considered to be a happy one. But it wasn't to last.

When yellow fever came knocking in 1793, Dolley watched helplessly as both her in-laws, her husband, and one of her young sons all died within weeks of each other. Devastated by these tremendous losses, Dolley filled the Todd House with friends as often as she could, in hopes of filling the void.

Future vice president Aaron Burr decided to attend one of Dolley's events at the Todd House and persuaded his friend, James Madison, to accompany him. The future president was instantly infatuated with Dolley when he met her. Just a few days after the party, James Madison came to call on Dolley. The two began to meet regularly, speaking on all manner of subjects while seated together in the parlor of the house.

Aware of the fact that Dolley's first husband had lived — and died — in the house, James Madison always noticed a certain degree of eeriness the moment he entered Dolley's home. He couldn't help but feel his every move was somehow being watched. Little did he know his concerns were well-founded. Dolley sensed John Todd's presence every time James Madison came to call on her, as if determined to protect her — even from the grave.

With time, John Todd found little ways to let Dolley know he approved of the relationship. In 1794, Dolley married Madison and eventually moved from the Todd House to the White House, where she made history alongside her husband.

John Todd still haunts his namesake house, especially the front parlor where Dolley and James's romance first began. Visitors often report feelings of eeriness and discomfort while exploring that room.

Many people question what might have been if John Todd's spirit had not given Dolley his blessing on her second marriage. Dolley played a crucial role in James Madison's election as the fourth president of the United States, and we may have a ghost to thank for that!

Todd House, Philadelphia, PA.

The Hill-Physick House

The Hill-Physick House, Philadelphia, PA.

Built in 1786, the Hill-Physick House once belonged to Philip Physick, who was considered one of the most successful surgeons throughout the country at the time.

Some of the doctor's most notable patients included Dolley Madison, Benjamin Rush, and Chief Justice John Marshall, who allegedly had 1,000 kidney stones! Andrew Jackson once received a vehement lecture on the dangers of smoking after suffering from significant lung hemorrhages.

Dr. Physick is credited for medical advances that laid the groundwork for modern-day surgical procedures, including the invention of the stomach pump. The doctor developed a reputation for conducting countless autopsies to learn more about the mysteries of death. He showed much care and compassion for his patients, but this temperament was rarely demonstrated at home. Dr. Physick and his wife, Elizabeth, found themselves entangled in a very bitter divorce during the late 1790s.

Fed up with his wife's alleged mood swings, Physick began dosing her with opium in secret, rendering her borderline catatonic. Once drugged, the doctor would leave his wife to wander unattended in the backyard. Elizabeth frequently took to lying beneath her favorite tree for hours at a time.

One day, when he was especially infuriated with his wife and the ongoing divorce, Dr. Physick cut her favorite tree down from the backyard. Elizabeth died not long after the prized tree was ripped out.

Two hundred years later, the legend of the Gray Lady of Physick House was born.

Three state employees were examining damage on the third floor when a sudden freezing wind rushed by them. One of the employees quickly blamed the nearby fireplace for the unexpected draft, but his coworkers knew the fireplace had been sealed for decades.

While the employees stood there dumbfounded, a shadowy figure walked past the open doorway right in front of them. Terrified, the three men begged the ghost to show them mercy, but she vanished seconds later. Now, this apparition has been seen by multiple witnesses ever since and is believed to be Elizabeth, back from the dead to keep watch on the house where her happiness was lost.

The Gray Lady roams through the house in a long, flowing gown, and frequently appears behind unsuspecting visitors when they go to look at their reflection in one of the household mirrors. Others have reported seeing her stare down at them from the windows.

Some locals are convinced that Elizabeth will haunt the house forever, in desperate search of her next opioid fix. But there's a growing theory amongst other locals that the Gray Lady isn't Elizabeth at all, but is the ghost of Elsie Keith.

After Dr. Physick died, the house was passed down to his great-great-granddaughter, Elsie. She moved into the house not long after but frequently complained to her friends there was something off about the place. Every room was perpetually caked in dust and seemed to possess an air of death no matter what she did.

Upon Elsie's death, the house was donated to the Philadelphia Society for the Preservation of Landmarks, and dust began to invade the property once more.

Now, a strange, inexplicable breeze frequently rushes through the house from no apparent source, and locals are convinced it is Elsie, still frantically trying to rid the house of all particles of dust. Elsie is reported to be kind to visitors, but even so, tourists are advised to be brief and don't leave any dirt!

Another spirit has been said to wander close to the Hill-Physick House and several other locations in the neighborhood. This nasty spirit has been deemed the Hag of Pine Street.

She once lived in a rowhouse along Pine Street and spent her days screaming at children and passersby as they walked past her property. Any child who wandered too close would be swiftly attacked with her cane.

After she died in the late 1800s, she chose to remain: she can be seen tormenting
 unsuspecting people who pass by her former home. Her wrinkled, wretched-looking face often appears at the window on the top floor, sneering at anyone who dares to look up at the house.

Locals complain of hearing disembodied shrieks and moans emanating from the house, and an apparition of the hag frequently appears on the lawn, still violently swinging her cane at anybody who dares to venture close.

The house sat empty for decades and was steadily avoided by locals who were too frightened of the hag to step foot inside the building. But a new owner has recently hired a voodoo priest in an attempt to banish the hag once and for all.

Some speculate that the hag never really left — she simply tricked the Voodoo priest into thinking she had, because, on a dark night, screams and shrieks can still be heard echoing from the house away into the night….

Gateway to Gettysburg

THE HISTORIC BRICKHOUSE INN

Enjoy Luxurious Rooms & Amenities

Live in luxury and convenience with a Heavenly Hot Tub, Romance Packages, EV Charger, Champagne and Cookies Social Hour, and More!

Experience Gettysburg in Any Season

Spring, Summer, Spooky, and Christmas. Winner of Gettysburg's Holiday Lights Award!

Mystery, History, Haunts, & Jaunts

Boos, Booze, Breakfast, and Foods. Enjoy homemade meals and a gift shop with one-of-a-kind merchandise. Visit historical hotspots, restaurants, battlefields, and stores on your choice of history tours, ghost tours, food tours, and more

Gateway to American History

Located on the main historic strip just a few hundred feet from the Gettysburg Battlefield and the site of Lincoln's Gettysburg Address.

BOOK YOUR GETAWAY NOW!

brickhouseinn.com

CHAPTER VI

The Ghosts of Pittsburgh

Nineteenth-century Pittsburgh was an industrial powerhouse. The clang of steel mixed with the flutter of cash, and magnates like Henry Clay Frick and Andrew Carnegie ruled like kings. Their names still brand the city's buildings — a lasting reminder of the industry that made "Steel City." But there's another, more sinister side to the story, and the spirits of the past are all too willing to tell it.

Workers waged deadly labor strikes. Diseases swept through the streets. Death lurked around every corner. It even knocked on Henry Frick's door. The trauma of those years is still etched into the city's most historic buildings, and it's produced plenty of restless souls.

The following chapters reveal Pittsburgh's most terrifying ghost stories, from the eerie corridors of the Allegheny County Jail, where the whispers of long-gone inmates linger in the cold cells, to the halls of the Pennsylvania Apartments — once the site of a deadly railroad strike.

Each one peels back a new layer of history, and offers a glimpse into the supernatural side of Pittsburgh. They may haunt you long after the pages are turned.

pittsburghghosts.com

The Ghosts of PITTSBURGH, PA.

U.S. Steel Tower

U.S. Steel Tower, Pittsburgh, PA.

Pittsburgh's most haunted begins with one of the city's most controversial figures. He was a hated man, but he's also at the center of a heartwarming ghost story — the story of a five-year-old girl who saved her father's life from beyond the grave. This is the story of Henry Clay Frick.

It starts in 1871, when Frick founded a company to turn coal into coke (a fuel used in the steelmaking process). He was a millionaire by the age of 30, and by 1891 he was living in Pittsburgh's illustrious Point Breeze neighborhood with his wife and three children: Childs, Martha, and baby Helen.

While his family adored him, Frick had plenty of enemies. He was partially responsible for a dam failure that killed 2,200 people in Johnstown, PA. His private club, the South Fork Fishing and Hunting Club, had lowered the dam by three feet to make the lake more suitable for recreation. The change weakened it, and it burst on May 28, 1889, sending a 40-foot-high wall of water racing toward Johnstown.

The club was never held responsible for the disaster, so many people called it "karma" when Frick suffered a personal tragedy two years later: His beloved daughter, Martha, died at the age of five.

When Martha was two years old, she managed to swallow a pin. Without x-ray technology, doctors couldn't find and remove it, so the child suffered for three years until, finally, the pin caused a deadly infection. She died on July 29, 1891.

Henry and Adelaide were heartbroken, and Henry doubled down on work to escape the pain. His business tactics were more ruthless than ever.

In June of 1892, the magnate announced pay cuts for hundreds of employees at the Homestead steel plant. When the employees went on strike, he shut down the mill and locked out 3,800 workers — going so far as to build a barbed wire fence around the building. He planned to fill their vacant positions with non-union strikebreakers, but the strikers armed themselves and sealed off the town. Furious, Frick countered by sending in an armed militia.

The violent squabble resulted in the deaths of 12 people. It would also fuel an assassination attempt.

One month later, Henry was working at his office in the Chronicle-Telegraph Building (now the U.S. Steel Tower) when a 21-year-old anarchist named Andrew Berkman burst through the door with a revolver and sharpened steel file.

Frick rose from his chair just as Berkman fired, causing the bullet to travel through the base of his skull and lodge in his back. The magnate fell to the floor and Berkman fired again, shooting the injured man in the neck. By this time, the other employees had heard the commotion and rushed in to stop the assassin — but Frick credited *something else* with saving his life.

When Berkman aimed, a blinding ray of light blocked his view of Frick. This happened both times he pulled the trigger, causing him to hit Frick at odd angles instead of straight on. Had he been able to see clearly, Henry Clay Frick would have been a dead man.

Henry claimed that as he looked up from the floor, he saw the light that was blinding Berkman. It looked like a glowing apparition of his late daughter, Martha. He credited the little girl with saving his life up until the day he died in 1919.

But Martha's ghost isn't the only Frick Family spirit. The others are found at their former mansion: Clayton.

The Ghosts of Pittsburgh, PA.

Clayton

Clayton, Pittsburgh, PA.

After Henry and Adelaide married in December of 1881, they purchased a house in Pittsburgh's Point Breeze neighborhood — once the richest neighborhood in the world. Known as Millionaire's Row, the streets were dotted with big names like Heinz (creators of the world-famous ketchup), Westinghouse, Carnegie, and a slew of others.

The house originally consisted of eleven rooms, but the pressures of society — and the arrival of their three children — led to a significant expansion. By 1891, it was a 23-room, four-story, chateau-style mansion. There were turrets, spires, and high, decorative chimneys. Doors breezed open to beautifully-trimmed balconies, and arched glass windows bathed the house in golden sunlight. Inside, the gorgeous woodwork was complemented by flocked velvet wall treatments and velvet drapes, friezes and other artwork.

The house was a dream, but the Frick Family would suffer several tragedies there. Little Martha died in 1891. Almost exactly one year later, Henry was shot by Alexander Berkman. Though he survived the shooting, another tragedy was waiting in the shadows.

The couple's newborn son, Henry Frick Jr., died two weeks after the attack. Henry and Adelaide were both bedridden at the time — Adelaide recovering from a difficult birth and Henry recovering from his injuries. They were so sick they couldn't even attend their own son's funeral.

The family hadn't made many happy memories in their Pittsburgh mansion, so it came as no surprise when they moved to New York, leaving behind all of their furniture and decor. But the move deeply affected their daughter Helen. She had far more happy times at Clayton than anyone else in her family. The house was her playground, her safe haven.

Fortunately, her parents never sold the family home. Henry stayed at Clayton during his frequent trips to Pittsburgh, and Helen visited often as an adult. When her mother passed away in 1931, she inherited the house, and she would maintain it as it faded into a historic relic. She moved back in in 1981 and died in the house three years later.

Today, Clayton is a museum dedicated to the Gilded Age, the Frick Family, and the Pittsburgh Steel Industry. And thanks to Helen's meticulous preservation, it looks almost exactly the way it did when the Fricks lived there. Maybe that's why their spirits remain in the house.

The spirits of Helen and Adelaide have appeared to numerous people over time. Are they spooky or ghoulish? No. Are they angry, thumping around and scaring people? Nope. The Frick ladies, when they are spotted, appear as genteel in death as they were in life. They don't seem to address the living, choosing instead to walk around their home as they would have in life, enjoying the family heirlooms inside and the grounds outside.

Security guards in the house regularly hear footsteps walking around on the third floor, long after Clayton House has been cleared of its visitors and employees for the night. The ladies seem to enjoy moving things around if they have been moved from a different spot than where they were when the Fricks lived there.

At various times, docents have observed one of the beds with a noticeable concave shape on top, as if someone is sitting on it. And the voices that echo from far away corners of the house seem happy, revisiting conversations of past or perhaps entertaining guests.

It seems the Fricks have found more happiness in death than they had in life.

Cindy Esser's Floral Shop

Cindy Esser's Floral Shop, Pittsburgh, PA.

At the corner of E Carton Street, you'll find a quaint store boasting the letters "Esser's Floral." Though the shop has changed hands — and names — many locals have fond memories of Cindy Esser's Floral Shop, which opened in 1982.

The shop had a solid group of regulars who would call in their orders over the phone: "I need a summer assortment for a graduation party" or "I need apology flowers for my wife…" But sometimes the calls were unsettling.

One Halloween, the shop received a call from a man named Chris.

"Do you have any peace lilies?" he asked.

When the receptionist confirmed they did indeed have peace lilies, Chris requested the order be delivered to a nearby church. The receptionist asked him if the arrangement was intended for a funeral — as many orders, sadly, were.

Chris quietly replied, "Yes, they are for my funeral."

All of the hair on the nape of her neck stood on end when the call suddenly disconnected. The receptionist went home that evening feeling thoroughly creeped out by the bizarre call. She barely slept, and when dawn broke she still couldn't get the encounter out of her head. She decided to call the church to ask about the mysterious man, Chris.

"I know this sounds odd," she said, "but I work for a florist, and we received a strange call from someone named Chris yesterday. He said he needed flowers for his own funeral, and he named your church."

The line was silent for a moment. Finally, the woman replied, "We're holding a funeral for Chris, but he died a week ago."

The receptionist hung up the phone, riddled with chills that she could not shake.

A few weeks later, the shop received another odd, late-night call.

"Hello," the man said. "I'd like to order a dozen roses."

He asked that they be delivered to the science teacher at his high school the following day. It was an odd request — maybe even inappropriate — but the shop didn't ask questions. They delivered the roses as requested.

A few days later, the science teacher showed up, her entire body trembling with grief and shock. She explained that her son had ordered the flowers. The employee interrupted, saying, "Well, that was very sweet of him."

"Yes," the woman agreed, "but he died two years ago."

Cindy Esser's Floral Shop, Pittsburgh, PA.

The Ghosts of Pittsburgh, PA.

Omni William Penn Hotel

Omni William Penn Hotel, Pittsburgh, PA.

Opened in 1916, the Omni William Penn Hotel is a Beaux-Arts masterpiece filled with gold, velvet, and crystal. It's hosted every president since Theodore Roosevelt. In fact, the 16th floor is home to the official Presidential Suite, which is closed off to the public when the president is in town.

Other floors are also inaccessible to the public, but for very different reasons... For decades, there have been rumors that the 21st and 22nd floors are haunted.

Those floors are said to be used exclusively for storage, but some say that back when there were guest rooms, someone was murdered up there. They also believe that because those two floors are haunted, they are no longer fit for guests to stay in. There are numerous reports of the sounds of people talking and laughing, as well as unexplained drafts and feelings of being watched.

Who are these entities? Well, there have been at least three deaths at the hotel.

In March of 1922, a fine lingerie salesman named Michael York took his own life in his room. In 1947, fashion designer and socialite Ruth Harkness died suddenly while staying at the Omni Penn. She had gained national attention for bringing the first baby panda to the U.S., and it's said guests and employees have heard "bleating" sounds coming from her old room — like a baby panda is trapped in there.

There was another wild incident in 1976, when a violent argument broke out between two men who worked as dishwashers in the hotel banquet hall. The men, 70-year-old Nelson Cooper and 65-year-old Samuel Bankhead, were actually lifelong friends. They had just finished their shift and were changing their clothes in the employee locker room when the fight escalated. Nobody knew what it was about, but as it happened, Cooper had a gun in his locker. He wound up shooting his old friend right in the head, killing him. Some believe the men might have been drunk, which is why those near the banquet hall claim to hear two inebriated men chatting in the outside hallway when nobody is there. But these stories are just a few of hundreds about how haunted the historic hotel really is.

On the 6th floor, one guest found himself battling an invisible entity. The closet door kept opening by itself, and the bathroom gave him the heebie-jeebies for some reason. The guest went so far as to close the bathroom door during his stay. On his last day there, he had a very early checkout — 4 a.m. Just before leaving, he went to open the bathroom door for a tissue and found it locked. After several minutes of rattling the doorknob trying to open the door, the guest finally let go — and heard an audible click as the door magically unlocked by itself. The guest wisely decided not to open it to see what was on the other side and vacated the room.

Then there is the 16th floor, the one with the Presidential Suite.

Of course, when someone important is staying on the 16th floor, it's closed off to the public; otherwise, guests are allowed to stay in the rooms on that floor. Some of them end up regretting it.

Guests staying on the 16th floor have reported feeling like someone is in the room with them, having nightmares, and getting feelings of an invisible evil presence when the lights are out. One woman said she dreamt that an elderly couple came into her room in the night with their luggage. The old woman became upset that "her" bed was occupied, since she had been murdered there. When the woman awoke, she wasn't so sure it had been a dream.

Angry spirits are a common theme at the Omni William Penn.

One couple reported that during their second night's stay on the 16th floor, they heard a knock on the door, along with a woman asking, "Can I come in?" When they asked why she wanted in, the lady replied through the door that she had a 6 a.m. wakeup call. The couple apologized for being loud and then left to go to an after-party.

When the couple returned with three other friends at 3 a.m., everyone knew to keep it down because of the woman next door, but then one of the guests noted that this particular room was at the end of the hall. So there didn't seem to be a real room next door, just an elevator shaft. But before they could open the door to verify what was behind it, the door swung open by itself and revealed an angry woman in her nightgown. She reminded the group that she had the 6 a.m. wakeup and promptly shut the door.

Everyone went to bed at that point. The next morning, the couple complained to one of the hotel employees, explaining that this woman had repeatedly scolded them. The employee just sighed and said, "Yeah… I'm sorry about that."

There was no room there, and there was no angry guest — just a very ticked off ghost.

Omni William Penn Hotel, Pittsburgh, PA.

The Ghosts of Pittsburgh, PA.

Pittsburgh University

Pittsburgh University, Pittsburgh, PA.

If you drive down Forbes Avenue, just past Schenley Plaza, you'll find a log cabin. The little house sticks out like a sore thumb — especially compared to the ornate Natural History Museum across the street — but it's an important part of Pittsburgh history.

Pitt University was founded in a simple cabin in 1787. It's since grown into 132 acres and over 100 buildings. Some were newly built, but many had past lives as businesses, hotels, and apartments. When the university purchased them, they unknowingly purchased some ghosts as well.

One of the largest buildings on the Pitt campus began as Schenley Apartments, a luxury apartment building that was completed in 1924 at a cost of $4.5 million dollars — over $77 million today. There were 238 apartments in all, spread throughout five buildings.

All was well, except for a series of odd mishaps that occurred in or near the Schenley within the first year.

In December of 1924, an unidentified female driver struck a man on the street in front of the apartments. She was able to rush the man to the hospital, but he died as they carried him inside. And when the orderlies turned around, the woman had vanished.

Just a week later, William Whigham, the president of Carnegie Steel, died in his apartment at the Schenley. And just days after that, a contractor working on an elevator shaft slipped and fell off his ladder, plunging several feet.

More tragedies followed. In 1926, movie promoter Hunt Miller shot himself in the head in his apartment due to financial woes and died at a local hospital. A while later, two women who lived at the Schenley were struck and killed by an automobile. Deaths and accidents continued to plague residents throughout the 1920s, but the most tragic death of all took place in what is today known as Bruce Hall.

There, in today's suite 1201, the apartment owner's mistress hanged herself. Since the university moved in in 1955, students and staff have routinely heard footsteps in the stairwells, as well as the disembodied voice of a woman talking. In addition, the fireplace in the suite has been known to light by itself. Also, napkins on a banquet table elsewhere in the building have suddenly unfolded all by themselves.

But Bruce Hall has nothing on the Cathedral of Learning.

A bedroom in the Early American Nationality Room on the third floor has been verified as haunted, by numerous people.

Once, a janitor who was cleaning the bedroom noticed that the quilt on the bed had been turned down. He remade the bed, turned away to clean another part of the room, and when he turned around the quilt was turned down again. And, there was a dent in the pillow as if someone's head had been resting on it. Another custodian reported a shadow gliding past him as he walked into the room to clean it. And yet another time, an entire Pittsburgh television crew was in the room shooting a sequence when the door slammed shut and locked them inside!

So who is the ghost of the Early American Nationality Room?

E. Maxine Bruhns, the former director of Pitt's Nationality Rooms Program, always claimed she knew who the ghost was: her grandmother, Martha Jane Poe McDaniel. It's her grandmother's quilt that lays across the bed. In fact, she made it herself.

Bruhns experienced her grandmother's antics the one time she decided to spend the night in the room. She was sleeping on the floor when her purse suddenly flew off of a nearby chair and landed with a thud right next to her head. Unfortunately E. Maxine Bruhns passed away in 2020. Perhaps she has joined her grandmother's spirit in the Early American Room.

Grandma McDaniel is not the only ghost of the Cathedral of Learning.

Group tours have often commented on the smell of fresh bread baking in the fireplace, which hasn't been used since the 1940s. And one Pitt alumnus said, as she studied late one night on the 26th floor, she and a friend distinctly heard a woman singing. The girls searched high and low for the singer but never found her. As they were looking, the elevator door suddenly opened and the singing got louder, but nobody was inside the elevator.

The alumnus believed the singer was probably Mary Croghan Schenley, a famous Pittsburgh philanthropist. The only problem is that Mary died in 1903.

Mary doesn't just spook around the upper floors of the Cathedral of Learning, she also haunts the Croghan-Schenley Ballroom on the first floor. The first floor originally consisted of two rooms and was located in the mansion of Mary's father, William Croghan. Although Mary moved to England after eloping with Edward Schenley, her father left her the extensive property that had been passed down through the family.

Because of her elopement, Mary never attended her own debutante ball in that ballroom, but today, they say, Mary's ghost comes to visit the ballroom where she moves the furniture around when the door is locked. Allegedly, the fireplace in the room had a secret entrance to a hidden chamber where Mary's ghost is believed to hang out. Some have even heard the sounds of a party going on, which falls silent if someone opens the door to see what's going on.

The Ghosts of Pittsburgh, PA.

Allegheny County Health Department

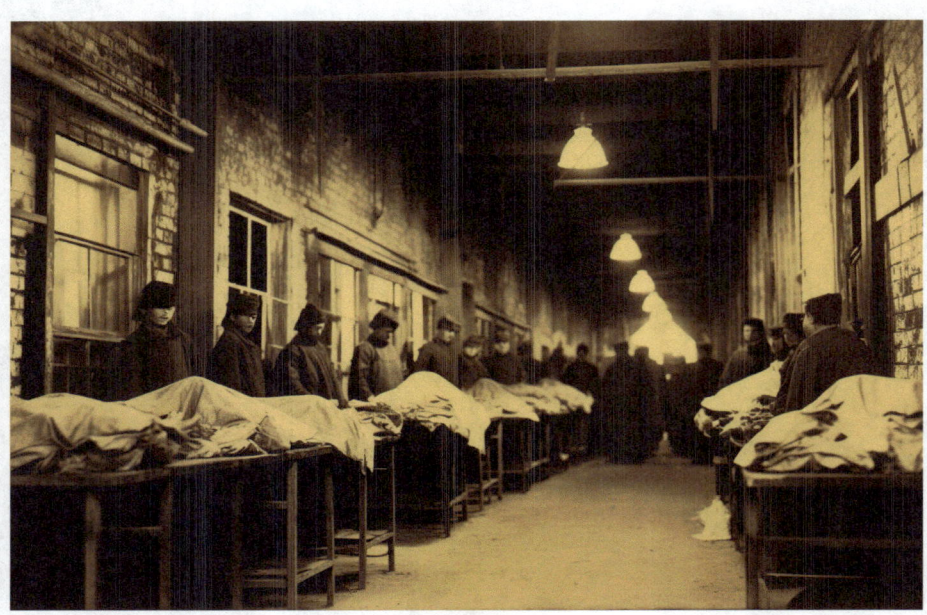

Allegheny County Health Department, Pittsburgh, PA.

The Allegheny County Health Department Headquarters has one of the weirdest histories in the city. It used to be the morgue.

Death was a constant presence in 19th-century Pittsburgh. There were accidents at steel mills. There were diseases. By the late 1880s, bodies were piling up faster than gravediggers could bury them. The city needed somewhere to keep them, so they constructed a morgue across the street from the courthouse and jail. It opened on April Fool's Day of 1903.

As Pittsburgh grew, there were times, like in any big city, that an unidentified body or two showed up. When this happened, the coroner would lay the dead person in the morgue's chapel for a time. In this way, families missing a loved one could come look to see if they could identify a body.

By the 1960s, they say, it was common knowledge that the chapel was open 24 hours for those wishing to pray, but also so they could come and take a look at the unidentified bodies if they wished. The story is that it became a gruesome tradition of sorts for the high school kids to visit the morgue on prom night to scare each other and their dates. New Year's Eve was another popular time to visit.

There are stories of voices echoing through the halls, strange unidentifiable sounds, and the occasional moving objects. One of the ghosts is even said to be Jake Freeman, who once worked as a janitor there. Mr. Freeman loved his job and loved a good joke, claiming that when he died, he would come back to haunt the morgue. Apparently he did just that.

Although the morgue itself was moved in 2008, the ghosts still linger in the Health Department building, terrorizing the staff from time to time. They've made it a point not to work too late, and who could blame them?

The Old Allegheny Jail Museum

The Old Allegheny Jail Museum, Pittsburgh, PA.

There's a limestone bridge looming over the 400 block of Ross Street. It looks like it belongs to a castle, but the reality is much darker: The bridge used to connect the courthouse to the old jail. It's where prisoners would look out at the city for the last time.

The assumption was that at least some of the criminals would emit an audible sigh of regret as they were led to serve their sentence… or face the noose. That's how it earned the nickname "Bridge of Sighs."

Today, the bridge is part of the Old Allegheny Jail Museum, where docents regale visitors with tales of affairs, escapes, hangings, and ghosts…

Between 1888 and 1911, 58 criminals were hanged at the old jail. There would have been more except some prisoners decided to cheat the hangman's noose by taking their own lives. Others cheated death another way — by escaping from the prison. That's what happened in 1891, after Detectives David Gilkinson and Patrick Murphy went to arrest a common burglar named Frederick Fitzsimmons.

Fitzsimmons and his wife, Lucy, knew the law was after them when they holed up in a cabin in a remote area known as Bull Run. When the detectives knocked on the door, Lucy refused to let them in. It was Gilkinson who pushed past the woman, only to be shot to death by Fred Fitzsimmons. Both Detective Murphy and Fred were wounded in the shootout, but both escaped with their lives.

The next day, Fred and Lucy were tracked down and finally arrested — but Fred quickly escaped the Allegheny County Jail using a saw and a rope provided by someone on the outside. Nobody seemed to notice him as he strolled right down the street and even penned a note to the local newspaper. The County Jail, he wrote, was not the grand hotel experience he was expecting, right down to the awful food. He also assured the paper that he would not go back to jail. And he didn't.

For weeks, Fred actually remained in Pittsburgh where he was even spotted attending a local circus. Not until early 1892 was he finally arrested, in New Orleans. But before the officials could bring him back to Pittsburgh, Fred managed to slit his own throat with a small knife. He had said he would never go back to the Allegheny County Jail, and he apparently meant it. Lucy, meanwhile, was sentenced to eight years for her part in the death of Detective Gilkinson. She was set free six years into her sentence.

From this wild tale came two ghosts: Detective Gilkinson, whose spirit remained in the cabin where he died at Bull Run, and Fred Fitzsimmons.

In 1901 William Phillis, who had aided in arresting Fred just after he killed Detective Gilkinson, swore that he saw the man's ghost in McKeesport. Phillis said that Fred's spirit, looking very much alive, walked right up to him and told him in a menacing voice that he would never forget him. The incident scared Mr. Phillis silly, and the story was run in several newspapers.

But that isn't the only ghost story associated with the old jail — not by a long shot.

In 1902, Warden Peter Soffel and his wife, Kate, lived at the jail. Kate was in charge of providing meals and other comforts for the prisoners, as well as praying with them. Of course, she got to know some of them well since she saw them every day.

It wasn't a very glamorous job, being the warden's wife. You would think that with the violent criminal history of the prisoners, Kate Soffel would have steered clear of making friends with them. But she didn't. Instead, she actually took pity upon brothers Ed and Jack Biddle, who were on death row for committing murder. They were held in the same jail cell once occupied by the ghostly Mike Ruminski and George Prescott.

Maybe it was something about that cell that created such a strange atmosphere, but for some reason Kate Stoffel felt sympathy for the Biddle brothers — so much so that she actually fell in love with Ed, and helped him and his brother escape. The trio didn't get far; the very next day the Biddle brothers were tracked down and shot to death on a remote road outside of town. Kate Stoffel was arrested for helping them escape and served time in the state penitentiary, during which time Peter divorced her. She died in 1909, but her spirit is said to haunt this building to this day.

Then there was William Culp, another death row inmate who was found hanging in his cell in 1907. But the man's ghost remained and terrified his fellow prisoners so badly that the warden actually agreed to move everybody on death row to another part of the jail.

The final ghost was never a prisoner. She was a victim.

In 1907, William McDonald was awaiting execution after slitting his lover's throat. Her name was Bessie Hyslop, and she was a spiritualist who had talked McDonald into leaving his wife for her. It didn't work out quite like she'd hoped. He killed her.

McDonald had pleaded with the governor for a reprieve from the hangman's noose, and most believed he would get it — until the spirit of Bessie appeared in his cell one night and told him there would be no sympathy for him. She was right; McDonald was hanged in 1908.

The last hanging at this jail took place in 1911. But in the years since, several more escape attempts have been made, and the spirits of the past have never left. Even after the jail was moved to another location in 1995, visitors here have reported hearing, and seeing, the many ghouls and ghosts who haunt this building to this day.

Extra Space Storage

Extra Space Storage, Pittsburgh, PA.

In business for over twenty-five years, Extra Space Storage has become a godsend for many Pittsburgh residents, thanks to the one hundred individual storage units inside.

Thousands upon thousands of objects have been moved in and out of the East Carson Street building over the years, and with them comes the occasional ghost. Numerous customers have reported having strange experiences they could not readily explain while on the property.

One day, a man named Bob drove up to the building to rent a unit. He was tired of lugging the supplies for his pool cleaning business in the back of his truck, so he wanted a small unit to store his additional chemicals. All seemed well at first, until Bob came to pick up a couple of bottles later that month.

When he opened the door, his supplies were strewn all over the floor. A few weeks later when he returned, the same thing happened. Every single time Bob came back to his unit, he always found the same mysterious mess.

One day, a facility manager happened to be driving past Bob's locker when he heard a crash loudly echo from the unit. Knowing the door was locked, the manager decided to inspect footage from the security cameras strewn throughout the property. He was shocked to see that the security footage revealed Bob's unit violently shaking in place. The moment Bob saw the footage for himself, he purchased and installed his own set of security cameras within his storage unit, determined to find the culprit once and for all.

The footage from Bob's interior cameras was far more chilling than he could have ever imagined. The man watched in horror as an eerie white mist took shape inside his locker and knocked his supplies all over the ground. Terrified by what he witnessed, Bob rented a different storage unit on the opposite side of the facility. He moved all of his supplies over, and then carefully set his cameras up once more. He patiently waited out the night, hoping nothing would happen.

But when the sun rose, he watched in dread as the phantom white mist appeared yet again in his new storage unit, wreaking havoc just like before. That was the final straw. Bob collected all of his supplies and put them back in his truck. He wanted nothing more to do with the spirit — or the chance of making it angry.

His experience wouldn't be the last.

One evening, all appeared to be quiet and calm at the storage facility, when the third-floor security alarm began to sound. Alarmed, a female employee left her office to investigate. She scoured the third floor but found nothing amiss. All seemed eerily quiet and peaceful once more. The employee went to review the security footage a few hours later, assuming it would show much the same.

But the woman was dreadfully wrong. Goosebumps pricked at her skin as she watched a bright light flash in front of the security camera the very moment the alarm began. Seconds after the bright light appeared, it was gone, and everything on the third floor went pitch black.

The woman watched in awe as another flash lit up the screen and lights in the room suddenly came back on. She watched as she appeared on the footage, hurriedly stepping off the elevator.

Many seasoned security guards employed at Extra Space Storage insist the area near the elevators is especially haunted. They repeatedly hear disembodied sounds and bangs from the elevators, especially late into the night. On one particularly chilling night, multiple security guards witnessed the elevator doors opening and closing by themselves over and over again on the third, fourth, and fifth floors of the building.

The guards searched the place from top to bottom. It was a ghost town.

S.W. Randall Toyes & Giftes

S.W. Randall Toyes & Giftes, Pittsburgh, PA.

S.W. Randall Toyes & Giftes is Pittsburgh's oldest and largest specialty toy store — a staple since 1970. It's a wonderland of dolls, trains, yo-yos, and board games, where kids and adults alike can let their imaginations run wild. And the fact that it's survived the technology boom and a global pandemic is a testament to its charm.

The business was founded by Jack Cohen, and there has never been any other owner. So who is S.W. Randall? The name is made up from the letters of Cohen's children's names: Sherry, Stacey, Wendy, and James, whose middle name is Randall.

Over the years, Cohen opened other branch stores in other parts of the city. Some closed while others have opened. At one point there were seven stores in all, but these days there are three. The Smithfield Street shop is the most famous — in part because it's haunted.

Admittedly, very little is known about this storefront, but it was built long before the toy store moved in. What is known is that some unseen presence has been felt here, especially on the third floor, where the store's many dolls are on display. Sometimes too, the apparition of a woman has been seen lingering near the merchandise, and those who have seen her have claimed that they can just feel the energy draining out of them when she is near.

A few years ago, two university students were upstairs trying to see if they could catch a ghost on film. The girls had their cameras all set up on the third floor. One of the girls turned to her friend to say something, and was shocked at what she saw: The other girl looked pale and terrified, standing perfectly still. She was able to mutter something about feeling like she was glued to the floor. Her arms felt like they were pinned to her sides.

It took several minutes before she could move, after which she felt as though the life had just been sucked right out of her. That girl was an exception; most visitors to the third floor report feeling strange cold spots, as well as getting the feeling that an invisible presence is standing near them.

Who are these mysterious entities? No one knows. But one thing is clear: They aren't interested in playing.

S.W. Randall Toyes & Giftes, Pittsburgh, PA.

The Ghosts of Pittsburgh, PA.

The Pennsylvania Apartments

The Pennsylvania Apartments, Pittsburgh, PA.

Pittsburgh's final chapter involves a railroad strike and a dead body hidden in a trunk. It's, of course, the story of Pittsburgh's Union Station — now the Pennsylvanian Apartments.

The 13-story, Romanesque building was completed in 1903. The upper floors housed hotel rooms for travelers, while the ground floor was accented by a dramatic, 40-foot-high rotunda that sheltered carriages coming in and out of the station. It was the third train station built on the site.

The first one burned down in a deadly skirmish.

In May of 1877, the Pennsylvania Railroad imposed its second 10 percent pay cut in two years. Workers had had enough. Since the Panic of 1873, railroads had laid off millions of workers and expected longer hours from the ones that remained — all for lower pay. Something needed to change, and it was going to take violence.

Baltimore was the first to strike. On July 16, workers blocked B&O trains in Baltimore and Martinsburg, West Virginia. One by one, the surrounding cities joined in. Philadelphia, Reading, Scranton, Columbia, and — yes — Pittsburgh halted all commercial train traffic.

Alexander Cassatt, a native of Pittsburgh who was also vice president at the company headquarters in Philadelphia, immediately came to Pittsburgh and demanded that the authorities remove the strikers off the tracks. When that didn't happen, Cassatt summoned the Philadelphia militia, which opened fire on the crowd.

Over 20 people were killed and dozens of others were wounded. As the fighting raged out of control, the militia finally sought cover in a roundhouse while looters on the outside burned the whole depot, as well as 1,200 freight cars, 100 locomotives, and a total of 30 buildings that included the main station. In the aftermath, a new station was built so quickly that people complained it looked "like a country barn or a fourth-class livery stable."

The new, elegant Beaux-Arts station came along a short time later.

For twenty more years, Union Station operated fairly smoothly, with one notable exception in 1885.

That May, workers unloaded a freight car full of trunks coming in from Chicago. Trunks were commonly used by travelers to keep their clothing, shoes, toiletries, and personal items in — plus anything else they wished to ship elsewhere.

According to legend, one of these trunks smelled absolutely rotten. The workers assumed it contained food that had gone bad. It wasn't unusual for people to stash fruits and bread in their luggage. But the smell continued to get worse as the day went on. It was so bad that they finally pulled the trunk out of the baggage room and set it on the open-air platform.

The trunk sat, forgotten, until later that day, when Union Station received a telegraph from the station in Columbus, Ohio, which said they had also received a smelly trunk… and it was bound for Pittsburgh. This was enough to catch the stationmaster's attention. He asked the baggage crew where they'd put the first trunk and they pointed outside, scrunching up their noses at the lingering stench.

There it was: Bound by heavy rope that seemed to say, "DO NOT OPEN." The stationmaster felt a cold lump of dread settle at the bottom of his ribcage. The smell was… distinct — the kind of stench you don't forget once you've smelled it. He hoped he wasn't right about what was inside.

He ordered a few employees to cut the ropes and jimmy the locks. As they pushed the trunk upright, something heavy slid to the bottom.

The stationmaster's dread grew. Finally, the ropes were cut and the locks had popped open.

The men peeled back the top to reveal exactly what the stationmaster feared: A rotting corpse.

The body had been bound up with rope, and he had been strangled. Some paperwork in the man's pocket revealed he was probably named Phillipe Caruso. With nothing to go on, the authorities were summoned and the trunk, and its grisly contents, were taken to Flannery's Undertaking Parlors for further investigation. The killers were eventually apprehended and tried in Chicago.

As for the Columbus trunk… It arrived later that day. The stationmaster rushed it through processing and placed it on a train bound for Philadelphia. Their crew could deal with it.

As the 20th century progressed and rail travel declined, the station faced demolition several times. In 1966, it was saved by the Pittsburgh History & Landmarks Foundation. In 1976, it was added to the National Register of Historic Places. It became The Pennsylvanian Apartments in 1988.

Today, there are 26 upscale apartments on the upper floors, while the waiting room inside is now the lobby. A small Amtrak depot continues to operate behind the complex, making Pittsburgh Union Station the oldest downtown train station still in use. And it isn't only the living who travel in and out…

The spirits of the past sweep through now and then. Misty figures vanish behind corners. Mysterious orbs float through the complex. Disembodied voices seem to travel on the wind. At night, there's a heavy feeling of being watched — even when the hallways are empty.

But the most disturbing occurrence at the Pennsylvanian is the rotting stench that occasionally rises up from the old train platform. Residents complain that it smells like rotten eggs, and no one can tell them where it's coming from.

Is it the smell of Caruso's body, still plaguing the former station? Or is it something else entirely? A reminder of some sinister crime lost to history?

There's no doubt the old station is scarred by secrets. Thousands of people have passed through its halls since 1903, and some of them decided to linger.

One woman noticed that her cats seemed especially skittish while living there, like they were always on alert and staring into thin air as though they could see something — or someone.

The Pennsylvania Apartments, Pittsburgh, PA.

The Pennsylvania Apartments, Pittsburgh, PA.

BONUS CHAPTER

Pennsylvania's Most Haunted Continued

You've explored the most terrifying corners of three Pennsylvania cities, and now it's time to take a detour.

Just north of historic Philly, a decaying relic of 19th century "prison reform" is nestled between modern buildings and parking lots. Eastern State Penitentiary could send a chill up anyone's spine — believer or not. Years of isolation, torture, and murder have drenched its long corridors in negative energy… but many visitors have experienced more than just a "bad feeling."

In Centre Hall, just off Route 192, you'll find a wildlife park that's home to an ancient cave — and a 300-year-old urban legend. Find out why visitors hear strange echoes and hushed whispers spoken in a Native American tongue.

And of course, there's the famously haunted Hotel Bethlehem, the best place to book "a room with a boo." Meet the hotel's four famous spirits: A singer, a town guide, a landlord, and the mysterious entity of Room 932.

These four stories may inspire you to take a road trip… or stay very far away.

Terrors of Pennsylvania

Eastern State Penitentiary | Philadelphia, PA

Eastern State Penitentiary, Philadelphia, PA.

Head a few miles north of Independence Hall and you'll find a decaying castle that was once the most famous prison in the country: Eastern State Penitentiary.

Throughout the prison's 142 years in operation, it was hailed as a model facility and branded a torture chamber. Today, the massive gothic structure is a museum and historic site. If the crumbling, solitary cells don't give you chills, the lingering spirits certainly will…

When Eastern State opened in 1829, it was a modern marvel. Prisoners were treated to central heating and indoor plumbing — luxuries that not even President Andrew Jackson had at the White House. But the physical comforts were quickly overshadowed by the psychological torture. It was called the "Pennsylvania System," and it operated on the belief that solitary confinement led to penitence and reformation.

Prisoners were completely isolated.

They spent 23 hours a day in a small cell with a skylight called the "eye of God," meant to represent the fact that God was always watching.
For one hour, they were permitted to enter another small room with an open roof. This was their "outdoor time." Meals were silently shoved through an opening in their cell door. Letters and social visits were forbidden, and recreation was nonexistent. Prisoners could read the Bible or do manual

labor like shoemaking. If they sang, hummed, or talked aloud — even to themselves — they were severely punished.

And punishment was inevitable. As the days stretched into weeks, months, and years, madness set in, and desperation overpowered fear. Men would tap on pipes to communicate with their neighbors. They would shout over the walls of their exercise rooms. Not long after the prison opened, the inmates trained a rat to carry messages between the cells.

First-time offenders were locked in an empty, dark cell for a day or two. They were denied meals and told to sit with their thoughts.

Repeat offenders were tortured. One man was locked in a dark cell for 42 days. In the winter, prisoners were stripped to their waists and chained to an outside wall before being drenched in water. As the hours passed, ice would form on their skin, causing severe pain and — at times — death.

In the warmer months, they were strapped to a chair so tightly that their circulation was cut off. They'd stay there alone for days without food or water until someone took pity on them. The chair eventually earned the nickname "the mad chair," but madness was the best-case scenario. Amputations and death were also common.

Still, nothing topped the iron gag.

The gag was a five-inch plate that fit over the prisoner's tongue. His wrists were tied behind him via chains that connected to the plate. If he pulled with his arms, the metal cut into his mouth, causing severe pain and bleeding. At least one inmate died fighting the device.

Between the physical and psychological torture, Eastern State became hell on earth. Suicide was common. Prisoners found ways to hang themselves or slit their own throats. Some spent their days plotting ways to escape. When the prison was renovated in the 1930s, crews discovered at least 30 incomplete tunnels leading out of cells.

By 1913, it was clear the Pennsylvania System wasn't working, but its downfall wasn't morality — it was money. Eastern State had a per-prisoner cost that was seven times greater than other prisons, and the price of expansion would be outrageous if they continued building private cells, so they scrapped the isolation method and allowed inmates to share a room.

This came with a new set of problems.

Overcrowding soon caused conditions to deteriorate. Two or three inmates were forced to share what began as tiny, solitary cells. Riots, fights, and killings scarred the "model facility".

In the midst of all of this, the prison received its first celebrity inmate: the infamous gangster Al Capone. Though he was only incarcerated for eight months between 1929 and 1930, Capone was treated like a king. He had a private cell with a desk, lamp, wall art, and a radio. It looked more like a lavish office than a dank prison cell. But Capone's stay at Eastern State wasn't a walk in the park. It's said he woke up screaming every night: "Go away, Jimmy! Leave me be!"

Of course, there was no one named Jimmy in Capone's cell. He was seeing a ghost.

James Clark had been shot to death during the St. Valentine's Day Massacre of 1929 — a mass murder that was likely organized by Capone. The iconic gangster was safe from retaliation inside the stone walls of Eastern State, but he wasn't safe from the ghosts of the past.

Dozens of paranormal teams have investigated the prison since it officially closed in the 1970s. Armed with flashlights, cameras, and recording devices, they venture through the prison's empty stone corridors in the dark. The eerie silence seems to stretch for miles — until it's broken by phantom footsteps or an errant cackle. They rarely leave disappointed.

In Cellblock 6, dark shadows slide along the walls, whispering, screaming, and laughing as they go. In Cellblock 12, the misty apparition of a prisoner appears behind cell doors. In Cellblock 4, the anguished faces of tortured prisoners show up in photographs.

Tradesmen have refused to go back to the prison after experiencing "intense, choking dread" while working. The dark outline of a guard looms over visitors from the old watchtower. Even when there are no visible spirits around, people have the strong sense that they're being watched — even if they're completely alone.

Imagine standing in the middle of an empty, stone cell, training your flashlight on the crumbling walls all around you. Your buddies are in another block and the silence is terrifying. Suddenly you feel a heavy tap-tap on your shoulder. The flashlight drops from your hand as you jump, and all you can do is run. The spirits cackle as you bolt down the corridor. Hardcore thrill seekers have ended up bolting out the doors of Eastern State, swearing they'll never return. And who could blame them?

Orbs float along the empty hallways. Whispers emulate from every corner. Phantom doors slam shut. Shadows whoosh past. Standing in the crumbling halls of Eastern State feels like going mad. It's exactly how the prisoners felt over a century ago…

Eastern State Penitentiary, Philadelphia, PA.

The Devil's Elbow | Altoona, PA

The Devil's Elbow, Altoona, PA.

On a crisp fall day, a leisurely drive through the Alleghenies can be a beautiful sight. The vibrant trees form a canopy, the foggy mountain tops loom in the distance… but when night falls, those same trees turn into looming monsters, and one sharp curve can turn a leisurely drive into tragedy.

Altoona locals know this all too well.

For over a century, the legend of the "White Lady of the Wopsononock" has been passed down through paintings, music, books, and campfire tales. But who is she? And why does she haunt the mountain roads outside of town?

Sometime around 1890, two young newlyweds were headed to the Wopsononock Hotel for their honeymoon. The mountaintop resort boasted a lookout tower where the couple could enjoy sprawling views and a cozy cottage where they could snuggle by the fire. They could hardly contain their excitement over the romantic getaway… but they would never get to enjoy it.

As they made their way up Wopsy Road, the pavement curved dangerously around the mountain. Today, the curve is a well-known hazard called "Devil's Elbow." Back then, it was a ticking time bomb waiting to claim its first victim. As the carriage careened around the turn, it flipped and plummeted over 1,000 feet down a ravine, throwing all three occupants from the vehicle as it fell. Cracks of wood against rocks and trees echoed in the air. Then — with a final, sickening crash — the carriage came to a stop. Silence fell over the mountain again. No one survived.

Rescuers were able to recover the bodies of the bride and the driver, but the groom was never found. The couple, who had hoped to be buried side-by-side in old age, were eternally separated before their marriage had even begun.

In the years since that fateful night, countless people have spotted a beautiful Irish woman in a flowing white dress walking along the side of the road. Descriptions of her are always the same: She's beautiful, radiant, sad. Her cascading blonde hair blows in the wind as she walks, lighting her way with an antique lantern.

The White Lady of the Wopsononock is still looking for her lost lover.

She will often flag down young men, asking for a ride. When they stop, she's all smiles, but doesn't say a word. She just climbs into the back of the car and sits quietly. Later, these men always report the same thing: That they looked in their rearview mirror and there was no one there, but when they turned around, there she was… still sitting in the back of the car — until they reached Devil's Elbow. The second they rounded the turn, she vanished.

Others have credited the spirit with saving their lives.

In the fall of 1987, a woman was speeding down Wopsy Road in the dark. She and her two friends were chatting, not paying attention to the dangerous curve up ahead. Suddenly a woman appeared in the headlights, her blonde hair shining in the bright light. The driver slammed on the brakes, eventually coming to a full stop just ahead of Devil's Elbow. The woman was nowhere to be found.

Years later, the driver admitted she had been going well over the speed limit that night. If she'd made the turn, she would have lost control of the car and killed them all. She owes her life to a 19th-century ghost.

Many things have changed since that night in 1890. The Wopsononock Hotel was lost to a forest fire in 1903. Carriages are long gone — replaced by high-speed cars. Even Devil's Elbow has changed. Today, the road is paved and outlined by a guard rail with hazard signs.

But tales of the Wopsy Road spirit span generations. Grandparents swap stories with their grandchildren, both still in awe that they'd seen a ghost. And perhaps a hundred years from now, drivers will still see her — the light from her lantern causing them to slow down and avoid the mistakes of the past.

Penn's Cave & Wildlife Park | Centre Hall, PA

Penn's Cave & Wildlife Park | Centre Hall, PA.

Just off Route 192 in Centre Hall, you'll find a 1,600-acre wildlife park dotted with bison, foxes, white-tailed deer, mountain lions, and wolves — and that isn't even the main attraction. Guests can board a flat-bottom boat and tour a natural limestone cavern with towering ceilings covered in glittering stalactites. The 1,300-foot-long cave formed millions of years ago and served various indigenous tribes before it was turned into a "show cavern" in 1885.

By then, it had already been haunted for a century.

The legend dates back to the early 1700s, when the majority of modern-day Pennsylvania was still unclaimed wilderness. It was springtime. A young Frenchman named Malachi Boyer was camping at Mammoth Spring, enjoying the peace and quiet of nature, when he noticed a beautiful Native American woman washing deerskin in the stream. Malachi immediately fell in love, but he knew that love was forbidden. This was Chief O-Ka-Cho's daughter, Nita-Nee. It was known throughout the land that she had seven brothers who guarded her fiercely, and that the tribe would never allow her to marry a white settler.

Still, Malachi couldn't resist being near her. He stayed in the area and the two stole glances whenever possible. Glances turned into loving smiles, which

led to whispered confessions. Soon, the two hatched a plan to run away to the eastern settlements, where they could be married and start a family. But Nita-Nee's seven brothers were waiting for them in the dark.
The lovers were captured and brought to the chief, who immediately locked his daughter away.

Malachi was brought to Penn's Cave — then a nameless, deep-water cavern. The green-hued water was deep, and there was only one way in and one way out. The brothers tossed the Frenchman in and watched him swim back and forth searching for an unguarded exit. Each time he'd try to escape through the cave's opening, they would beat him back, injuring him further. It took over a week, but exhaustion and hunger won out. Malachi crawled to the back of the cave, where the brothers wouldn't see him die, and breathed his last breath. It was a heartbroken whisper: "Nita-Nee."

The brothers eventually collected the man's body, weighed it down with stones, and dropped it into the deepest part of the cave. Nita-Nee was never told what happened to her love, and she lived out the rest of her life as a pale shadow of the woman she once was.

This tale was passed down to folklorist Henry W. Shoemaker from Seneca Indian Isaac Steele in 1892. Shoemaker published it in 1903. By then, Penn's Cave had been a tourist attraction for almost a decade, and both staff and visitors had encountered Malachi's ghost without realizing what it was.

On summer nights, a mournful echo rings through the caves: "Nita-Nee… Nita-Nee…"

Countless people have heard the Frenchman's call, but it seems he isn't alone in the cave. Tourists often find misty, distorted figures in their photographs. Voices bounce off the limestone. Guides have heard female voices calling out as well as hushed whispers spoken in a Native American language.

The cave was already millions of years old by the time Malachi Boyer was thrown into its depths. It's possible others have died there. Perhaps Malachi exists in peace with spirits of the same tribe that killed him.

Though the lovers were never reunited in life, they exist together in nature. The waters of Penn's Cave have been dubbed Lake Nitanee. One can imagine the native princess wrapping her arms around her love as he sank to the bottom. She still holds him to this day.

Terrors of Pennsylvania

Hotel Bethlehem | Bethlehem, PA

Hotel Bethlehem, Bethlehem, PA.

In 1741, Moravian missionaries built a modest log cabin at what's now 437 Main St. in Bethlehem, PA. It was the first house built on the settlement, and it would become one of the most haunted hotels in the United States.

Today, Hotel Bethlehem towers over Main Street. The stately, nine-story building boasts floor-to-ceiling palladium windows and elegant 1920s decor, transporting visitors back to the day it opened in 1922. It was much fancier than the previous hotel built on that spot, the Golden Eagle. By 1918, the wood-frame structure was almost a century old and falling apart. The town wanted a larger, fire-proof hotel, and Charles M. Schwab had no problem paying the bill.

Schwab was a wealthy steel magnate who had grown Bethlehem Steel into an industrial powerhouse. A new, elegant hotel would impress businessmen who regularly traveled to the town to meet with him — so Hotel Bethlehem was born. The list of notable guests racked up quickly. Amelia Earhart attended a banquet at the hotel, Winston Churchill stayed there when he toured Bethlehem Steel, and Eisenhower booked a room so he could mediate the Steel Strike of the late 1950s.

But Schwab's guests were in for a unique experience when they unlocked the doors to their rooms… The Bethlehem is haunted by four famous spirits: A singer, a town guide, a landlord, and the mysterious entity of Room 932. All four seem to be left over from the Golden Eagle Hotel, and they're not shy.

May Augusta Yohe

May Augusta Yohe was born at the Golden Eagle in 1866, and she spent her childhood singing and dancing in the hotel lobby. She was a charming, confident little girl. There was no denying she had talent. In fact, the Moravians were so impressed by her that they sent her to an arts school in Paris, where she won over teachers and classmates.

By the time she was 25, she was a traveling singer, but her romantic escapades often overshadowed that talent. She married at least seven times before she died in 1938.

At 28, she married Lord Francis Clinton Hope, the owner of the 45-carat Hope Diamond — but the novelty of the diamond (and their marriage) wore off rather quickly. She left him for a "dashing" U.S. Army Captain named Putnam Bradlee Strong in 1902. Strong fought with her and fled with her jewelry. The two divorced in 1905.

After that, Yohe returned to Bethlehem to marry a childhood friend named Newton Brown, but their marriage lasted less than a year. By 1908, she was living in Portland, Oregon, with a new husband — and she gave up a baby boy for adoption. The baby's father is still a mystery.

From Portland, Yohe moved to Seattle, where she wed husband number five: Frank Reynolds. One year later, she was in Chicago living in poverty with husband number six: Jack McAuliffe.

In 1914, she wed another captain: John Addey Smuts. This one stuck, and the two remained together through World War I, the 1918 Influenza epidemic, and a mysterious shooting at their Boston home. Smuts would be the one to sprinkle her ashes in the Atlantic Ocean after she succumbed to heart and kidney disease in 1938. He followed her in death a few months later.

Though she traveled the world and blew kisses to crowds of adoring fans, Yohe was never truly happy as an adult. She was always chasing money, chasing men… Her happiest days were spent as a carefree little girl at the Golden Eagle Hotel.

Staff members at Hotel Bethlehem believe Yohe's spirit returned to her childhood playhouse after she died. The player piano will turn on randomly, bellowing out a jaunty tune, and guests have reported seeing a woman with dark, curly hair and vintage clothing lingering in the third-floor hallway late at night.

Francis "Daddy" Thomas

Long before May Yohe was a twinkle in her mother's eye, Francis Thomas immigrated to Lancaster, PA, from Germany.

At six years old, he found himself influenced by the morals and work ethic of the Moravian Bishop Spangenberg, and he carried those values throughout his life. He remained faithfully married to the same woman for 53 years, he happily fostered three children who had been sent to Bethlehem by missionaries, and he made sure anyone who visited town was well taken care of. He became the unofficial town concierge.

Though Thomas died in 1822, he's still caring for guests at Hotel Bethlehem to this day. Visitors have spotted him in the boiler room, peeking over people's shoulders as if to say, "Do you need anything?"

Mrs. Brong

The Bethlehem's restaurant, "1741 On The Terrace," offers a rotating menu of farm-to-table dishes and romantic views of the surrounding town. It's the perfect place for a date night — but be warned. You may be rudely interrupted by a barefoot ghost.

In 1833, the landlords of the Golden Eagle Hotel — Mr. And Mrs. Brong — were fired by the owners. They had only been in charge of the building for six months, yet they'd managed to destroy the hotel's reputation with their behavior. Mr. Brong spent almost every evening in the bar, drinking until he couldn't stand without falling over. Mrs. Brong liked to greet guests completely barefoot. That might be viewed as unprofessional today, but in the 19th-century it was a social death sentence.

The couple was lectured and fired. Mr. Brong was able to move on, but Mrs. Brong seems to have some unfinished business with the hotel. Dinner guests, cooks, and servers have all reported seeing a woman in 19th century clothing lurking in the restaurant area. How do they know it's Mrs. Brong?

The ghost is always barefoot.

Room 932

The final spirit of the hotel is a mysterious entity that's taken over Room 932. Management cheekily calls it a "room with a boo."

One night, a couple awoke to a man standing over their bed asking, "Why are you in my room?" Terrified, they fumbled around for the light switch. As soon as it turned on, the man disappeared.

Other guests have spotted floating orbs zooming through the room late at night. Figures appear in the mirror, only to vanish when someone does a double-take. But the most chilling experiences involve the room "changing." There have been several reports that the decor, the wallpaper, and the furniture in the room change at night. One man woke up to find he was in a completely different room altogether.

Is the room transporting guests back in time?

In 2007, a paranormal investigator arrived at the hotel to sort out the mysteries of Room 932 once and for all. He recorded voices saying, "It's Mary," "What a beautiful bathroom," "I've locked myself in the closet," and "Look out the window."

The identity of the "boo" in Room 932 may never be revealed, but one thing is certain: Hotel Bethlehem is teeming with spirits who are ready to tell their stories.

A Night at The Welty House

The Welty House Ghost Hunt
If You Dare

Spirit still linger at **The Original Welty House Site:** Crowds return soldiers' national cemetery dedication, November 19, 1863, Gettysburg, PA.

Spirits of Soldiers

Hunt for Ghosts → *A Night to Die For*

Ghost Hunt in the Heart of Haunted Gettysburg

Explore the haunted and historic home that played a role in the Battle of Gettysburg.

Dive Into Real Civil War History in Gettysburg

Uncover Gettysburg's fascinating Civil War history during the hunt.

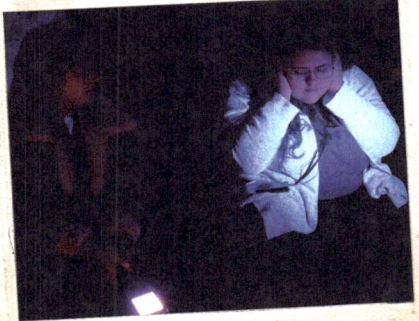

Investigate with Custom-made Equipment

Use EMF detectors, Spirit Boxes, Thermal Detectors, and more to connect with potential spirits.

Ghosts in the Shadows

Interact with Ghosts of the Past

Photograph anomalies and get evidence of paranormal activity.

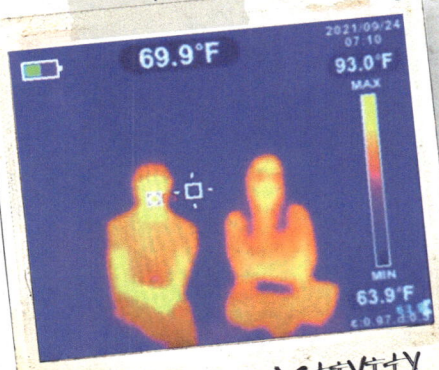
Paranormal Activity

Dare to Book Your Ghost Hunt Now!

usghostadventures.com/welty-house

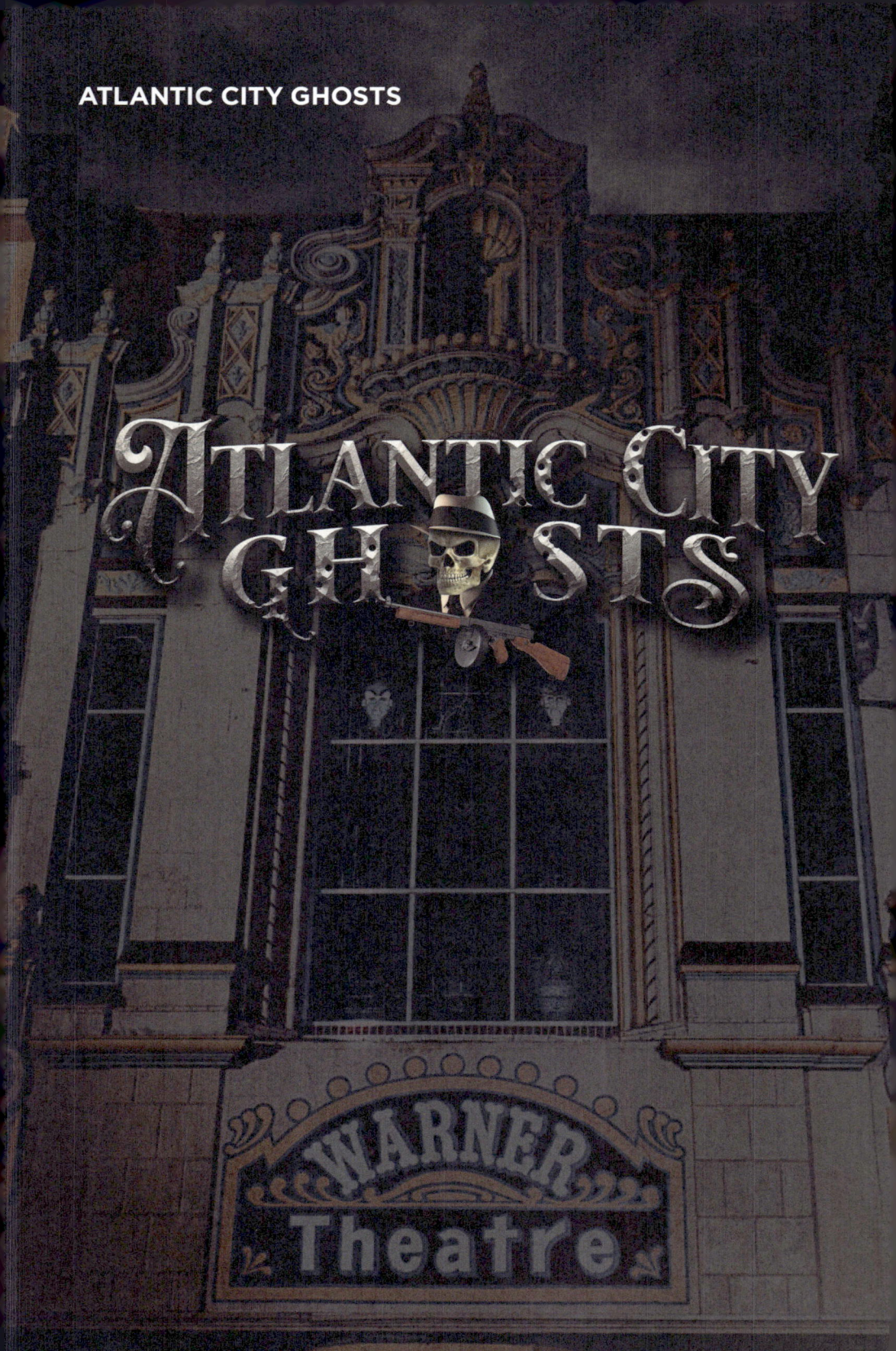

CHAPTER VII

The Ghosts of Atlantic City

Atlantic City has been a popular tourist destination since the 1880s, when the railroad began delivering city-weary crowds to the seaside boardwalk. Kids skipped down pleasure piers with fistfuls of saltwater taffy while their parents lounged in the sand. Broadway wannabes put on flashy shows. By the 1920s, it had become "America's Playground."

But Atlantic City's glory days are interwoven with tragedy, turmoil, and death. During Prohibition, violent mobsters lurked in the shadows of the city's towering hotels. Nucky Johnson pulled puppet strings from the ninth floor of the Ritz, and blood flowed through the streets just as often as liquor.

In the 40s, war came to the Jersey Shore. Thousands of World War II vets were treated at Thomas M. England General Hospital, and some of them never made it home. Now their spirits linger on the property, terrifying guests at the Resorts Casino Hotel.

These days, the struggling city is better known for vices than vacations. High rollers rake in chips as they sip cocktails on vibrant casino floors. A good night in Atlantic City can make you feel invincible. A bad one can end your life. Plagued by tragic suicides, the Colosseum Parking Garage has become a hotbed of ghostly activity… and a reflection of the city's darkest moments.

The following chapters detail the legends, hauntings, and best-kept secrets of New Jersey's most famous city. You'll never look at Park Place and Boardwalk the same way again.

usghostadventures.com/atlantic-city

Playground Pier

Playground Pier, Atlantic City, NJ.

In 1906, an entrepreneur named Captain John L. Young announced he was going to build a pier that "cost a million dollars" at the end of Arkansas Avenue. Today, it's known as Playground Pier, and all that remains of Young's dream are the spirits left behind…

The Million Dollar Pier was 1,900 feet long, jutting over the Atlantic Ocean. It claimed the "world's largest ballroom," a 4000-seat Hippodrome theater, a roller skating rink, an aquarium, a reproduction of a Greek temple, and an exhibit hall.

To great fanfare, the pier opened on July 26th, 1906, right in the midst of the summer heat. The Million Dollar Pier hosted circuses, dance marathons, western shows, big bands, and other entertainment. There were even daily fishing net hauls brought in that were directed by Captain Young himself.

Visitors to the pier gathered twice daily for the best show around, nets upon nets of fish being hauled up from the salty waves and spilled onto the deck. The crowd gawked, but the most striking view was that of Captain Young, in his puffy pantaloons and straw hat, lecturing on the wonders of the ocean.

But time moves on, and business at the Million Dollar Pier didn't last. After bankruptcy, the Pier changed owners multiple times. Attractions came and went. To stay afloat, they charged admission to the pier, then they dropped the admittance charge to attract visitors, then they added it again.

Like so many things, the Pier fell into neglect and disrepair. Captain Young died in 1938. The Pier suffered two fires, both under suspicious circumstances. Arson destroyed the aquarium, the skating rink, and the ballroom in 1949. In 1957, a short in an electric sign damaged the Hippodrome.

While that electric short seems like a case of bad luck, arson certainly points to something more insidious. Though no one was ever charged with a crime, it seems a bit unlikely that someone would burn down an area set for demolition for no good reason. It would certainly save on some of the costs of tearing down a structure if you let a fire do for free what a team of men might charge a lot to do. As in many Atlantic City mysteries, it seems like we'll never know the full story.

In late August and early September of 1960, Hurricane Donna swept up the Eastern coast. The storm was responsible for millions of dollars in damages and the loss of hundreds of lives along its path from western Africa, through the Caribbean, and along the United States's shoreline. Among her casualties, Donna claimed 50 feet of the Pier that had been hanging over the ocean.

With no one to support the efforts, the Pier fell into severe disuse, with wide gaps between sections. A third fire, even more suspicious than the first two, destroyed what was left while the pier was being demolished in 1981.

Fire. Destruction. Decay. It's little wonder that this area has attracted attention from the spirit world — because it's been largely abandoned by the living. Walking through the Pier mall today is like strolling through a ghost town. The vast majority of the shops and restaurants are empty, their storefronts serving as reminders of a commercial center that thrived just a few years ago.

But dare to walk through the mall at night, and you will realize that you are not alone. Shadows stir in the corners, peek out from darkened doorways, and follow closely with the sound of invisible feet scuffling.

Locals have also reported seeing phantom fishermen standing at the edge of the pier, perhaps looking for the net haul and Captain Young. Maybe they are wondering what has become of the Million Dollar Pier they once knew. The number of fatal accidents involving fishermen on the pier over the years is unknown. These apparitions could be the ghosts of the unfortunate ones who now haunt where they used to haul.

Across the water, strange lights illuminate the way for these ghostly fishermen. Glowing orbs appear in the ocean like impossible bobbers. Some say these lights may simply belong to bioluminescent fish. But why are they always spotted on the same nights as the phantom fishermen?

And when the shops are closed and the people have all gone home, unmistakable sounds echo from the pier. The circus barkers. The old dance hall music. Children laughing across the ice rink. Conversations that no longer make sense for our time, in this place. Memories of better days, or perhaps sadder days, still lingering over the ocean's waves.

Playground Pier, Atlantic City, NJ.

Warner Theatre

Warner Theatre, Atlantic City, NJ.

Atlantic City is constantly changing, racing to keep up with the next big thing. The city's been torn down and rebuilt so many times that it's rare to see a surviving relic of the old days — but Warner Theatre is just that. The ornate facade has avoided the bulldozer for almost a century, and it seems to be a safe haven for the spirits of the past.

The elegant Warner Palace Theatre opened for business in 1929. A marvel of design, it boasted more than 4,000 seats and details borrowed from Spanish-Moorish design. Its first screening was the 1929 musical *On With the Show*, the first talkie film released completely in color. It was a worldwide hit, taking in more than $2 million globally — nearly $35 million today.

Through the 30s, the Warner was a highlight of Atlantic City's vibrant entertainment culture. It played the classic movies from Hollywood's Golden Age, and music from the theater's massive Wurlitzer organ wowed the audience between pictures.

In the 50s, the theater changed focus and changed names. As the Warren Theater, the venue focused solely on live entertainment. Ella Fitzgerald. Mel Torme. Ricky Nelson. At one point, the owner was offered the chance to showcase a new, rising talent. He declined, however, reportedly saying to the talent agency, "Who's going to go for a guy with a crazy name like 'Elvis'?"

By 1966, the venue had changed again, this time into a bowling alley that hosted all the famous pros. In 1979 the theater was demolished to make room for a car park, but the facade remained. Through the 1980s and 90s it stayed there, with a tiny building behind it operating as a burger stand.

By the early 2000s, it seemed like the Warner's number was finally up. Caesars and Bally's had plans to combine their casinos, but the old facade was standing in their way. It was a woman named Florence who rallied to save it. She was heartbroken that another piece of Atlantic City history was going to be destroyed, so she talked them out of their plans, and the casinos worked the old facade into their new construction.

It still stands today, now hosting Atlantic City's first permanent entertainment residency, continuing the tradition established 100 years ago of bringing the latest, greatest talent to the boardwalk.

It seems the change has stirred up some ghosts as well.

Late at night, the faint sound of organ music floats on the wind, though the theater's Wurlitzer was hauled away long ago. Witnesses have spotted the apparition of what appears to be a homeless man in the balcony area at night. The man is very thin with raggedy clothing and disheveled hair. His identity is a mystery, and he vanishes from sight as soon as anyone begins to approach him. Some speculate that it may be the ghost of a homeless person who lived on this site — and possibly died here as well — after the theater was demolished.

Others claim to have seen hazy figures of people in old-style clothing, standing on the walkway where they would have waited for someone. Maybe it is the lingering impression of a rondez-vous that never happened, and now the longing ghost spends every night hoping their special someone will give them a second chance, even all these decades later.

During World War II, some soldiers would spend their last nights at the theater before shipping out to war. Their bodies didn't make it home, but their spirits remember their last happy memory. This place was busy for a long time. Many people came through the theater's doors. Perhaps some of them never left.

Caesars Atlantic City

Caesars Atlantic City, Atlantic City, NJ.

When people think about Atlantic City, most imagine a place like Caesars, where a steady stream of cash and booze keep the party going all night long. High rollers show off at the blackjack table. A single dice roll can make or break you.

It's one of the city's oldest casinos — opened in 1979, three years after gambling was made legal. Of course, gambling had been happening in Atlantic City for decades by then. Before Vegas was Vegas, there was Atlantic City.

And, like Vegas, Atlantic City had ties to the mob.

In 1929, the nation's leading gangsters descended on the boardwalk for a three-day summit now called the "Atlantic City Conference." It was led by Enoch Lewis "Nucky" Johnson, a New Jersey politician who had become the Crime Boss of Atlantic City. He gathered the hoard of gangsters — which included Al Capone — at the President Hotel to discuss the future of organized crime, then retired to the Ritz-Carlton Hotel, where he spent his nights. He was known as the "Czar of the Ritz," because he leased the entire ninth floor.

Johnson was at the height of his power then. The U.S. Government had enacted Prohibition in 1920, but Johnson made sure the liquor never stopped flowing in Atlantic City. In return, he received a cut of every gallon of booze sold — and there were many gallons of booze sold. Over 40 percent of the illegal alcohol coming into the country came through, or near, Atlantic City.

The glittering allure of liquor, prostitution, and gambling made the Jersey Shore a premiere destination, a true adult playground. And the 1920s became Atlantic City's Golden Age.

But the boom was about to end.

The first nail in the coffin came in October of 1929, when the stock market crashed and plunged America into the Great Depression. The second came four years later, when F.D.R. repealed Prohibition. With booze available everywhere, Atlantic City lost its allure.

The final nail came a decade later, when Americans shipped out to fight in WWII. Though the city buoyed itself by turning hotels into military barracks, it wasn't enough. The city floundered through the 50s and 60s. By the 1970s, journalists reported that it was on "life support."

The city needed to go back to the 1920s… but they had to do it legally this time. Alcohol was already legal, and prostitution was out, so the last bastion of hope was gambling. The issue was placed on the November 1976 ballot and approved by a slim margin of 56 percent. Casinos were coming to Atlantic City — but there were concerns about the mob getting involved.

After signing the Casino Control Act into law, New Jersey Governor Brendan Byrne issued a stern warning to organized crime bosses in the area: "Keep your filthy hands off Atlantic City and keep the hell out of our state!" The only problem was that they'd already moved in.

Nucky Johnson had died in 1968, so there was a new boss in town: Nicodemo "Little Nicky" Scarfo. Standing five-foot-five inches tall, he had a severe Napoleon Complex that resulted in a murderous temper, and he unleashed that temper on the businesses moving into Atlantic City. He bullied them into choosing his company, Scarf Inc., to pour the foundations for their casinos — including Caesar's.

Soon he had the Atlantic City mayor, Michael Matthews, in his back pocket. Politicians were easily bribed. Anyone who wasn't easily bribed was threatened… or worse. By the time he was arrested for extortion in 1987,

Scarfo had played a part in at least 20 murders. He was sentenced to 69 years in prison, which ended up being a life sentence. He died in 2017 at the age of 87.

Since then, Atlantic City hasn't had any more mob bosses. The FBI cracked down on organized crime in the 1980s and 90s, removing the most influential bosses and their number twos. While mobsters still exist, they're nowhere near as powerful as Nucky or Nicodemo… not the living ones anyway.

Guests at hotels across Atlantic City report seeing ghosts in vintage suits lurking in the shadows, watching, waiting… At Caesar's, there's a man in black who floats through the halls. When people try to get a good look, he disappears.

Sometimes a phantom hand jiggles the door handles of the guestrooms. When people call out, "Who is it?" they're met with silence. When they finally open the door, there's no one there, but the strong smell of cigarettes lingers in the air despite a years-long ban on smoking in hotels.

Some think the spirit is one of the countless gamblers who've come and gone from Caesar's. He's hit it big, and he wants to cash out just one more time. But others claim he's one of Nucky or Nicodemo's men — a hazy reminder of Atlantic City's roots and a bloody history it will never fully escape.

The Colosseum Parking Garage

The Colosseum Parking Garage, Atlantic City, NJ.

On its face, the Colosseum Parking Garage is a pretty typical parking structure. Ten levels, open air, and it's been in Atlantic City as long as Caesars, so it's become a pretty familiar landmark. Most people don't give the place anywhere close to a second thought, even though they should.

Parking garages are the perfect place for modern paranormal activities. They are dark, with a lot of corners that stay just outside our vision. They're cold, too, even in the summer. Even in Atlanta City's heat, the Colosseum Garage feels like it has never seen sunlight. Sound behaves strangely too. It's like noises come from everywhere and nowhere all at once. It's hard to find the source of voices or footsteps until they're right on top of you. And smells linger, even in a breeze. Like a memory you can't forget.

One of those memories was made in April 2021. The winds coming off the Atlantic Ocean are chilly, but there's a hint of Spring in the air and the undercurrent of warmer weather soon to come. It's a Wednesday, lunchtime, and everything is business as usual, until, as witnesses later recount, a man takes to standing at the edge of the parking garage's highest level.

That's pretty high up there. And there's no good reason to be that close to the edge.

As the people at ground level watch, without any indication or sound, the man steps off the building, falling ten stories and meeting his demise on the asphalt below. He was 62 years old. The man's identity was never released, and no one knows why he stepped off the ledge. Maybe he lost all his money gambling and subsequently lost his will to live.

But that wasn't the only dark day for the Colosseum Garage. On October 19, 2010, an investigator from New York City died of a self-inflicted gunshot wound on one of the levels. No one knows what exactly he was doing there, but he'd been missing for several days before passing authorities discovered him in his car. That man was 49.

These situations are, unfortunately, common in Atlantic City. The city itself seems to breed the kind of loss and desperation necessary for such drastic decisions: either through financial loss at the gambling tables or the sort of personal loss that rising and falling fortunes tends to enhance.

Negative energy feeds into itself, creating an emotional cycle that increases over time. The cumulative impact takes its toll and can leave an imprint upon a place where such terrible events have occurred.

What terrible voices did these men hear to cause them to take their own lives? We can't say. Sadly, we'll never truly understand what pushed them in those final moments.

What we do know, however, is that people often feel an ominous presence in and around the parking garage. Visitors to Caesars have returned to their cars and reported seeing a shadow darting between the vehicles, as if searching for the perfect place to hide until it's time to jump out and catch someone by surprise.

Others have heard a disembodied voice within the concrete walls, the eerie speech undefinable as it bounces off the walls and ceilings like a chattering spirit surrounding you as you try to make it to your vehicle.

Witnesses have also seen someone looking over the edge of the garage as they stood on the outside. Photographs taken near the garage often show hazy orbs floating around the structure. One visitor even reported seeing a bright light falling from the top of the garage onto the cement below, only to vanish at the final moment. These creepy visual phenomena are undoubtedly supernatural manifestations of the people who have died there, the sorrowful souls that still haunt the place where they ended their own lives.

Jim Whelan Boardwalk Hall

Jim Whelan Boardwalk Hall, Atlantic City, NJ.

Constructed in 1926, Jim Whelan Boardwalk Hall is one of the oldest buildings in America's Playground. As such, the former convention center is rich with the history of Atlantic City corruption.

Then-Mayor Edward Bader, one of Nucky Johnson's best-connected political cronies, lobbied for the purchase of land to develop the hall.

It's where Arturo "Thunder" Gatti and "Irish" Mickey Ward battled in the third bout of their legendary trilogy. It's where a young fighter by the name of Mike Tyson fought and dismantled Larry Holmes in 1988. Later that year, Tyson destroyed and retired previously undefeated Michael Spinks in 91 seconds. It was Spinks's first loss, and it scared him so much that he retired almost immediately after the fight.

The Jim Whelan Boardwalk Hall has hosted many other sports as well, such as hockey, football, and basketball. In fact, the hall was even the home of the Atlantic City CardSharks, a now-defunct indoor football team. It was also once home of the college football Liberty Bowl and later, the Boardwalk Bowl. And most notably, it's a concert hall.

It boasts the largest pipe organ in the world, according to Guinness.

Its incredible acoustics have supported some amazing performances. The Beatles stopped there on a tour a week after the Democratic National Convention in 1964. The Rolling Stones, Bruce Springsteen and the E Street Band, Bon Jovi, Phish, Madonna, Brittney Spears, Jennifer Lopez, Lady Gaga, Beyonce, and others have all performed there.

And in 1961, Judy Garland performed two shows in the hall. They went so well, she may have never left.

The Hollywood icon and "It girl" had been performing since the age of two. She had a career as a singer, dancer, and actress that spanned forty-five years. Sadly, she died tragically from an accidental overdose of barbiturates at age 47.

She had a very tumultuous life and career, battling inner demons and the studio system through the entirety of it. Garland was 16 when she rose to national prominence after starring as Dorothy in *The Wizard of Oz* in 1939. Despite her cheery public image, Garland was institutionalized after a suicide attempt while filming *The Pirate* in 1948. Her life would continue to be full of turmoil, including struggles with substance abuse, several failed marriages, and a poor self-image as a result of movie executives criticizing her appearance.

She found peace on the stage, however, and used her voice to move audiences everywhere she performed. That includes Boardwalk Hall, where it's said she gave one of her most powerful performances. Garland sang there in 1961, and that night, as she sang "The Man That Got Away" from her movie *A Star is Born*, audience members reported feeling unexplainable cold spots, psychic energy, and phantom touching. Like someone was reaching out to them.

Garland's voice was always described as memorable. Powerful but also fragile. Beautiful but tinged with a sense of hurt and loss, like the broken shards of a stained glass window. The people in the Hall were lucky to have shared such an experience.

These days, Garland is gone, but the presence people felt that night still lingers. Visitors still experience odd impressions that someone is there, just out of view, watching and trying to communicate. It could very well be the emotional energy of Judy Garland's magical voice. But there seem to be other entities at Jim Whelan Boardwalk Hall as well.

Construction workers doing repairs on part of the hall have reported seeing their tools move across the floor on their own as if pushed by an unseen force. One worker approached what he initially thought was a co-worker until the shadowy figure dissipated before his eyes. Some believe this to be the ghost of a past employee who perished under a falling stack of pallets that crushed him to death.

Other stories claim that if you peer into a certain mirror in the building, in the dark or by candlelight, bad luck or even death may soon follow you. People even say they sometimes see *someone else* in the mirror with them. Who is the spectral face in the glass? A past visitor? A phantom performer?

After Michael Spinks's 91-second knockout loss to Mike Tyson at the Hall in 1988, he famously said, "Fear was knocking at my door, big time." How could a man, previously undefeated, whose career had spanned 12 years, suddenly lose himself so badly going into the biggest fight of his life?

Maybe he was getting prepared for his match, hyping himself up, staring at his own reflection in the mirror. Then that ghostly face appeared next to him, gazing back from the glass, looking into Spinks's eyes and striking fear into his heart. That would be enough to throw anyone off their game, and perhaps it was this spirit that scared Spinks into retirement.

The Ghosts of Atlantic City, NJ.

Atlantic City Beach

Atlantic City Beach, Atlantic City, NJ.

Perhaps the most haunted place in Atlantic City is its oldest feature — a place that predates every hotel, restaurant, and casino: The beach. It was a summer home for the Lenni-Lenape Indians, who fished and hunted on the shore. It witnessed European exploration in the 16th and 17th centuries. And it became a healing retreat in the 1800s.

That's when tragedy struck.

On April 16, 1854, the wooden schooner *Powhatan* sank just off the Jersey Shore after being battered to splinters by a storm. Around 300 people were on board, mostly German immigrants hoping to start a new life in New York. They would perish before they ever reached land.

Near the end of its journey, the ship encountered a monstrous, hurricane-like storm. Huge waves and biting winds unloaded on the floundering *Powhatan* while the crew fought to reach land. People watched from the shore, unable to do anything more than pray — but their prayers went unanswered. Around 5 p.m., the ship was dashed upon the shoals. The rocks tore a hole clean through, the ship broke apart, and everyone on board drowned.

It gets worse.

Even before the ocean completely claimed the ship, bodies of passengers began washing ashore. Locals frantically searched for signs of life, but it was hopeless. Over the next several days, the tides continued to bring victims onto the beaches.

The manager of the nearby "Mansion of Health" — a healing retreat — headed down to the shore to examine the bodies. His name was Captain Edward Jennings, and he'd been appointed wreckmaster by the State of New Jersey. He was tasked with salvaging any belongings and making sure the bodies were properly stored until the coroner arrived.

Items were scattered for miles. There were trunks with names inscribed on the sides. There were little socks and bonnets. There were books and letters, waterlogged and covered in sand. The hopes and dreams of hundreds of immigrants had been thrown onto the beach, never to be realized.

Jennings began the arduous task of collecting everything and, by the time the coroner arrived, he'd managed to get most of it in order.

A curious thing, though, was that no money had been found on the beach. This was very unusual because immigrants typically brought their life savings on these journeys, safely tucked away in money belts. All eyes immediately turned to Jennings, but there was no proof he had stolen anything, and he reacted in outrage when accused. The state let it go.

A few months later, another violent storm hit the coast. This one caused massive waves to crash onto the shore, licking at the foundations of Jennings' Mansion of Health. When it was over, the waters had eroded a nearby cedar tree, where locals found piles of leather money belts. They'd all been cut open and emptied before being stashed in the tree trunk.

Jennings left New Jersey in disgrace, but he was never able to escape his crimes. He suffered from guilt-ridden nightmares for the rest of his life — the ghosts of the *Powhatan* wreck tormenting him night after night until he died in a barroom brawl in San Francisco. The rest of the spirits remained on the Jersey Shore, where they're still seen today.

At night, when the crowds head home and the only noise is the soft swoosh of the waves coming in and out, people report hearing loud sobs rise over the water. It sounds like hundreds of souls crying out at once, yet there's no one there.

As people walk the beach, they'll catch a hazy apparition in the distance —

a woman in 19th-century clothing, holding her toddler close to her chest. She looks terrified and lost, but anyone who tries to help her is left shocked and confused. As they get closer, she vanishes into the night air.

Perhaps she's looking for her husband. Some families were separated during the burial process, dooming dozens of restless souls to an eternal search. Some wander the beaches, and some linger near the Absecon Lighthouse.

Atlantic City Beach, Atlantic City, NJ.

The Absecon Lighthouse

The Absecon Lighthouse, Atlantic City, NJ.

Jonathan Pitney, considered by most to be the "father" of Atlantic City, had been begging for a lighthouse for almost a decade when the *Powhatan* sank. It wasn't the first ship to perish in the dangerous waters off the Jersey Shore. Over 50 wrecks had occurred since 1847.

But the *Powhatan* tragedy finally motivated Congress to appropriate the funds, and construction on the brand new Absecon Lighthouse began in 1855. Perched at the north end of Atlantic City, it would become one of the most haunted lighthouses in the country...

The most well-known spirits are that of the German shipwreck victims — many of whom were buried close by. They always look worried, like they've lost something important. Some walk in circles. They flicker from one place to the next. These are the spirits who are searching for their families. Buried in two separate places, their spirits are doomed to spend eternity in purgatory, endlessly searching for their missing loved ones.

Others search for the items Captain Jennings stole. They pat their pockets. Some have even been spotted digging in the sand. When visitors approach them to ask if they need help, they don't respond. They just keep digging. Staff members have found disturbed sand and mysterious footprints on days when the lighthouse is closed to visitors.

But the *Powhatan* ghosts aren't the only entities at the lighthouse.

Inside, the strong aroma of cigar smoke fills the air, perhaps left over from an old lighthouse keeper. A few members of the staff swear they've seen him — a big burly man with a bushy beard and 19th-century clothing. One employee says he locked eyes with the ghost before he disappeared.

One of the former lighthouse keepers witnessed a few oddities himself. In 1909, Frank Adams was burning the midnight oil when he heard a loud *thud* above him. The light began to flicker in odd patterns, like something was being waved in front of it. Concerned for passing ships, Adams grabbed his gun and went outside to inspect the tower. There, he found a massive creature "like an ostrich with less feathers." Its massive wings were waving over the lighthouse beacon, blocking the light.

Adams aimed his gun and fired a single shot, hitting the creature dead-on. Later, he said the scream the animal emitted was absolutely "spine chilling," like nothing he'd ever heard before. It flew away, injured but still alive.

Many people believe it was the infamous Jersey Devil of the Pine Barrens.

Nothing quite that dramatic has happened at the lighthouse since then, but it remains a top haunted spot for New Jersey ghost enthusiasts. Orbs are said to float around the tower, and disembodied voices are often heard in the distance. The long, spiral staircase acts as an amplifier, carrying the voices of the past up to tourists standing at the top.

Paranormal investigators rarely leave without collecting some new, bone-chilling piece of evidence, and adding another layer of mystery to the 160-year-old structure.

It's likely to last another two centuries. After Hurricane Sandy pummeled the New Jersey coast in 2012, the lighthouse stood strong and unshaken while the rest of Atlantic City was under water. Though it's dwarfed by towering casinos and flashy hotels today, the lighthouse serves as a steadfast memorial — a reminder that no corporation, no politician, no gangster holds more power in Atlantic CIty than the ocean it's named for.

The Claridge Hotel

The Claridge Hotel, Atlantic City, NJ.

In the early 1940s, Atlantic City had a very different clientele than it does today.

Over 40 Atlantic City hotels signed up to become military barracks after the attack on Pearl Harbor. It was the perfect deal. The city got a steady stream of cash and the military got a readymade encampment, complete with beaches, booze, and broads to entertain servicemen.

Compared to other military camps, it was the lap of luxury, but the horrors of war soon cast a dark shadow over America's Playground — and the Claridge saw it all.

Opened in 1930, the 24-story hotel had earned the nickname "Skyscraper by the Sea" because of its Manhattan-esque design and 370-foot-tall tower. From their rooms, recruits could see the entire city. Yet — instead of seeing a vibrant-neon resort town — they saw shadowy buildings bordered by a pitch-black sea. Why? The lights were cut off at night to prevent a German attack.

During the day, it was easy to ignore their fears. They were training — constantly moving, listening for the next order. But at night, as the military's strict curfew went into effect, they were left with nothing but darkness and their own thoughts. The city's hotels absorbed the fears of over 300,000 troops, and they would soon see those fears become a reality.

By the fall of 1943, the world knew the Axis powers had lost the war. Atlantic City transformed from a training base to a redistribution center for the veterans returning home. Families reunited on the boardwalk, relieved and elated that the hell was finally over. But for some veterans, the hell of war would linger like a dark cloud.

Many returned home with horrific wounds — missing limbs, third-degree burns, embedded shrapnel… and that was only what others could see. Post-Traumatic Stress Disorder (PTSD) was rampant, yet soldiers were expected to mask their feelings.

How many veterans experienced horrific nightmares at the Claridge? How many contemplated ending their lives, if only to stop the voice in their heads saying, "Why should you get to live when your brothers died on the battlefield?"

According to staff members and guests, dozens of World War II vets haunt the hotel to this day. Misty figures walk the halls. The distant sound of wartime music echoes through the building.

Most disconcerting, guests have jolted awake to find barely visible apparitions floating at the foot of their bed. They are always dressed in specific, historic clothing. Some are from the 1930s. Others are 1940s airmen. They always have downcast eyes, seemingly apologizing for disturbing the sleeper, but unable to resist reaching out.

While it's rare to see these apparitions, people who are sensitive to the spirit world report feeling a sense of dread while lounging in their rooms at the Claridge. The feeling is sometimes accompanied by phantom knocking, as if a soldier is being roused by an officer shouting, "It's time to go!"

Those four words would send sixteen million Americans into the bloodiest war in human history. Though we've lost almost all of them in the decades since, their dreams and fears are imprinted on places like the Claridge, where the spirits of the past serve as a constant reminder of the sacrifices of war.

The hauntings are even worse at the Resorts Casino Hotel.

The Ghosts of Atlantic City, NJ.

Resorts Casino Hotel

Resorts Casino Hotel, Atlantic City, NJ.

As soon as voters passed the 1976 gaming referendum, the race was on to see which company would open the city's first casino. Hoping to beat the competition, Resorts International opted to renovate an existing hotel rather than build a new one.

That decision earned them the title of "Atlantic City's most haunted casino."

The hotel they chose was Chalfonte-Haddon Hall, which had served as Thomas M. England General Hospital during the war years. Over 60,000 soldiers had passed through those doors, and some never made it home. The hospital received its first patients on August 15, 1943. On September 3, doctors pronounced their first patient dead.

The veterans at England General had been suffering for weeks by the time they reached American soil. Injured soldiers were treated on the field first, then sent through a chain of hospitals. Sending troops back to the U.S. via hospital ship was a last resort. The journey was long and arduous, accompanied by the constant threat of enemy attack. Only vets who needed long-term rehabilitation were sent home… and some succumbed to their injuries before they ever reached the shore.

These soldiers were recovering from burns, infections, spinal cord injuries, severed limbs. Some had shrapnel embedded in their bodies. Shrapnel wounds were so common that infantrymen coined the phrase, "I'm not so worried about the bullet with my name on it; it's the shell addressed: 'To Whom it May Concern.'"

But the most common injury wasn't physical. Nearly 40 percent of medical discharges during the war were for psychiatric conditions like "combat fatigue," which could turn into a more severe disorder called PTSD. Headaches, irritability, violent outbursts, excessive worry, depression, and loss of appetite were all treated at England General.

While PTSD was better understood in the 1940s than it had been during World War I, treatments were severely lacking. Throughout the late 40s and 50s, veterans would be subjected to experimental treatments like electroshock therapy, insulin-induced comas, and lobotomies. Others would self-medicate with alcohol and drugs, hurting themselves and their families.

It's likely England General was a place of both healing and torment.

By January of 1946, the war had been over for five months. The Army announced it would close England General and return all Atlantic City hotels to their owners — despite protests from patients and business owners. The wounded veterans felt abandoned and the hotels felt cheated. They had been counting on the Army for a steady paycheck through the slow winter months.

Still, the military packed up and left town. By the summer of '46, Atlantic City looked exactly like it had before the war. The only artifact from that time is a plaque on the Resorts Casino Hotel… and the spirits that remain there.

Guests who stay in the Ocean Tower — the oldest part of the complex — report feeling uneasy in their rooms. A few years ago, a couple staying in Room 646 had a harrowing experience. They swore they heard someone bumping into their door and jiggling the handle. When they went to investigate, the hallway was empty and quiet.

Later that night, the couple felt like "someone or something" was in the room, watching them. Even when the presence left, there was an overwhelming feeling of unease — like someone had died there.

Fearing that they'd be laughed at, the couple left without telling the staff what they'd heard and felt. If they had, they would have been assured that they weren't alone.

Dozens of people have reported seeing, hearing, and feeling odd things at Resorts. Some have even witnessed full-bodied apparitions in the hallways and registration area. These misty figures are usually dressed in casual, 1940s clothing — the kind recuperating veterans would have worn. They flicker like an old movie, silently floating through space.

It's possible these are residual hauntings. When a certain action is repeated over and over again — like physical therapy exercises — it can become embedded in the fabric of time. Now those actions are being replayed on a loop, and guests are catching little snippets of them.

The ghost on the 12th floor is most certainly not a residual haunting.

It's said the second the elevator doors open to No. 12, people feel an overwhelming sense of dread. It doesn't help that the entire floor is plagued by a dark entity — a "shadow person" that lurks around corners and vanishes through walls. No one knows who, or what, it is. It doesn't have distinguishing features like the ghosts downstairs. But the prevailing theory is that it's the spirit of a soldier who never made it out of Thomas M. England General.

The 12th floor served as the hospital's morgue.

The Psychic Shop

The Psychic Shop, Atlantic City, NJ.

Atlantic City's most haunted ends with a famed magician, a writer, and a psychic's curse.

In June of 1922, *Sherlock Holmes* author Sir Arthur Conan Doyle held a séance at at Atlantic City's Ambassador Hotel. The goal was two-fold: To connect with the dead, and to prove to Harry Houdini — famed magician and skeptic — that spiritualism was real.

Houdini had his suspicions. Spiritualism had grown into a lucrative industry after the Civil War, as grief-stricken families struggled with the deaths of 620,000 soldiers. They turned to psychics and mediums who claimed they could speak with their dead loved ones, but Houdini — an expert illusionist — believed these people were nothing but table-rappers.

Conan Doyle disagreed. He had plunged headfirst into the world of spiritualism after he lost his son to WWI and the 1918 epidemic. He believed his wife, Jean, was a medium, and he believed Houdini had psychic powers of his own (even though Houdini fervently denied it).

So the two sat together in a darkened room with a Ouija board between them. Jean, Conan Doyle's wife, led the séance. She closed her eyes and tried to connect with a woman who had died nine years earlier: Cecelia Steiner Weiss. Why this woman? She was Houdini's mother.

Houdini had worshiped his mother, and her death had devastated him. That was the one thing Conan Doyle and Houdini had in common: the pain of grief. Houdini wanted to believe in spiritualism because he wanted to believe his mother was still alive in some way — that there was an afterlife, that he would see her again. But he had attended several séances. All he ever found were tricks and lies.

This one was no different.

Jean claimed Cecelia was speaking through her, but nothing she said made sense to the magician. His mother had been a Hungarian immigrant who spoke broken English, yet the messages Jean was "receiving" were all in perfect English. She had also drawn crosses on the tops of each page — something his Jewish mother wouldn't have directed her to do.

Houdini expressed his disbelief, angering the couple, and they parted ways.

Their friendship unraveled over the next few years, as Conan Doyle dug his heels in on the subject of spiritualism, and Houdini denounced the whole movement as a fraud. He went so far as to testify in front of Congress, hoping to regulate the industry. But his arguments had little effect — then and now.

Today, the old Ambassador Hotel is the Tropicana, and it shares the boardwalk with psychics, crystal shops, and palm readers. Houdini would roll his eyes at them. Others will tell you they possess incredible powers.

According to one legend, an Atlantic City psychic once cursed a newlywed couple from Baltimore.

The couple had taken a train into the city for a much-needed weekend away, as they were already experiencing trouble in their marriage. But the change of scenery didn't do much to quell their arguments. While the groom stormed off to find a drink, the bride walked the boardwalk alone, racking her brain for some way to save her relationship.

She found it in the neon lights of a boardwalk psychic shop. As she entered — the little bell above the door ringing loudly — she found an elderly, eastern European woman sitting alone at a table. A sign boasted:

PALM READING - 50 CENTS

She paid the fee and laid her hand, palm up, on the table. The woman got to work following the creases in her skin with a haggard finger. She would hum every so often, as if she were learning something heavy and significant about the young woman's life. After a few minutes, her eyes snapped up abruptly.

"You have a hex," the fortune teller said. "You are in grave danger."

The woman was skeptical.

"A hex?" she asked.

"Yes," the fortune teller shot back. "I can remove it for $100 dollars. $100 dollars to remove the hex!" And the woman traced her long, gnarled finger down the newlywed's wrist. "Or that wedding ring and bracelet should do!"

The bride snatched her wrist from the palm reader and left the shop as quickly as she could. Before she could make it out, however, the fortune-teller cackled, "Or I can make the hex worse!"

The terrible cackle followed the newlywed all the way back to Baltimore.

One week later, the young woman found herself alone in bed. Her husband had left for a business trip in New York City, and she wondered if he even planned to come back. Their marital troubles had worsened since the Atlantic City trip. It was like a dark shadow was hovering over them constantly.

As she lay there, staring up at the ceiling, the strong smell of incense filled the room. It smelled exactly like the psychic shop on the boardwalk — thick and smoky. The woman sat up and, just as she did, the bedroom door flew open to reveal a tall man in a formal suit. He had sunken eyes and pale skin, and he floated into the bedroom carrying a tray of burning incense.

The woman froze. She was too terrified to scream. She was too terrified to even move. The figure stared directly into her eyes and then floated away, out the window. When she looked out into her backyard, there were two freshly dug graves, side by side. And the graves had markers, but they were old and worn out, so she couldn't make out the words on them from the bedroom window.

Then she heard it again: the fortune-teller's harsh, cackling laugh coming from somewhere in the night sky. She slammed her window shut and resolved to book the next train to Atlantic City.

With over $100 and a box of fine jewelry stashed in her purse, the woman scurried down the boardwalk toward the psychic's shop. But when she finally reached the little building, it was boarded up. A man approached her then — the saltwater taffy salesman from the shop next door.

"She was a swindler," he said. "The cops came and shut her down for taking people's money."

If she was such a con artist, though, where did those graves come from? And who was the man floating towards her? The woman never found answers. But for the next several years, any time the night was particularly still and cold, she would smell the thick, smoky scent of incense. She never visited a psychic again.

The Psychic Shop, Atlantic City, NJ.

BONUS CHAPTER

New Jersey's Most Haunted Continued

It's time to venture into the Pine Barrens, where the infamous Jersey Devil has been terrorizing nearby towns for centuries. If you don't encounter the winged beast, you may come face to face with a ghostly pirate, or the heartbroken woman he left behind.

Head north to Bernards Township, where a mysterious oak tree wards off threats with "devilish," supernatural powers. Many have tried to chop it down. None have succeeded… or lived to tell the tale.

But maybe you'd rather visit Jersey's sandy beaches. In that case, head out to Cape May, America's oldest seashore resort. There you'll find the Emlen Physick Estate and all of its odd spirits. The 18-room mansion is a relic of the Victorian Age and the Spiritualism craze that swept the nation after the Civil War. Seances and Ouija Boards unleashed an army of ghosts on the seaside town… and they don't plan to leave any time soon.

Explore the hidden, haunted corners of the Garden State. Atlantic City was only the beginning…

Terrors of New Jersey.

The Pine Barrens | Pemberton Township, NJ

The Jersey Devil, NJ.

Some of America's most haunted locations are not well-known outside of their local area. However, that's not the case for the cryptid from New Jersey's Pine Barrens. The Jersey Devil is so famous that the state's NHL hockey team is named after it. But don't let their cartoon-like mascot fool you. This is a real legend that has been terrifying people for over a hundred years. And it's only one of several weird stories connected to the same area.

The Pine Barrens, sometimes just called the Pines, is a protected area of woodlands. This coastal region of New Jersey is full of dense coniferous forest. It was given the name barrens by early European settlers who could not cultivate their crops in that land, though the ecosystem actually offers a diverse range of plant life.

Some say that the Pine Barrens also spawned a rather unique creature that has become known as the Jersey Devil. Descriptions of the cryptid vary, but common features include a bipedal creature with leathery, bat-like wings and the face of a horse or goat. It is often described as having antlers or horns on its head, clawed hands on small arms, cloven hooves on long legs, and a pointed or forked tail.

Interestingly, the Lenape tribe, the original people of the Pine Barrens, believed in a spirit they called M'Sing who could take the form of a "deer-like creature with leathery wings." While this sounds very similar to the Jersey Devil, folklore seems to have its own origin for the creature.

In 1735, there was a Pine Barrens resident named Jane Leeds who had twelve children and was hence given the nickname "Mother Leeds." Some say that her husband was an alcoholic and rarely home, leaving the poor woman to take care of all those children largely on her own. When she got pregnant for the thirteenth time, Mother Leeds cursed in frustration and exclaimed, "Let this one be a devil!"

When Mother Leeds went into labor, it was an unusually stormy night. Flashes of lightning intermittently lit up the small room while her cries of birthing pain intermingled with the howling winds and clapping thunder from outside. After much travail, she finally delivered a baby boy through a painful but routine birth.

The newborn seemed perfectly normal at first, but things began to change within minutes. Mother and midwives watched in frightened disbelief as the baby grew in size right before their eyes. Horns sprouted from the top of its head, talons grew from its fingers, and wings spread from its back. The monster child's eyes began glowing a fiery red as it stared at the horrified woman who had just birthed it.

It is said that the creature attacked and killed its mother. Then it flew toward the midwives with slashing claws and gnashing teeth, causing more death and dismemberment before flying up the chimney to escape. It flew into the dark desolation of the Pine Barrens, which it has called home ever since. And it is from this stretch of untamed wilderness that the creature continues to terrorize anyone who wanders near.

The earliest documented sightings of the Jersey Devil go back to the early nineteenth century. Commodore Stephen Decatur, an American naval hero, once visited Hanover Mill in New Jersey. He was there to inspect how the cannonballs his navy would be using were forged. While at the mill's firing range, Decatur spotted a strange flying creature in the sky overhead. He fired a cannon directly at the airborne thing. The shot had no effect, and the creature simply flew away.

In 1820, a similar beast was reported by Joseph Bonaparte, Napoleon's older brother. He had purchased 800 acres in Bordentown, New Jersey, and built a home there in order to live between the two busy ports of New York and

Philadelphia. One snowy evening, as Bonaparte was hunting in the woods that surrounded his estate, he came across some strange-looking tracks in the snow. They resembled donkey tracks but if the animal only had two legs. Bonaparte followed the tracks until they abruptly stopped as if whatever made them had just flown away.

A sudden hissing sound caused Bonaparte to jump and spin around. He was now facing a rather large winged beast with bird legs and a horse's head. For uncounted minutes, Bonaparte stood frozen in fear. When he remembered that he had a rifle in his hands, he pointed it at the creature, but it flew away before he could take the shot.

There were several accounts of raided chicken coops and unexplainable livestock deaths in the 1800s that were attributed to the Jersey Devil. But in January 1909, it seems that the Devil went on a week-long rampage. During this time, hundreds of encounters were published in local newspapers. First came the sightings of unidentifiable footprints in the snow. The weird tracks seemed to go under fences, through backyards, and across the roofs of houses.

Then the creature began popping up in places all over South Jersey and even into the Philadelphia area. Multiple witnesses claimed that the Devil attacked a trolley car full of passengers in Haddon Heights. Police in Camden and Bristol, Pennsylvania, fired their weapons on the flying beast but failed to bring it down. It appeared on a house's roof in West Collingswood; people described it as a kangaroo with wings. Firemen attempted to spray it with a high-pressure hose, but it flew away with a loud screech that pierced the night air.

A wave of animal attacks coincidentally occurred in that same week. Many area farmers reported the slaughter of their livestock, especially chickens. One woman said that she came outside to find the Devil trying to eat her dog. She charged the creature with a broomstick, causing it to flee and hence rescuing her pet from a gruesome death.

The Rampage of 1909 caused so much panic that several schools and places of employment closed and urged people to remain home. It is said that the Philadelphia Zoo offered a $10,000 reward for the creature, which was never claimed.

No other period of time has produced as many Jersey Devil sightings in only one week, but people have reported many other encounters throughout the twentieth century. Reports that may be years apart are linked by a similar description of the monster.

The Jersey Devil is by far the most well-known and pervasive legend of the Pines, but it is by no means the only strange story connected with this part of New Jersey. One of them is even intertwined with the Devil.

Captain William Kidd was a Scottish privateer from the late seventeenth century who was commissioned by the English to protect their interests in North America. He was hired to take down enemy ships and pirates, but it seems he became a bit of a pirate himself. Tales of his exploits include numerous treasure hunts as well as the plundering and capturing of other ships in the Atlantic Ocean.

In 1698, Captain Kidd captured the *Quedagh Merchant*, a 400-ton Armenian merchant vessel captained by an Englishman. For this act, Kidd was accused of mutiny and denounced as a pirate. He was eventually arrested, tried, and found guilty of murder and five counts of piracy. He was publicly hanged on May 23, 1701.

Ever since his death, speculation has run rampant regarding the locations where Captain Kidd had buried his many treasures. One of these spots is said to be Barnegat Bay in New Jersey. During the seventeenth and eighteenth centuries, numerous reports told of locals spotting the ghost of Captain Kidd walking along the beach of the bay. Sometimes the Jersey Devil walks alongside the spirit, perhaps as extra protection for his buried treasure.

Another apparition often seen in the same area is known as the "Golden-Haired Girl." It's believed that she was a farm girl who Captain Kidd may have met while in the area waiting for his ship to be repaired. According to the legend, Kidd became infatuated with her. He even considered trading in his untamed buccaneering lifestyle for a more settled and peaceful existence as a coastal fisherman with a lovely wife. This may be the reason he stowed away treasure in this particular location: a deposit put down on their future together.

When three British ships came into the bay looking for him, however, Kidd quickly boarded the ship and made an escape without his new love. The girl, abandoned and betrayed, disappeared into the dark vastness of the Pines. It is not known if she dug up the treasure or even knew where it was. Most people believe that she committed suicide in the woods and that Kidd's treasure remains buried in Barnegat Bay to this day.

Also still roaming those shores is the ghost of the Golden-Haired Girl, who can be seen on a moonlit night staring out at the sea as if mourning the loss of a loved one. Her white dress ripples in the breeze, even on a windless night. Eager treasure hunters have wondered if her appearance marks the spot where

Captain Kidd's stash was buried, but no one has found it yet.

The final story involves a tragic hit and run.

On the fringes of the Pine Barrens runs a road that was never finished being laid. It's called Burnt Mill Road, and this is where a young boy met his untimely demise on Christmas Night. The boy was outside playing with a basketball when a car came speeding down the road, hitting the child. The driver decided not to stop and instead kept driving, only to arrive at a dead end. They had to do a U-turn and drive back past the body of the young boy they had just killed.

Many locals still take the drive down Burnt Mill Road to catch a glimpse of the boy's ghost. There are varying directions people might give to make the apparition appear. Some say you must go there at midnight, honk three times, and flash your lights three times. Others say you need to turn your lights and engine completely off, then wait in the vehicle. You might have to get out of your car and walk away about twenty feet, then turn around.

One way or another, the boy's spectral form is said to emerge from the darkness of night and start walking toward your vehicle. He'll inspect your car thoroughly as if trying to determine if it's the one that hit him. Even if you don't stop and just drive slowly by, people say you may still spot the spirit of the boy chasing a bouncing ball, heading into the street in front of you.

Between the Jersey Devil and the myriad of supernatural entities that dwell in the same area, there is no doubt that the Pine Barrens in New Jersey is one of the most haunted places in all of America.

The Jersey Devil, NJ.

The Devil's Tree | Bernards Township, NJ

The Devil's Tree, Bernards Township, NJ.

Anyone driving down Mountain Road in Bernards Township, New Jersey, is likely to notice a solitary oak tree protruding from an undeveloped field near the corner of Emerald Valley Lane. It looks like your average oak tree except for the fact that no matter the season, a portion of its limbs always seem to be dead. As the sun sets, it turns into a skeletal silhouette against the darkening sky, as trees tend to do.

Passersby might notice it but not think much of it. Locals know better.

They call it the Devil's Tree because the ominous oak is believed to be cursed with powers that could only be described as hellish. It's said that if anyone tries to harm the tree, harm is soon returned to them sevenfold.

Nobody is quite sure how old the Devil's Tree is or how it acquired its evil energy, though there are a few origin stories. Bernards Township hosted the central headquarters for the New Jersey division of the Ku Klux Klan in the early twentieth century. Some say the Devil's Tree was used many times to lynch rebellious slaves in colonial times, and those lynchings continued all the way to the 1920s when the KKK was hanging free African Americans. The oak tree could be tainted from the terrible tragedies that have occurred upon its branches.

Another story involves a farmer who, for unknown reasons, snapped and killed his whole family. Rather than face the authorities, he came to this lone tree in an open field and hanged himself. His last words before he died proclaimed that anyone who ever tried to cut down the tree would "come to an untimely end."

The Devil's Tree still stands today, though many have attempted to chop it down. Axe-wielding men have tried to take it down only to find their blade can't penetrate the wood. Each one who made an attempt seemed to meet an untimely demise of one kind or another. Teens trying to prove their courage have taken axes to the trunk, set it on fire, and tagged it with graffiti. The marks can still be seen, yet the oak remains standing. As for the so-called brave teenagers, no one knows where they are today…

For some inexplicable reason, the curse of the Devil's Tree often manifests itself as car troubles. A twenty-something man who will remain anonymous recounts a tale from when he was in high school. He says that he and his friends all knew about the legend of the tree, and it was time that they paid a visit to check it out for themselves and see if there was any truth behind the stories.

"I'll prove once and for all," the driver said, "that the stories are all fake and that the stupid Devil's Tree is nothing!" He pulled the car over right in front of the spot where the oak tree stood, its leafless branches spread wide as if to beckon him near. As he marched toward the tree, he shouted challenges at the ghosts to show themselves. Nothing happened. Then, as if expressing a sign of dominance, he urinated all over the base of the trunk. Still, no consequence.

"I told you so," he said in a cocky voice as he got back into the car. His friends looked a little relieved, and he decided it was time to take the "wimps" home. As he drove down the road, the gas pedal suddenly floored itself, causing the car to speed up tremendously. The driver was caught off guard and lost control of the car, which skidded sideways with a terrible screech before colliding into a tree. Luckily, the teens sustained only minor injuries, but the oldest friend's car was totaled.

People who visit the Devil's Tree usually get more than what they bargained for. Locals generally believe it is best to avoid the area altogether, but that doesn't stop the curious minds and thrill-seeking ghost hunters from stalking this very haunted location.

Terrors of New Jersey.

Union Hotel | Flemington, NJ

Union Hotel, Flemington, NJ.

Built in 1814, the Union Hotel originally served as a stagecoach shop and gathering place for wealthy passengers and socialites. The exterior, a unique French/Victorian design, was added on in 1878. Shortly thereafter, the Union began operating as an upscale hotel.

In 1935, the Union Hotel became part of the "trial of the century," as it was dubbed by the media. Richard "Bruno" Hauptmann, "the most hated man in the world" (again, media's choice), was accused of kidnapping and murdering the infant son of Charles Lindbergh Jr. The trial took place at the courthouse across the street from the Union. As such, the fifty-two rooms of the hotel were filled with sequestered jurors and world-famous journalists who were covering the story. Hauptmann was eventually found guilty and executed in the electric chair.

Within decades of that spectacle, the Union stopped taking guests to spend the night but continued operating as a restaurant for another fifty years. In 2008, the Union Restaurant closed its doors to the public, and the building has gone into disuse ever since.

While it is true that the grand old hotel's last guest checked out in the 1950s, some say that certain guests have never left the building at all. They still haunt the upper rooms and corridors, which have been vacant and sealed off from the public for nearly half a century. A whole host of spirits have even come down to the main floor while it was operating as a restaurant.

Employees have reported seeing children running around late at night who seem to just giggle and vanish before anyone can get to them. Other staff members claim to have witnessed the ghostly figure of a little girl bouncing a red ball down the hall near the restrooms. One night, while a night shift worker was locking up after closing time, the doors he had just locked suddenly flew open on their own. As he approached the doors to close them again, he noticed on the stairs beyond the doors a pair of black children's shoes walking up the steps with no body attached to them. The employee ran out of the building, telling his coworkers as he fled that they should "get out of the building."

In a similar staff member departure, a waitress said that while counting the register, she heard a strange voice humming like an eerie lullaby. It scared her so badly that she dropped the drawer full of money, rapidly exited the building, and never returned to work.

Another supernatural encounter comes from a manager who would sometimes stay late to clean up and look over the books. One early morning around 3:00 a.m., she suddenly felt a dark presence in the room with her. It seemed to wrap around her body. "I could feel the pressure of it right up against me," the manager explained, "pushing on my chest. It was making it hard for me to breathe." Internally panicking, she gently asked whatever it was to please stop and leave. Much to her surprise and relief, the unseen force complied and never returned.

Other paranormal incidents at the Union include staff members hearing voices coming from an empty dining room after the restaurant is closed. It sometimes sounds like at least two people are still in there, dining and talking in whispers, yet no one can be seen. In that same dining room, a waiter who was fairly new on the job once thought he saw something and asked the bartender on duty, "Whose kid is that playing in the dining room?"

The bartender looked confused at first.

"What did she look like?" the bartender asked.

"Probably about nine or ten," the waiter replied, "with long dark hair, wearing a fancy dress." At that description, the bartender laughed. "Oh yeah," he said, "that's one of our ghosts!" The waiter didn't know how to take it at first, but he soon learned that the only employees of the Union that stuck around were the ones who were able to accept that they shared their workspace with the dead.

We cannot be sure why so many ghosts of children, or spirits of any age for that matter, continue to haunt the Union Hotel. It was once a place of splendid grandeur that is now a shell of its former glory, minimally maintained, with dirty doors and cracked paint on the inside walls. Perhaps these deceased souls enjoy spending their afterlife in a place with which they share fond memories, recalling the good old days of the past. Or maybe there were many horrible deaths that occurred at the Union, dark secrets of history that the building has yet to tell about.

The Cranbury Inn | Cranbury, NJ

The Cranbury Inn, Cranbury, NJ

One of the oldest eateries in the state of New Jersey, the Cranbury Inn has actually been open to the public since before the colonies declared independence from the British. People had been gathering there to eat and drink for decades before the inn was officially established in 1780.

What were originally two eighteenth-century stagecoach taverns standing side-by-side converged in 1800 to create a lavish dining destination. The addition of the main dining hall in 1930 brought it all together. The Cranbury Inn provided rooms for overnight guests until the 1980s. Despite no longer serving in a hotel capacity, the inn remains in business today and is as busy as ever. It seems especially active with paranormal activity, some of which may be connected to its historical roots.

Town records indicate that there was a stop for the Underground Railroad in Cranbury. Many locals believe that the Cranbury Inn would have been the ideal choice for a safehouse at which to hide and help escaped slaves. The inn's own website describes "an unusual amount of wear on the steps to the attic of the innkeeper's house and remnants of a door to a room and a shelf below which are nails to hang your cloak on," suggesting that the attic space was used for more than just storage.

Enoch Middleton wrote about his service as an Underground Railroad agent decades after he ceased in the activity. Enoch had said that, "he kept enough to make a load and under the cover of darkness he would load them into his wagon and take them to Cranberry, the next stop on the road to freedom in Canada." Cranberry was the original spelling of the town until the official change to Cranbury around 1886.

Was the Cranbury Inn their safe house? The spirits of the inn may hold the answer.

Patrons and employees alike have witnessed weird and eerie occurrences that can only be described as supernatural. The good news is that most of the spirits seem to be friendly and helpful — perhaps a little mischievous — rather than violent or dangerous.

Some of the doors inside the inn will swing open all on their own. A pregnant employee had this happen to her just as she was coming through with her hands full. She couldn't open the door herself, and she became convinced that a ghost got the door for her. Other staff members have claimed to receive telepathic messages from unknown voices warning them about electrical failures in the inn and giving them advice on how to deal with the potential emergency.

In one rather peculiar incident, a woman staying at the inn had an interesting and heartwarming message for owner Tom Ingegneri before she left. She told Tom that the mirror in the bathroom of the room she stayed in "has great love for you." Then she paid and left without ever explaining herself. Tom, however, understood the sentiment, and he smiled warmly even with a tear in his eye. The mirror in that bathroom was a keepsake from his deceased mother.

In 2011, the Cranbury Inn invited a group of twenty-four psychics and ghost hunters to investigate the building and premises. It was a mixture of paranormal experts and amateurs, with many bringing their tools of the trade: electromagnetic field (EMF) meters, electronic voice phenomenon (EVP) recorders, temperature readers, and night vision cameras. Several people took photos that exhibited ghostly orbs in certain rooms, the fuzzy spheres seemingly floating around the heads of the curious guests. A faint voice that did not belong to anyone present was captured on the audio recorder; it sounded like words being spoken but was not clear enough to make out what might have been said.

If the Cranbury Inn is truly haunted, the question remains: Who are the spirits seemingly tethered to this location? One story from yesteryear revolves around a regular customer of the inn who was hit and killed by a stagecoach in the 1790s. Some believe he is one of the many ghosts that have decided to linger on the property. They say that he isn't happy with all the renovations that have been made over the years, but he does seem pleased that the inn is still in use and appreciated by the public.

When people enjoy their time at the Cranbury Inn, they often talk about how warm and friendly the place is. What many don't realize is that the nice, fuzzy feeling they got was in part from the energy of the kindhearted spirits that still live there.

Terrors of New Jersey.

Emlen Physick Estate | Cape May, NJ

Emlen Physick Estate, Cape May, NJ.

On the southernmost tip of the Jersey Shore lies an area designated as the "nation's oldest seashore resort," called Cape May. The quaint seaside town has become a very popular vacation destination for people on the East Coast. It also once attracted an almost obsessive interest in spiritualism and the occult as well as its fair share of supernatural phenomena. It may be a place so relaxing and lovely that people never want to leave.

At 1408 Washington Street stands the Emlen Physick Estate, a weird and beautiful example of Victorian "stick style" architecture. The best description of the edifice: It resembles a giant nineteenth-century dollhouse. This 18-room mansion was built in 1879 for the family of Dr. Emlan Physick Jr. After the doctor's death in 1916, the home passed through several owners but went largely unused and soon fell into disrepair. It wasn't until 1973 that the city of Cape May purchased the property and subsequently placed it under protection through the Mid-Atlantic Center for the Arts and Humanities, who are headquartered there to this day and are credited with rescuing the mansion from the wrecking ball.

The Emlen Physick still stands, and millions of people visit Cape May every year. Most of these folks don't know the dark secrets related to the region's history, including an obsession with spiritualism, the belief that people can communicate with the spirits of the dead. People believed that their deceased loved ones were still with them but on another plane, and that through proper methods — séances, Ouija boards, psychic mediums — they would be able to make contact and speak with them once again.

In the late 1800s and early 1900s, there was an intense interest in spiritualism in the Cape May area. Some think this has to do with the high level of quartz found in the sands of Cape May's beaches. Quartz is said to act as a conduit for spiritual energy, which would make the surrounding area a natural hotspot for supernatural activity.

Spiritualism was practiced frequently in Cape May until the trend started to die down in the late 1930s. By that time, locals say that thousands of entities from the other side were invited into their town. Some were the ghosts of past residents who were harmless, simply appreciating the opportunity to be reunited with their family and earthly home. For those not adept at contacting the dead, however, they run the risk of summoning more malevolent entities, demonic spirits that portray themselves as dead souls in order to infiltrate people's homes, cause chaos, and perhaps even possess the living. Certain paranormal experts believe that this may have opened up a portal to other worlds that may still be open to this day.

In the wake of the spiritualism frenzy, it is no surprise that Cape May is one of the most haunted places in all of New Jersey. Tourists and residents have spotted a shadowy figure walking along the shores at night who dissipates into the ocean mist once anyone gets too close. He is believed to be the spirit of a man who committed suicide by drowning himself on the beach. At other times, the apparition of a mother and child walking hand-in-hand can be seen. Their identity is unknown. Beachgoers have also complained about receiving scratches on their backs from unknown sources.

The Emlen Physick Estate itself has spawned a large share of the Cape May ghost stories. There have been three confirmed deaths in the house, including Dr. Physick himself. According to the stories, another doctor once purchased the mansion but refused to live in it because of the strange experiences he had within its walls. The doctor heard disembodied footsteps every night but could never discover a reason. His scientific mind simply wouldn't allow the notion of ghosts, but he moved into a downtown apartment anyway until he had resold the house.

Workers doing maintenance on the property have reported numerous strange incidents. They have seen hazy figures walk in and out of rooms that seem to be gone in the next moment. Near one of the staircases hangs a full-size mirror, and it is there that the apparition of a pale woman has been seen peering into the glass. One worker claimed to see the page of a book standing straight up in the air as if someone were holding and reading it. As soon as they walked into the room, the page dropped down with a slight gust of wind heading toward the entering worker that chilled his blood.

A medium who visited the Emlen Physick Estate claimed to have identified several of the ghosts who dwell there, all relatives of Dr. Physick. Outside on the mansion's grounds, the medium felt the presence of two women; one was friendly and gentle while the other came off as quite miserable. He said that the former was Aunt Emilie, known to be a jovial party girl in life who was very sociable, and the latter was Dr. Physick's mother, Frances Ralston, who rumors say "ran the house with an iron fist."

This was further confirmed when the medium entered the mother's bedroom, where she had died. Despite the large size of the room, the medium immediately felt claustrophobic and oppressed. The feeling washed over him like a wave and soon weighed him down like a dark depression. Mrs. Ralston may have been mean, but perhaps she was suffering from her own torment that nobody knew about.

The medium was surprised at the other ghosts he encountered — a pack of dogs. They were just barely visible, but he could sense their presence, circling around him, panting and wagging their tails as if expecting dinner. Later, the medium would learn that Dr. Physick was the head of the *Society for the Prevention of Cruelty to Animals* and had kept many dogs at his home that might have otherwise been bound for the pound or euthanasia.

Indeed, Cape May is so nice that nobody wants to leave — not the happy ghosts, sad spirits, evil entities, suicides, poltergeists, not even the dogs. The Emlen Physick Estate is a miniature symbol of the rest of Cape May. It's a beautiful but tainted place that hosts all types of the living and the dead, from the happiest to the most miserable. What a wonderful location to visit, and an even better place to stay… forever… and ever… and ever.

DARE TO VISIT US ON YOUTUBE?

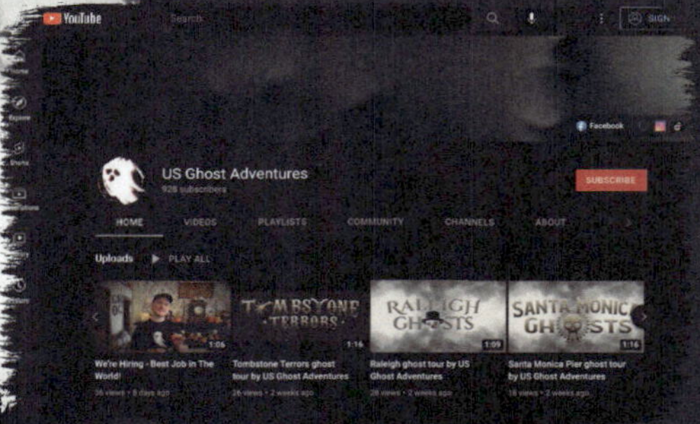

HAUNTING
CAPTURED INSIDE THE LIZZIE BORDEN HOUSE

GUEST TOUR
LIZZIE BORDEN HOUSE TOUR GUEST EXPERIENCE

VOICE
BEHIND THE COUCH

LIZZIE BORDEN HOUSE 3RD FLOOR EXPERIENCE

WITNESS ACCOUNTS FROM THE MORSE ROOM

US Ghost Adventures

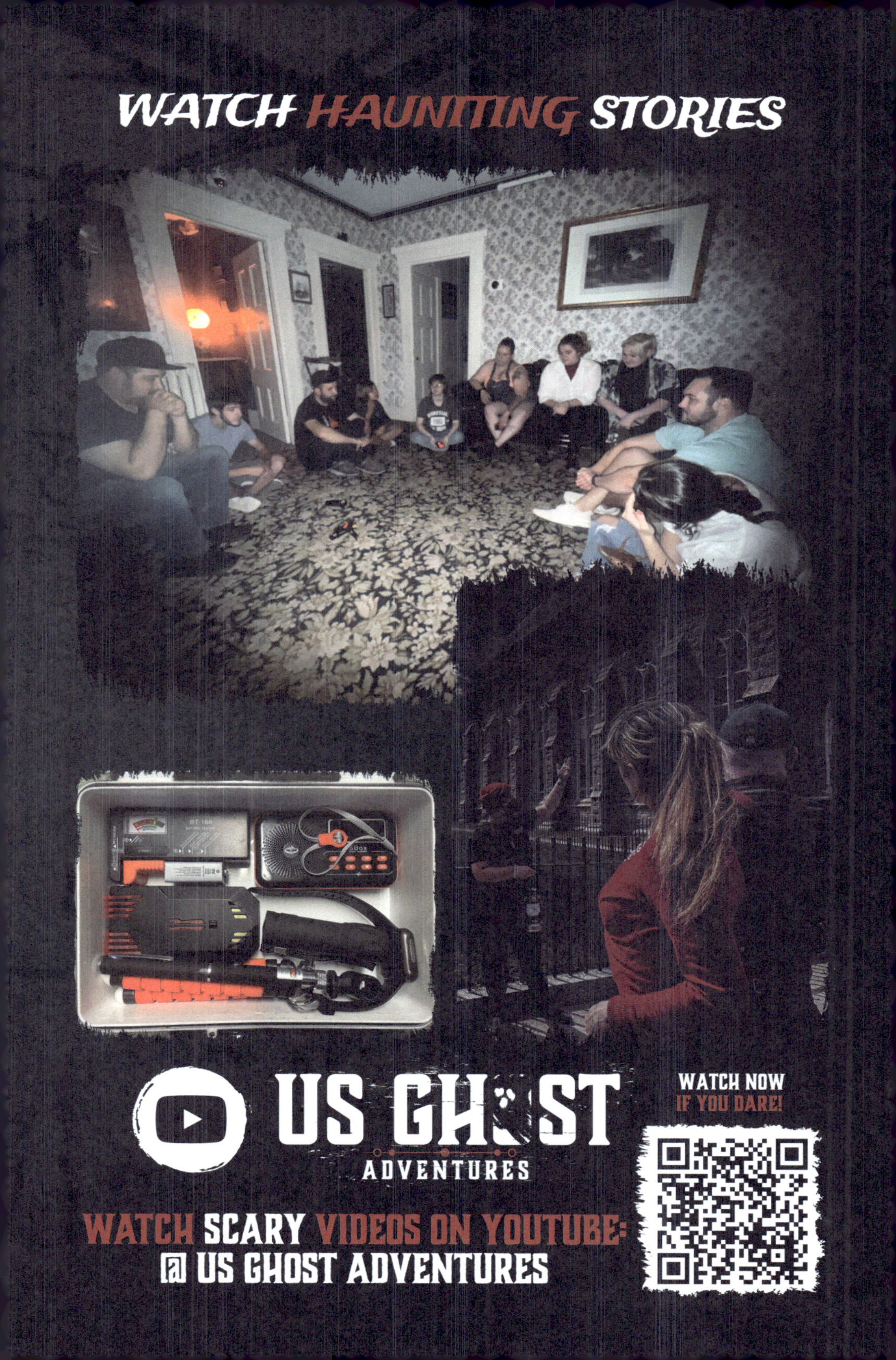
WATCH HAUNTING STORIES
US GHOST
ADVENTURES
WATCH NOW
IF YOU DARE!
WATCH SCARY VIDEOS ON YOUTUBE:
@ US GHOST ADVENTURES

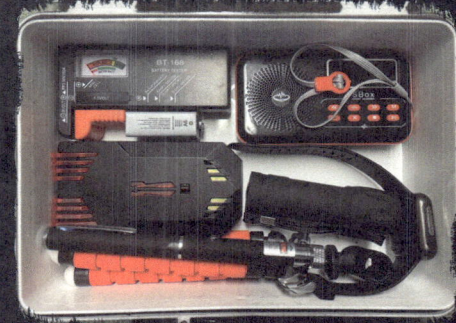

NYC GHOSTS

CHAPTER VIII

The Ghosts of New York City

There are few places in the world like Greenwich Village. This vibrant, New York City neighborhood is a haven for outcasts and artists — a freethinker's paradise wrapped in historic charm. But beneath its rainbow exterior lies a dark history.

Executions. Yellow fever. AIDS. Murder. Death is the village's oldest and most loyal resident, so it's no surprise the historic, cobblestone streets are teeming with ghosts.

Misty figures jump from the Brown Building, where the infamous Triangle Shirtwaist Fire claimed 146 lives. Yellow fever victims roam Washington Square Park. Mark Twain lingers in his former sitting room, and the infamous Gay Street phantom lurks in the shadows…

The following chapters dive into some of New York's most disturbing, nightmare-inducing ghost stories. You may think you know Greenwich Village, but you've never heard this side of the story. Pull up a chair and let the dead fill you in.

usghostadventures.com/new-york

The Ghosts of New York City, NY.

Washington Square Park

Washington Square Park, New York City, NY.

Washington Square Park is steeped in over 300 years of history. It was present for the inauguration of George Washington on April 30, 1789, and it's witnessed every American war, milestone, and protest since then.

- Labor unions marched there after the Triangle Shirtwaist Factory fire.

- In the 1930s, 100,000 people gathered there to protest the rise of fascism in Europe.

- Bob Dylan and other "beatniks" were beaten with billy clubs for interfering with the "peace and tranquility of the park" during a 1961 folk festival, but the advocates petitioned the city and won.

- Anti-war protests broke out in the park during the Vietnam War, and Bella Abzug held a 1970 rally to commemorate the first anniversary of the Stonewall riots.

Hundreds of famous faces have protested, sang, danced, and filmed there. Spiderman has swung over the park. The Glee kids jammed out there. And the ghosts of *Ghostbusters II* flew through the famous arch.

When you walk into Washington Square Park, you're walking onto a stage that embodies the values of Greenwich Village: free expression, free love, and unity. But there was a time when this park represented something very different.

For three decades, the land was tainted by death.

Early Americans were well-acquainted with the grim reaper. In 1780, the average life expectancy was around 64 years old, and that was if you made it past the age of five. The child mortality rate was almost 50% for much of the 18th and 19th centuries, which meant parents often had to bury more than one child.

So death was constant, but that didn't make it any less terrifying.

When the grim reaper arrived in New York City in 1795, the wealthy fled, the poor huddled in their houses, and doctors and nurses accepted their fates. The gruesome disease that had ravaged Philadelphia two years earlier had finally arrived on New York's doorstep: yellow fever. It seemed to kill at random. Some victims would come down with a headache and a mild fever before making a full recovery. Others would bleed from their eyes, nose, and ears. Bloody, black vomit would erupt from their throats, and their skin would turn sickly yellow.

Those patients were sure to die, yet doctors tended to them anyway, risking their own lives in the process. When the disease struck again in 1798, Dr. Sandy Anderson abused alcohol and opium to get through the summer. By September, he'd lost his parents, brother, and wife to the disease, and Bellevue Hospital had become a revolving door for doomed New Yorkers. As soon as one patient died, another would fill their bed.

The disease claimed 3,000 lives between '95 and '98. Bodies piled up all around the city. Men peddled coffins "of all sizes." But the victims who didn't have money or families ended up at what's now Washington Square. In 1797, the square was purchased and used as a crude dumping site for the city's untouchables. Initially, the city planned to bury 5,000 people, but yellow fever upped that number quite a bit.

Yellow fever victims had to be buried quickly. No one knew how the disease was spread, and they feared the corpses would infect anyone who came near them. So bodies were thrown into shallow, mass graves. Often, gravediggers would crash through an existing grave while digging a new one. They would sever a limb or scatter bones, leaving the graves a mangled mess of body parts.

Decades later, construction crews began stirring up the dirt, and they mangled the remains even more. The city didn't try to rectify their mess until 2021, when bone fragments collected between 2008 and 2017 were reinterred in a special plant bed near the Sullivan Street entrance, but the act hasn't stopped the hauntings...

The greatest irony in ghost hunting is that cemeteries are almost never haunted. People who are buried in cemeteries are laid to rest in a respectful and loving way. Their souls transition into the afterlife peacefully, and they have no unfinished business to attend to. Places like Washington Square Park, where bodies are dumped into mass graves, are a different story.

The park is filled with tens of thousands of restless souls. Some people believe the land is cursed because of it — eternally tainted by despair and disease.

Locals have seen shadows limping through the park late at night. Some are missing arms, legs, or heads... They're searching for their lost body parts. Rumors of these shadows began as early as the 1830s, not long after the potter's field was turned into a parade ground. And they aren't the only ghosts to inhabit the park.

There's a 340-year-old English Elm on the square. Most elderly trees like that are called "witness trees" because they've witnessed significant historical events, but this one has a much darker name: Hangman's Elm.

In the 18th and 19th centuries, execution by hanging was a common punishment. It was cheap, simple, and it could be done safely around a large crowd (and they wanted a large crowd). Executions were held out in the open so the public could see what would happen to them if they committed a crime.

There are a few different legends about Hangman's Elm. They say Revolutionary War traitors swung from its branches. There's also a rumor that the famous general, Marquis de Lafayette, witnessed the execution of 20 thieves. But the city has poured over historical documents, and they haven't found evidence to back those stories. If you ask New York history buffs, only one person was ever hanged in Washington Square Park: Rose Butler.

Rose was an enslaved woman who had been owned by several New York families. In 1817, she was sold to William Morris. The move would prove to be a death sentence. Two years later, Rose was tried for arson, which was a capital offense at the time.

The family claimed Rose intentionally set a fire in the middle of the night and tied a string to the kitchen door, preventing them from escaping. No one had died — in fact, the fire was so minimal that it barely caused any damage to the house — but this was the 19th century, when everything was built out of wood. A single spark could burn down the entire city.

In 1776, a fire broke out at Fighting Cocks Tavern and spread north and west, engulfing 10% to 25% of the city before it was stopped. This was during the British occupation of New York, and both sides pointed fingers — the British blamed the patriots and the patriots blamed the British. If the fire was intentionally set to get rid of the redcoats, it didn't work. They tightened their hold on the city and turned it into a prison. They took over the remaining buildings and left the charred remains to the Americans.

The city was still scarred by those days. Terrified of another inferno, New York State made arson a capital crime in 1808, which meant Rose's case made it all the way to the New York Supreme Court.

During the trial, Rose told the court she had been threatened by four white men who were urging her to set the fire, but their names were erased from the records. The reason behind the arson didn't seem to matter anyway. Rose's confession sealed her fate. She was sentenced to death.

On July 9, 1819, Rose was led to Washington Square Park, where an ominous wooden gallows loomed over the field. It stood where the famous arch stands today. Over 10,000 people had gathered at the bottom of it, eager to watch Rose's death. The ravenous crowd had tagged the area with racist graffiti. One read:

Rose Butler sat upon a bench —
Down drop't the trap and hanged a negro wench.

The noose was tied, the shouts of the crowd filled the air as the door opened under her feet, and then it was done. It was a terrible, traumatic way to die. She was only 19 years old, and she shouldn't have been sold to William Morris in the first place.

Rose was enslaved during a confusing transition period when New York was abolishing slavery in stages. She was chained to the Morris family while free blacks roamed the streets. Slavery was officially abolished in New York eight years after her death.

Rose may not have been the only person hanged at the park, but she was certainly the last. In the 1820s, the wealthy began constructing homes on the outskirts of the potter's field, and they weren't keen on having people executed and buried on their front lawns. The field was turned into a parade ground and pedestrian park in 1827.

But no amount of happy memories can erase the violence, or the fear, or the roar of a blood-thirsty crowd.

That kind of trauma will imprint on a place, leaving behind a sinister, dark energy. Some people report seeing ghostly white figures swinging from the branches of Hangman's Elm. Others say the air hovers — stock-still — even on the windiest of nights. You may hear a phantom snap or the sickly sound of a heavy trap door banging against the gallows.

And then there's Rose.

NYU students have reported seeing her shadowy form dangling in the air. When they get closer, she disappears. Other students have actually walked through her. They were strolling through the park on a warm summer night when all of a sudden the air turned ice cold and they felt something — like a chilly breeze — pass right through them.

Her presence is accompanied by strong feelings of sadness, fear, and anger — a reminder of one of New York's darkest moments.

House of Death

House of Death, New York City, NY.

In the middle of W 10th Street, you'll find a charming, Greek Revival row house with pretty windows and an arched doorway. It blends in with the other houses on the street — so much so that most people pass by it without a second look — but "Number 14" is no ordinary Greenwich residence…

It was built in the 1850s, when Washington Square Park attracted high-society elites, so it's no surprise that one of its first occupants was the wealthy widow of a railroad magnate.

Mary Johnston lived there with her daughters in the late 1880s — the peak of New York's Gilded Age, when women like Lina Astor ruled the city. Back then, the four-story townhome was probably a glamorous setting for tea parties and fancy dinners… but it wasn't long before it became tainted by tragedies.

Leanna Renee Hieber wrote: "Just walking by it gave me a sinking, troubled, pressed, and fraught sense; the sense that the building is, in and of itself, a distinctly negative presence and that something is deeply wrong there."

According to legend, 22 people have died in the house, and many of their spirits remain trapped inside. By the time the most famous resident —

Mark Twain — moved in in 1900, there were already rumors that it was haunted. But Twain was a renowned skeptic who laughed at the idea of ghosts. And he had fallen into such a deep depression by that point that he probably didn't care.

Twain was well-known for his humor and sharp wit. He charmed the world with vibrant tales of life on the Mississippi River, publishing *Tom Sawyer* in 1876 and *Huck Finn* in 1884 — but behind the scenes, the beloved author was struggling.

He'd lost his father to pneumonia, his brother to a steamboat accident, and two of his children to disease. By 1896, he'd sunk most of the family's savings into bad investments, and he was out on the lecture circuit trying to dig them out of debt. While he was away, he received a letter saying his daughter, Susy, had contracted spinal meningitis. Thinking she would recover, he stayed put so he could continue making money. She died a short time later.

That seemed to be the last straw for him.

After burying Susy, Twain became a bitter, hopeless man who claimed humans were inherently greedy and evil. His writing turned dark and sinister, and his days of penning American classics were over. His friend Joe Twichell said, "With all his brilliant prosperities he had become a lonely, weary-hearted man, and the thought of his departure hence was not unwelcome to him."

Living in a haunted house certainly didn't help.

There's only one recorded incident from Twain's time at Number 14. One night, he saw a piece of wood floating over the fireplace. This was the early 20th century, so he shot at it with a pistol. The wood fell to the floor. When Twain went over to inspect it, he found a few drops of blood on it. He thought that was odd, but he insisted there was a logical explanation for it... he just couldn't think of one.

If the author experienced any other hauntings, he didn't record them, but he moved out of the house shortly after the incident. He only lived there for a year.

Not long after moving, Twain's wife died, leaving him a heartbroken, isolated man. He told friends he envied the dead and wished he could join them. It wouldn't be long before he did. He died of a heart attack in 1910. But... that isn't the end of Twain's story.

In the 1930s, a young widow and her daughter moved in. By then, the townhouse had been split into separate apartments to rake in cash, and the pair lived on the floor that used to serve as a sitting room for the wealthy.

One evening, the mother walked into the darkened living room and found a white-haired man lounging in a chair, looking out the window. She jumped and demanded to know who he was and what he was doing in her house. The response was chilling.

"My name is Clemmons, and I got problems here I gotta settle."

When he turned to face her, she saw the wild, mustachioed face of Mark Twain (also known as Samuel Clemmons). He was dressed in his classic white suit — a steely look of determination in his eyes.

It's been almost 100 years since that night, but Twain's ghost still lingers at 14 West 10th. Current residents have claimed to see his stark white hair disappearing around corners on the lower levels. Whatever problems he has to settle remain unsolved… but that's not surprising. This house seems to thrive on chaos. Even one of the most famous ghost hunters in the country couldn't banish the spirits that reside there.

In the late 1950s, an actress and poet named Jan Bryant Bartell moved into the top floor. Bryant was an off-broadway actress married to a World War II veteran. She had severe depression and anxiety. He had PTSD. Their marriage was rocky, and they spent a lot of time apart. With no children, Jan spent most of her time with the couple's dogs.

Just like Twain, Jan Bartell moved to Number 14 during one of the darkest periods of her life. The house seems to attract people like that.

A few weeks after moving in, Bartell felt a "monstrous moving shadow that loomed up behind" her. When she whipped around to see who it was, she was met with an empty room. She said she felt like the house was closing in around her, like a noose… but there was a housing shortage in New York, so she was stuck there. As the years passed, the chaos of the house became routine.

She would hear the sound of footsteps sneaking up behind her. She would hear glass shattering in the next room. She'd feel someone's hand brush the back of her neck.

Jan tried to make peace with the spirits, but they didn't seem interested in peace. One day, a shadowy figure appeared directly in front of her. When she reached out to touch it, she felt a "chilly, damp" sensation. It was accompanied by a sickly sweet smell... and then it disappeared.

Desperate for answers, the Bartells hired Hans Holzer, the renowned psychic who would later investigate the Amityville Horror House. He was handsome, confident, and unafraid. He often said ghosts were only "fellow human beings in trouble," and that there was no reason to fear them.

He hadn't met the ghosts of 14 West 10th yet.

The second Holzer stepped into the house, he was accosted by several spirits: a little girl, a woman, a gray cat... Suddenly, his eyes went wide with a dramatic gasp. He had been possessed by a young woman named Reenie Mallsion, a 19-year-old whose husband died in the Civil War. She was distraught over her dead husband and her aborted child. When he demanded that she leave the house, the spirit shot back, *"Never! I will never leave here! They will have to go! This is my home!"*

When Holzer came to, he packed up his things and told the Bartells their New York townhouse was a lost cause. They moved out in 1973, settling into a quiet home in New Rochelle... but the curse of 14 West 10th Street seemed to follow them. Jan Bartell thought of the house day and night. Miles away, she was still haunted by it... so she wrote a book.

Spindrift: Spray from a Psychic Sea details Jan Bartell's experiences in this house. It might have relaunched her career and saved her marriage... if she hadn't died by suicide right before it was published.

That isn't the end of the story. The final chapter is the most disturbing.

In 1987, Joel Steinberg lived at Number 14 with his girlfriend, Hedda, and their two adopted children: 6-year-old Lisa and 18-month-old Mitchell. From the outside, they looked like the perfect family. Hedda edited children's books for Random House, and Joel was a lawyer. They had a boy and a girl and a beautiful townhome in one of New York's most desirable neighborhoods. All they were missing was a white picket fence and a dog.

But all of it came crashing down in November of '87.

In a cocaine-induced rage, Joel beat Lisa into a coma in front of Hedda and Mitchell. He left his wife on the bathroom floor for 10 hours before police arrived and rushed her to the hospital. She died of a severe brain hemorrhage four days later.

Mitchell was found tethered to his playpen, soaked in urine, and Hedda was bruised and bloodied. The Steinbergs had been living a double life. In public, they were prim and perfect... but behind the walls of Number 14... something seemed to take hold of them. They had illegally adopted both children, and Lisa's murder had followed years of abuse.

Joel served 17 years in prison, but he was let out in 2004. When he talks about Lisa, he rolls his eyes. Asked if he had anything he wanted to say to his daughter, Steinberg answered in a cold tone that dripped with sarcasm: "Yeah, I'll never kill you again, and I'll never beat you up every day, and I'll never make you a torture tot in a house of horror."

The only silver lining to the story is that Lisa seems to be happy now. Her spirit laughs and plays with the other children who are trapped in the house, and residents have spotted a sweet little girl wandering through various rooms. For the ghosts of 14 West 10th, the house isn't a prison. It's a safe haven from the horrors on the other side.

Emma Lazarus House

Emma Lazarus House, New York City, NY.

Over a dozen famous writers have called the Village home over the last 200 years. Mark Twain, EE Cummings, Robert Frost, Oscar Wilde, and Edgar Allan Poe usually make the Top 5, but this story is all about Emma Lazarus.

Most people have never heard of her, but they're familiar with her most famous poem:

> "Give me your tired, your poor, Your huddled masses yearning to breathe free, The wretched refuse of your teeming shore. Send these, the homeless, tempest-tost to me, I lift my lamp beside the golden door!"

Those lines are from an 1883 piece titled "The New Colossus", and they're inscribed on the Statue of Liberty. Lazarus was a fierce advocate for Jewish immigrants. She was born to a wealthy Portuguese–Jewish family that had immigrated to America before the Revolutionary War, when New York was still a British colony, so she had a soft spot for the refugees who were fleeing persecution in Europe.

From 1866 to 1887, she wrote a novel, a short story, and several poems calling attention to the plight of immigrants. When she wasn't writing, she volunteered at the Hebrew Immigrant Aid Society and helped connect them with vocational training.

She was mentored by Ralph Waldo Emerson and adored by critics. By the time she was 30, she was already accepted into New York's high society and art circles… but her glowing career was about to be cut short.

The Lazarus Family moved into 18 West 10th Street in 1883, when Emma's father, Moses, retired. Her famous poem was penned there, but that isn't what the house is known for. Two years after moving in, Moses Lazarus succumbed to "a complication of diseases," as the papers put it. They didn't know it at the time, but he had contracted a rare form of cancer… and Emma was next.

The same year, Emma sailed to Europe to advocate for social reform. She swept through the continent, chatting and charming her way through rooms of men. She was rich, famous, childless, and unmarried. She had built a life most 19th-century women couldn't even dream up, but there was an invisible assassin waiting to take her down.

When she returned to New York in September of 1887, something was very wrong. She was weak, exhausted, and her lymph nodes were swollen. She had developed a rare form of cancer called Hodgkin's Lymphoma, which eventually cuts off the body's ability to fight infections. Within two months, she was dead. The funeral was at the house the next morning.

Over the years, many ghost sightings have been reported by owners and

Emma Lazarus House, New York City, NY.

passers-by. Emma Lazarus is said to look out the windows of the upper floors, and various creaks and slammed doors are often attributed to her spirit moving about the house.

For the most part, encounters have been relatively harmless. Sometime in the 90s, the basement was converted into an apartment, and one of the tenants — we'll call her Colleen — moved in with her husband. They had moved to New York from the Midwest after landing great jobs that could rent them a gorgeous place in the Village, but there was something off about their new home… At night, they heard loud coughing, an incessant hacking that continued for hours on end.

After a few days with little sleep, they complained to the owners. However, they claimed that they had never heard of such a thing. As Colleen did more research on Lazarus and the house, she became convinced that it was the ghost of Lazarus who was coughing. Her suspicions were confirmed one night when Colleen was awoken again by coughing, but this time it was her own. Just like the ghost, she could not stop. Her husband tried to get her a drink, but nothing helped. Then, she started to cough up blood.

They decided to call an ambulance, but before they could dial the number, Colleen started violently seizing. When the ambulance arrived, Colleen had coughed up enough blood to soak through her sheets. They rushed her to the hospital, but the minute she left the house, she stopped. It cleared up immediately.

At the hospital, the doctors couldn't find anything wrong with her, and although she apparently had lost a lot of blood, she was showing none of the signs of extreme blood loss. Colleen and her husband stayed in the house for the remainder of their lease, but as soon as it was up, they found a new place and moved out. They never had another issue like that, but Colleen remained convinced that she was somehow touched by Lazarus' ghost.

Jefferson Market Library

Jefferson Market Library, New York City, NY.

The Jefferson Market Library, commonly called "Old Jeff," has seen its share of history. The main attached building was completed in 1877 and served as the courthouse for New York's Third Judicial District until 1945.

Everyone from petty thieves to murderers have been tried and convicted there, including abortion doctor "Madame Restell" in 1878 and millionaire heir Harry Thaw in 1907.

When Ann Trow Lohman, better known as Madame Restell, began her practice, only surgical abortions after the quickening (when a pregnant person can feel the fetus move) were illegal in New York. However, the success of her work attracted copycats and competition. This, in turn, brought with it attention from the American Medical Association, which began a campaign in 1857 to end abortion.

Madame Restell arrived at the Jefferson Market Courthouse in a fashionable carriage, dressed in fine clothes as she was escorted inside to be arraigned. Bail was set at $1,000. She was said to have reached into her purse to pull out $10,000, but the judge would accept only regular bail bonds, so Restell had to pay a bondsman. On the eve of her trial, a maid discovered her in the bathtub at her home on Fifth Avenue where she had run her practice; she had slit her own throat on the morning of April 1, 1878.

Thirty years later, the "Trial of the Century" took place at the courthouse. Harry K. Thaw, heir to a 40 million dollar coal and railroad fortune, shot the famous New York architect Standford White in front of more than 300 witnesses.

Thaw was obsessed with the fact that his wife, actress and chorus girl Evelyn Nesbit, had been assaulted by White when Nesbit was a teenager. Thaw believed this to be an act of chivalry, as he was devoted to the idea of female chastity and purity, which he believed White had robbed Evelyn of.

Thaw's first trial resulted in a hung jury, leading to a re-trial where he pleaded not guilty by reason of insanity. His second trial succeeded in him being committed to the Matteawan State Hospital for the Criminally Insane in Fishkill, New York. Thaw later escaped Matteawan and fled to Canada in 1913, only to be extradited back to New York.

This was during the heyday of yellow journalism, so sensationalist articles about the trial and Thaw himself had convinced a contingent of the population that he was justified in his murder of White and that he was a defender of "American womanhood." A new trial found Thaw to be no longer insane, setting him free once again.

Though few people remember the "Trial of the Century" today, it may have had an eternal impact on the courthouse. When the building was reopened as a library in 1967, people began seeing a woman in a blue gown smiling and waving at them. As soon as they would lift their hand to wave back, she would disappear.

Could it be Evelyn Nesbit, still trying to drum up support for her husband? Or is it someone else? According to one witness, this spirit has the power to drive people mad…

A daughter and her mother, who walked by the building each morning for their daily exercise, reported some strange activity around the tower. Every time they passed the building, the younger woman would wave. After a week of waving, the mother finally asked her daughter who she was waving at. The daughter said she was waving at the woman on the tower. Her mother laughed and said that there was no one up there. The daughter was incredulous. She thought her mother was pulling her leg, because the woman on the tower was so obvious, with her frantic waving and blue gown, no one could miss her.

The next time the daughter saw the waver, she tried to point her out to her mother, but by the time they looked up together, the woman had disappeared. She even tried dragging her mother into the library to ask about the mysterious female. The workers at the library were, of course, aware of the sightings but instead told the local woman that practically no one went up to the tower, and certainly never a woman in a blue dress.

It probably should've ended there, but it didn't.

The daughter could not stop arguing with her mother about the mysterious waver. Their rift grew until the daughter just stopped going for walks with her mom. The mother stopped for a few days too, but then one day she started up the habit again by herself. On her walk, she saw the tower in the distance and, to her surprise, a figure standing there. She started jogging toward it, driven by her newfound feeling that her daughter hadn't made up the story.

But her relief was short-lived because when she drew closer, she saw that the woman on the tower was actually her daughter. The daughter gave her mother a wide, high-up, welcoming wave just as she hopped over the side and fell to the sidewalk. But she didn't die instantly. She was taken to the hospital, where she died from her injuries several weeks later.

The strangest part was that she was wearing a blue dress — an antique from the early 1900s.

12 Gay Street

12 Gay Street, New York City, NY.

The story of 12 Gay Street starts in the 1920s, with the city's corrupt, womanizing mayor, Jimmy Walker.

Walker was nicknamed "the Night Mayor" because he spent his nights partying and sleeping around while his wife stayed home. He escorted his mistress, Betty Compton, around town in a $17,000, silver-trimmed black Duesenberg — a gift from some unknown lobbyist who wanted political favors — and rolled into work around 3 p.m., often leaving three or four hours later.

As Prohibition raged on, Walker leased an apartment at 12 Gay Street so he could throw lavish, booze-drenched parties. Liquor, laughter, and music filled every room. He had a beautiful woman on his arm and an endless stream of cash. For Jimmy Walker, life was one long party — but all parties come to an end eventually. Walker had been embezzling hoards of money, and the New York legislature eventually found out. He was forced to resign in 1932, and he fled the country with Betty.

His exile didn't last long though. He came back to lead the Majestic Records Company and died in New York at the age of 65 — but he wasn't the same man. Betty had divorced him and moved on to husband number four, and his reputation never recovered from the 1932 scandal.

His best days were spent at his Gay Street apartment.

Some people still hear the clicking of flapper heels on the basement floor, as if the party continues. Others report the appearance of female ghosts in full 1920s attire, complete with a feathered headband. These are likely residual hauntings — actions or images that become embedded in the fabric of a place itself. The spirits aren't really there. It's just a recording of them, and it's playing over and over like a broken record.

But there's at least one ghost that's more than just a residual haunting: the legendary Gay Street Phantom.

The phantom began appearing after Frank Paris and his partner Ted Lewis bought the property in 1956. The men were both puppeteers, so they converted the basement into a workshop and puppet theater. That's where Paris crafted the very famous (and very creepy) puppet "Howdy Doody," who had his own TV show from 1947 to 1960.

One night, around 3 a.m., the men were working downstairs when Frank smelled a strong floral fragrance. The couple's black spaniel lifted his head — signaling that he smelled it too — but Ted was oblivious.

Months later, the couple was hosting a dinner party when they heard a loud thump overhead, like someone jumping. Footsteps moved across the floor above them, loud enough that the guests asked if anyone lived upstairs. After a long pause, Frank responded with a knowing smile, "No, not a living soul."

Frank often heard footsteps climbing the stairs or objects moving around. The dog would bark ferociously at strange corners of the house and tilt his head at phantom noises... but Frank wasn't afraid of the ghosts. He was intrigued by them. Maybe that's why the Gay Street Phantom decided to appear to him.

One day, an older woman named Mary paid the couple a visit. She was sitting in the second-floor living room when she spotted a man with dark hair dressed in full evening clothes and cape standing near the stairs. She turned to get Frank's attention. When she turned back, the man was gone.

Frank thought she was imagining things. The house may have been haunted by strange noises and smells, but the couple had never seen a full-bodied ghost. Time passed, and he forgot all about the strange man... until he walked downstairs early one morning. The dog trotted happily behind him, ready for his breakfast.

When Frank looked up, he saw the same man. His face was obscured by the shadows of the hallway, but he was wearing evening clothes and a cape, and he had a young, handsome appearance. The dog wagged his tail and walked over to greet him... but by the time he reached the man, the specter disappeared.

Stories of the Gay Street Phantom spread throughout the Village. No one could agree on who it was. Was it Jimmy Walker? Or someone from the Gilded Age, when Gay Street was still a narrow path in between horse stables? A few deaths had occurred in the area back then — a murder and a carriage accident — and there was a morgue nearby. The well-dressed phantom could have been anyone.

Desperate for answers, Frank called the one and only Hans Holzer to investigate the house. This time, Holzer brought a medium named Betty Ritter. She sensed that a crime had been committed in the house. There was a man reaching out to her who said he'd been tortured to death for keeping a secret. He was a French diplomat. Unable to get the man's name, this story has never been verified... but with so many powerful men frequenting the parties held there, who knows what could have happened within those walls?

After Frank's death from lung cancer in 1984, Gay Street's haunted reputation faded with time. It became better known as a backdrop for music videos like Cyndi Lauper's "Girls Just Want to Have Fun" and movies like *A Night to Remember* — but the locals never forgot what happened there.

In 2009, the house was listed for $4.2 million. One of the neighbors tried to warn interested buyers about its chilling reputation, telling *New York Magazine*, "I wouldn't go in there right now — it's legendary that ghosts live there. That place would be like moving into *The Shining*."

Rumor has it that the legendary Gay Street Phantom still appears from time to time. Folks have caught a flash of his cape billowing behind him as he disappears behind a corner, off to his next party.

12 Gay Street, New York City, NY.

Marie's Crisis Café

Marie's Crisis Café, New York City, NY.

The quaint little piano bar at 59 Grove Street hides quite a bit of history: One of the most important American revolutionaries and political rabble-rousers died on the site.

In the early 1800s, Thomas Paine's modest wooden house sat there. Paine was a prolific pamphleteer who authored fiery calls to action. A few of his most famous pamphlets include *Common Sense* and a series called *The Crisis Papers*, both published in 1776. They played an important role in mobilizing people to revolt against King George III. Historians have said that the revolution would not have succeeded without Paine's influential and widely distributed publications.

But by the time Paine died in 1809, he was an outcast. Only six people attended his funeral, and the *New York Evening Post* reported that he had "done some good and much harm."

What caused the country to turn on him? He spoke out against organized religion. Paine wrote that organized religion was "set up to terrify and enslave" and to "monopolize power and profit", and that Christianity was too "absurd for belief."

That didn't go over well, so Paine was penniless and alone when he died of a "mysterious illness" in his little house. He was buried at his farm in New Rochelle. No one gave any grand speeches, and no one visited. His neglected grave was quickly suffocated by overgrown weeds. It would continue to decay for the next ten years, until William Cobbett came along.

Cobbett had once been Paine's arch nemesis. He was a fierce loyalist who wrote papers opposing Paine's democratic views… but, when he returned to England after the war, he decided the patriot had been right about everything.

Cobbett sailed back to the U.S. in 1817. By then, Paine had been dead for almost a decade, and it was too late to make amends, so the former loyalist decided to visit his grave instead. He expected to find a well-kept tomb — something befitting of Thomas Jefferson or James Madison. Instead, he found a shabby, overgrown mound. Outraged by the lack of respect, he did something drastic: He stole Thomas Paine's bones.

His grand plan was to rebury the forgotten founding father with honors, but no one would donate to his cause. He was a laughingstock in England and a criminal in America, where body snatching (or in this case, bone snatching) was illegal. When he died in 1835, Paine's bones were sold at auction to pay off Cobbett's lingering debts.

The remains were scattered over the years. Some were destroyed, some were fashioned into decorative buttons, some were put on display in different countries. The only remains left in New Rochelle are a mummified brain stem and a lock of his hair, which were buried in a secret location by the historical association.

Marie's Crisis Café is the closest thing we have to an actual gravesite for Thomas Paine. They've honored him with a plaque next to the front door, displaying a direct quote: *The world is my country, All mankind are my brethren, To do good is my religion, I believe in one God and no more.*

That short passage does a great job of illustrating the confrontational nature of Paine's writing, but it also shows his contagious passion for freedom and liberty. He was a man who could be contained by no other, and it seems that his revolutionary spirit followed him into the afterlife…

Paine rallied against authority figures, so it makes sense that most of the ghostly activity has revolved around managers of Marie's Crisis Café. Important papers show up in strange places (like under the refrigerator or high up on hard-to-reach shelves), and phantom footsteps sneak up behind them when they're working after the café is closed.

Several people have reported seeing Paine's spirit sitting or walking around. He is dressed in colonial garb, and he doesn't really interact with anyone before vanishing in seconds.

There is another presence that is decidedly less benign than good ole Thomas.

One of the piano players tells a particularly chilling tale about coming into contact with this entity. The night was coming to a close, and he was packing up his things and getting ready to leave. As he walked out the back door, he saw something but wasn't exactly sure what it was. It seemed like a red ball that wasn't fully there. It was translucent, and it gave off a faint heat as he was standing just a couple of feet away from the thing. He admits that he had been drinking, but he says this was an especially slow night, so he didn't waste his few tips on heavy liquor.

Well, the orb moved slowly toward him, and as it did, he froze completely. But it was not because he was scared (although he was terrified). Something was stopping him from moving.

This orb then got about a foot away before it burst into flames. The man described the heat as being so intense it felt like the skin on his face was starting to peel away. Luckily, he had forgotten his wallet inside the bar, and another employee burst out of the back door to catch him before he left. As soon as the door popped open, the orb disappeared, and the piano player crumpled to the ground.

The employee helped him up, but when the man tried to explain, he got a blank stare. The piano player believed he was temporarily living out the death of a past fire victim. What's odd is that the building has no recorded history of a fire ever happening.

Some have speculated the entity is left over from the property's brief time as a brothel, when a woman was allegedly murdered in the basement. Sadly, her story has been lost to time.

Whatever this thing was, the piano player likely would've been hurt in some way had his coworker not interrupted. He claims that the feeling of helplessness has stuck with him, even after all these years.

The Ghosts of New York City, NY.

One if by Land, Two if by Sea

One if by Land, Two if by Sea, New York City, NY.

Opened in 1973, "One if by Land, Two if by Sea" honors Paul Revere's midnight ride. Before he left Boston, Revere ordered the lighting of two lanterns in the belfry of Old North Church, signaling that the "British were coming" by sea (across the Charles River), instead of marching out of Boston Neck.

But the legend surrounding the bar has nothing to do with Revere. Instead, it centers on Aaron Burr, the infamous vice president who shot and killed Alexander Hamilton.

Long before the bar was constructed, there was a carriage house on the property. Burr began keeping his horses there in the 1790s, and he was often spotted there with his young daughter Theodosia. The girl's mother had died in 1794, leaving Burr to care for her. She was his world. No one had any doubt he was a loving father, but there were rumors that he was too loving. Some historians believe those rumors are what led to the duel between Burr and Alexander Hamilton in 1804.

Though Burr was never convicted of murder, karma eventually came for him…

On December 31, 1812, Burr's 29-year-old daughter boarded a ship named the *Patriot* in Georgetown, South Carolina. She was never seen again.

Theodosia had boarded the *Patriot* to visit her father in New York. She was ill at the time in addition to grieving the death of her son, and the country was still embroiled in the War of 1812. British ships patrolled the coast, and pirates were known to frequent the Carolina waters. There were countless reasons she shouldn't have been traveling. Her husband, Joseph Alston, had warned her against going — but nothing could stop Theodosia from making her father happy, and he very much wanted to see her.

But the *Patriot* never arrived. Burr was wracked with guilt and spent the last years of his life in a haze. Theodosia's biographer wrote that, "For the rest of his life, only the broken-hearted shell of Aaron Burr walked the streets of New York."

The newspapers went wild with speculation. Had the ship capsized in a storm? Had it been taken by pirates? Some theories pointed to the "wreckers" of the North Carolina coast — nefarious men and women who would use lanterns to confuse ship captains, causing them to run aground. The tricksters would then loot the ship's cargo.

But the *Patriot* hadn't run aground. It had disappeared. Even today — over 200 years after its doomed voyage — no one knows where it is or what happened to the passengers on board.

Theodosia's husband Joseph believed that the *Patriot* sailed into a severe storm and sank to the bottom of the Atlantic Ocean, taking his wife down with it. But many others speculated that the ship fell into pirate hands, and later testimonies may corroborate this story. In 1820, two men being executed for crimes on the seas claimed that they plundered and sank the *Patriot*. In 1833, another pirate explained with much detail how he forced Theodosia to walk the plank. Of course, there was no way to verify either story.

There have been a number of other theories put forth with varying amounts of evidence. Some say Theodosia was taken captive and made a pirate's mistress, then murdered when she resisted said pirate's advances. She has even been linked to another east coast legend: Could Theodosia be the "Female Stranger," the mysterious spirit that haunts an unmarked grave at St. Paul's Episcopal cemetery in Alexandria, VA?

We may never know, but One if by Land, Two if by Sea claims Theodosia found her way home eventually.

Occasionally the lights within will flicker on and off for no apparent reason. This has even happened during a busy dinner service, with diners looking around at each other wondering if the next person just saw what they saw. One woman sitting at the bar had one of her earrings fall out — she could have sworn it was pulled out by an unseen hand — and then never found it again.

Pictures hanging on the restaurant's walls have fallen when nobody was around to touch them. Some of the paintings simply go missing when staff members aren't looking, only to show up in some random place later. And in the kitchen and food prep area, plates have been known to go flying all on their own.

These strange happenings could be attributed to one of the other dozens of ghosts said to haunt the property, but the "woman on the stairs" is undoubtedly Theodosia Burr. Multiple witnesses have seen the apparition of a young woman dressed in all black walking down the staircase. Some have said that upon seeing the spirit, they suddenly felt deeply depressed, as if an unseen cloud of sorrow emanates from the spectral sight.

Other times, she is spotted in the mezzanine walking with an older gentleman that could only be Aaron Burr. It seems that Theodosia finally made it home to her father after all, and now they can spend the afterlife together forever.

The Ghosts of New York City, NY.

Brown Building

Brown Building, New York City, NY.

Completed in 1901, New York University's Brown Building got its start as the Asch Building, an iron and steel structure known for its "fireproof" rooms. Today it's known as the site of the deadliest industrial fire in New York history.

The Triangle Shirtwaist Factory was housed on the 8th, 9th, and 10th floors. This factory produced women's blouses known as "shirtwaists" and employed 500 people — mostly Jewish, Italian, and German immigrant women, some as young as 13 years old. The women worked nine hours a day on weekdays, plus seven hours on Saturdays. They earned about $10 each week, equivalent to making about $5 per hour in today's economy.

When the workday came to an end on the evening of March 25, 1911, an employee may have accidentally thrown an unextinguished match or cigarette into a waste bin. Beneath the wooden bin, hundreds of pounds of scraps had piled up, leftovers from thousands of pounds of shirts that had been cut at the table. As a result, the highly flammable material quickly caught fire.

The workers on the 8th floor tried to warn the ladies on the other floors. They managed to warn the 10th floor with a phone call, but they had no way of speaking to the women on the 9th. As the fire began to spread, everyone jammed into the elevators while they still functioned or ran to nearby stairwells.

Unfortunately, the emergency escape doors were all locked. The factory had a policy of checking all the women's purses as they left, to make sure no one was stealing clothing. Due to this policy, most of the doors were kept locked until the workers could be checked at the end of their shift. Trapped, the panicked women began pounding on the doors.

Unfortunately, the foreman who had the keys had made a run for it as soon as he noticed the smoke, leaving everyone trapped on the upper floors.

Two elevator operators continued working the elevators as long as they could. The first of these elevators stopped running when the heat buckled the guide rails. The second elevator continued running until the operator began hearing loud thumps and bangs coming from above. People looking for a way out of the fire started to jump down the elevator shafts, in the hope of landing on the elevator roof. The roof did, in fact, catch the jumpers, but the distance proved to be too great. These jumpers fell to their deaths, buckling the elevator and causing it to also stop running.

Within minutes, the fire had spread and trapped hundreds of women. Terrified, some of the remaining employees scrambled to a crowded fire escape. Horrifically, the flimsy iron structure twisted and collapsed, throwing 20 victims nearly 100 feet to their deaths on the concrete pavement below.

Once firefighters finally arrived, their ladders could only reach as high as the 6th and 7th floors. With the fire escapes all blocked by fire or collapsed, the elevators not working, and the other exits locked, people made their way to the roof or windows in order to put distance between themselves and the fire. Soon, as the fire spread to the outer reaches of the buildings, people had two choices: allow themselves to be overcome by smoke and fire or jump 100 feet and hope to be caught by the firemen's nets below.

The first few jumpers made it safely. A man was seen helping women out of a window, and so they dropped safely to the net below. Unfortunately, the nets could take only so many impacts and soon started to break. At times workers jumped in twos and threes, which was too much for the nets to handle. William Gunn Shepard, a reporter at the scene recalled, "I learned a new sound that day, a sound more horrible than description can picture — the thud of a speeding living body on a stone sidewalk."

The oldest fatality was a woman aged 43, and the youngest was only 11 (some sources say 14). This event would draw upwards of 20,000 spectators as 146 people perished in the flames or on the sidewalk below.

Today, the building serves New York University, but the trauma of that day lingers.

Students at NYU say that they can sometimes make out shapes of women jumping from the upper floors of the building. They've seen the famous kissing couple, a pair who kissed each other goodbye before jumping from adjacent windows. Screams are often heard throughout the old building. The echoes of a phantom crackling fire will interrupt lectures. Students also report seeing a woman fleeing down one of the hallways of the 8th floor and appearing out of nowhere in one of the bathrooms.

On the 9th floor of the building, a tall, rectangular mirror hangs just across from the elevator. Sometimes, people who look into the mirror will see someone other than themselves in the reflection. Generally, it is a woman wearing clothes from the early 1900s. Then in an instant, the face flickers and wavers as though viewed through rising flames before the viewer's normal reflection returns to stare back at them from the glass.

There are many spirits who haunt the Washington Place building, but none as memorable as Yetta. She was an 18-year-old Austrian immigrant looking for the American dream while working in the factory. When the fire broke out, Yetta fled to the edges of the building until there was nowhere else to go. She stood at a window, feeling the rapidly growing flames lick at her skin. Desperate, she looked at the pavement below and decided that it was one way or the other, and then jumped.

Her body collapsed in a heap of blood on the streets below. It would be discovered that she broke her spine and both femurs. Later, she would die in the hospital.

Yetta's ghost is typically seen walking down the stairs and heading out the door toward the street. She is described as having beautiful long brown hair, twinkling sultry eyes, and a look of elegance about her. Yet, as she passes living spectators, they're quickly reminded that she isn't really there.
Her presence is always followed by the alarming scent of burning flesh and the sound of hellish screaming. No matter how much time passes, the screams sound just like they did in 1911.

Brown Building, New York City, NY.

Fire Patrol No. 2

Fire Station No. 2, New York City, NY.

Before 84 W 3rd St. was a fire station, it was a popular brothel run by Matilda Herman, also known as the French Madame. Lawmen, emergency workers, soldiers, police and the like all came to see the madam and her associates. It was a very lucrative business for a woman who understood how much New York's elite enjoyed their various nocturnal pleasures.

Matilda was apparently as savage as she was savvy and handled her business in more ways than one. Journalist and writer Herbert Asbury has described Matilda as a woman large and in charge who "acted as her own bouncer, and acquired great renown for the manner in which she wielded a bludgeon, and for the quickness with which she seized obstreperous women customers by the hair and flung them into the street."

But, in 1895, following a scandal regarding police corruption, she was called upon to tell what she knew. And, against her better judgment, she testified against the police. Later she disappeared, never to be seen alive again.

In 1906, the building became a firehouse for an independent firefighting group that specialized in fighting commercial fires rather than residential ones. And it served in this capacity for a hundred years.

It wasn't long after Fire Patrol No. 2 first began operating that firefighters started reporting strange occurrences and encounters with ghostly entities. Many have spoken about seeing a man with a mustache in his 40s. He is said to drift through the hallways, wearing full firefighting gear from the 1930s, but he is also sometimes spotted wearing casual pants and a red double-breasted shirt.

A psychic was brought in one day to investigate the presence. The psychic called him by name: Schwartz. According to the psychic, Schwartz was around just before WWII in the 1930s. The story goes that Schwartz hanged himself on the 4th floor after discovering that his wife had cheated on him. Sightings of Schwartz have occurred frequently since then. And they say that the fourth floor is the most haunted area of all.

In the basement, a fireman saw Schwartz slide down a coal chute, which is too small for an adult to fit into. In 1992, one fireman had an experience with Scwartz that was actually frightening. He claims that as he woke up one morning, he opened his eyes to see Schwartz standing right beside his bed, looming over him. But before the fireman had time to shake the shock and scream or say anything, Schwartz just disappeared.

Other than Schwartz and Matilda Herman, there is at least one other famous spirit that spends its time in the vicinity of the old fire station: Aaron Burr.

Many locals have reported seeing an affluent-looking gentleman wearing 19th-century clothing walking down the sidewalks around the area of Fire Patrol No. 2. Some believe that this is the ghost of Burr, casually taking a stroll and still flaunting his avoidance of a conviction even today.

Fire Station No. 2, New York City, NY.

The Ghosts of New York City, NY.

Edgar Allan Poe House

Edgar Allan Poe House, New York City, NY.

Now part of NYU's Furman Hall, 85 W 3rd Street was once occupied by Edgar Allan Poe and his 13-year-old bride and cousin, Virginia, for eight months between 1844 and 1845. During this time, Poe wrote his classic story, "The Cask of Amontillado," and part of his masterful poem, "The Raven." These days, the only part of the original residence that remains is the banister and maybe Poe's ghost, which has been seen by many spooked law students.

The renovation of the old house into Furman Hall began on September 28, 2001 — only 17 days after the attack on the World Trade Center. In fact, it was the first construction project to begin in all of Manhattan after 9-11. The doors opened in 2004, and the only thing you could recognize from the old house was the aforementioned banister.

Eventually, a study lounge was constructed inside Furman that became known as the Poe Room. This room contains many different artifacts related to the old house. A semiannual event is held in the Poe Room "in honor of the life, times, and works of Edgar Allan Poe."

In addition to his terrifying fiction and gloomy poetry, Poe also wrote some nonfiction while living in New York. He reported on the "Witch of

Staten Island" story, one of the most sensational news events of the day. The story revolved around the trial of Polly Bodine, who was being accused of murdering her sister-in-law and niece, then setting fire to the house to destroy all evidence of her crime. Eventually Bodine was acquitted, though nobody ever identified a different perpetrator.

During this time, Poe was also rumored to be a notorious adulterer. Many of the women he was involved with were also poets, such as Fanny Osgood. Osgood mothered an illegitimate child with Poe. The child suffered from breathing complications and was physically deformed. However, Poe's affair with Elizabeth Ellet was perhaps the most notable of them all. Allegedly, Ellet was a hateful mistress who wanted Poe's wife, Virginia, out of the picture. She cursed Virginia with a "poison pen letter."

All of this wore on Virginia.

As she sat at the piano picking at the keys one night, she began coughing up blood — the first sign of tuberculosis, then called "consumption." The illness progressed slowly. Poe moved his dying wife to a cottage in the Bronx, hoping that the open air and large living space would help. Nevertheless, Virginia died on January 30, 1847, at the young age of 24. Ellet's letters had affected Virginia so much that on her deathbed, she claimed Elizabeth had succeeded in murdering her.

It's said the poor woman still lingers in Furman Hall — forever staring helplessly out of a window on one of the floors. It is believed that she suffered so greatly because of tuberculosis, and the emotional strain of her husband's many affairs, that her sorrow may have been "imprinted" upon the home. It may have even affected Poe.

The writer's drinking habit increased when Virginia got sick. But after her death, it spiraled out of control. When he wasn't posted up at one of the local bars, he was sitting at home, drinking alone. Looking across the street, Poe was able to see Washington Square Park, which he knew was the site of mass burials caused by disease. Surrounded by death, disease, and betrayal, it's no wonder that Poe was influenced to write about the horrors of the human condition.

He would follow his wife in death two years later.

Though he died in Baltimore, New York University students have spotted his apparition in the old Poe House. They've watched in a combination of amazement and fright as his ghost slowly descends the stairs, holding on to his old banister. He steps carefully and seems unstable, perhaps in one of his drunken stupors. And just when you catch a good glimpse of his face — those deep-set eyes peering out from a hazy malaise — that's when the apparition simply vanishes.

Furman isn't the only place in Manhattan where the ghost of Poe has been spotted. There is an Italian restaurant at 47 Bond Street with a very famous wine cellar. In Poe's day, that basement was an underground bar, one where he spent many nights drinking his sorrows away. People say that his spirit still haunts the cellar from time to time, as if he is frequenting his favorite places to drink even in the afterlife. Restaurant employees say that they sometimes find wine bottles taken off the racks and placed on a table when no one was around. They believe that it is Poe letting them know which wine he prefers that day.

As the master of the macabre said himself:

"The boundaries which divide life from death are at best shadowy and vague. Who shall say where the one ends, and where the other begins?"

BONUS CHAPTER

New York's Most Haunted Continued

There are enough New York ghost stories to fill several books. Centuries of war, betrayal, and tragedies have blanketed the state with restless souls — some more active than others.

Journey to Sleepy Hollow, where Washington Irving's Headless Horseman chased Ichabod Crane across the Church Bridge. Is the tale a myth? Or is there a headless soldier stalking the Old Dutch Burial Ground…

Travel back to December 8, 1980, when John Lennon was shot and killed outside The Dakota. In the decades that followed, Yoko saw and heard his ghost in their penthouse apartment — but the hauntings started long before that. Lennon often saw the spirit of a crying woman floating through the hallways. Was she trying to warn him?

If that isn't enough to fuel your nightmares, head north to the old Utica State Hospital — a 19th century asylum that patented a torture device called the "Utica Crib." If you aren't familiar with the spine-chilling punishments inflicted on the "patients" here, the spirits are more than happy to fill you in…

The following four stories are some of New York's most dramatic, bone-chilling tales. Buckle in, because we've saved the best for last.

Terrors of New York State.

The Dakota | New York City, NY

The Dakota, New York City, NY.

The Gothic Revival grandeur of The Dakota is an atmospheric example of great architecture — a throwback to medieval European style even when it was first built in 1884. The impressive edifice looks like it is straight out of a British murder mystery. Its peaked roofs and dormer windows, designed for class and prestige in the late nineteenth century, lend it an ominous facade today.

The imposing appearance of the Dakota has earned it a place in movies such as *Vanilla Sky* and *Rosemary's Baby.* While the exterior oozes with history and atmosphere, the walls inside have literally dripped with blood, and paranormal forces are said to flow freely within.

The Dakota is known as New York's first luxury apartment building and remains the city's oldest still in use. When it first opened, it offered residence for the upper middle class, housing local workers from lawyers to launderers (of clothes, not money — though, with the organized crime New York would soon become known for, who could say?).

Sometime in the 1960s, the Dakota became a co-op. Once that occurred, the building primarily existed to host celebrities. Among the rich and famous to reside at the Dakota were Judy Garland, Boris Karloff, Connie Chung,

Joe Namath, Rosie O'Donnell, and Maury Povich. Even Peter Tchaikovsky is believed to have had a room there, though he may have lived there before construction was complete considering he died a year before the building officially opened.

The most famous Dakota resident, however, was John Lennon.

On December 8, 1980, a self-proclaimed Beatles fan, Mark David Chapman, approached Lennon for an autograph. The rockstar obliged and then got into a limousine with his wife, Yoko Ono. When the limo returned about six hours later, Chapman was still waiting outside, hidden in the shadows of the Dakota. He walked up to Lennon from behind and shot him four times in the back. The wounds were fatal, and the news rocked the entire world.

Yoko Ono spread Lennon's ashes over a part of Central Park, an area now called Strawberry Fields in his honor. Until February 2023, she remained living in the Dakota apartment she once shared with her husband. At ninety years old, Ono finally sold the apartment and moved to a farm in upstate New York where her son, Sean Lennon, could look after her.

Long before she moved out of the Dakota, however, Ono told multiple stories of seeing the ghost of John Lennon after his death. It seems that in the afterlife, he chose to continue living with his beloved wife in the apartment they shared for seven years. Ono claimed to have seen Lennon sitting at his famous white piano as if ready to compose his next hit song. One night, he looked at her with much compassion in his eyes and simply said, "Don't be afraid. I am still with you."

Lennon may have been joining a whole host of ghosts that had made the Dakota their permanent home. Ono also confessed that at one point, Lennon told her that he saw the spirit of a woman who always seemed to be crying. The sorrowful apparition roamed the hallways, floating to and fro as if searching for an end to her misery.

Numerous other apparitions have appeared within the Dakota's walls over the years. Some residents have reported seeing a couple of children — a boy and a girl — who wander around the complex. The young ones are dressed in nineteenth-century garments, and people say they must have been the children of the building's earliest tenants. They are usually spotted out of the corner of one's eye and seem to disappear completely as soon as they turn a corner. Sometimes their bone-chilling giggling is still heard even after they vanish.

Some say that the Dakota is so haunted with unfriendly entities that it may have cursed the crew of one of the movies filmed there. *Rosemary's Baby* is a classic film that terrified and shocked audiences when it was released in 1968. However, the horror of the movie pales in comparison to the real-life events that befell director Roman Polanski and the rest of the film's crew for decades after its production.

One year after the release of *Rosemary's Baby,* Polanski's wife, Sharon Tate, was attacked in her home by followers of Charles Manson's "family." The horrific and infamous event resulted in the brutal murder of Tate, eight-months pregnant, and three house guests. During the killing spree, one of the Manson followers is quoted as saying, "I am the devil, and I come to do the devil's business." They also wrote the words "Helter Skelter" and "Piggies" on the walls in their victims' blood. Both are names of songs by the Beatles. Was there some unexplainable connection between these murders and a demonic spirit from the Dakota?

When the murders hit the news, some fans noticed a resemblance between the gruesome acts of Manson's followers and the plot of *Rosemary's Baby*. In the film, a Satanic cult targets a young woman and wishes to sacrifice her unborn baby to the devil. The character is, of course, Rosemary — a role that Polanski originally wanted his wife to play.

Shortly after the movie's release, a number of people connected with the film died.

Within months, composer Krzysztof Komeda fell off a cliff at an LA party and suffered a fatal cerebral hemorrhage. Producer William Castle was so anxiety-ridden from believing that the film was cursed that he was stricken with severe kidney stones. While he physically recovered, his mind only got worse. Castle confesses in his autobiography to having disturbing hallucinations about certain scenes from *Rosemary's Baby*. He was haunted by the film for the rest of his life and never had another hit movie again.

Even people who know nothing about these events take one look at the Dakota and know that something from the other side must dwell within…

The Dakota, New York City, NY.

Terrors of New York State.

Sleepy Hollow | Sleepy Hollow, NY

Sleepy Hollow, Sleepy Hollow, NY.

While the name Sleepy Hollow is an international household name, most people outside the small village know very little about the actual place that inspired Washington Irving's classic tale of terror. In real life, appropriate to the legend it has inspired, it is considered one of the most haunted places in the world.

Sleepy Hollow is nestled along the east bank of the Hudson River, approximately thirty miles north of New York City. The original people who lived on the land were natives from the Delaware and Mohican Tribes. When Dutch explorers first sailed up the Hudson in the early 1600s, they encountered unfamiliar landscapes that inspired wonder but also fear. Every dense patch of forest could be hiding a native ambush or something much worse. Many Dutch settlers brought superstitious beliefs with them to the New World. Back home, they feared imps — goblin-like forest-dwelling tricksters — also known as "Hidden People." How many imps were hiding in the mountainous hills, thick woods, and deep waters of the Hudson Valley?

Initially, relations between the Dutch and the natives were relatively peaceful. By 1643, however, the Dutch were at war with the tribes of the region. Twelve years later, the Dutch settlement was named Slapershaven — literally, Sleepers' Haven — which (when Anglicized) became known as Sleepy Hollow.

Over the centuries, farms and mills were built in the area, work that brought Dutch, German, French, and Swiss colonialists to the area in addition to their African slaves. While commerce and industry continued to expand in Sleepy Hollow, it never grew into a large city. To this day, it is a quaint village with a population of less than 10,000.

Certain acts of government, such as the Indian Removal Act of 1830, relocated many of the natives of the Hudson Valley. Ask around, however, and you shall learn that some locals believe their ghosts still linger, the restless spirits of displaced people that forever haunt the lands from which they were forcefully removed. And they aren't the only supernatural forces that call Sleepy Hollow home.

One of the village's most famous real-life hauntings fittingly comes from Sleepy Hollow Cemetery. This is, of course, where one can go to visit the grave of Washington Irving. Several other famous people have been buried in the same graveyard, including Civil War General Samuel Thomas. Across from Thomas's mausoleum sits a larger-than-life statue known as the "Bronze Lady." She sits facing the tomb of General Thomas with downcast eyes, as if contemplating the state of the one interred.

The Bronze Lady is said to be imbued with supernatural forces from beyond the grave that can extend to people who perform a certain ritual. The actions and consequences of this ritual have varied over time. Some say that if you touch the Bronze Lady's face, you'll be cursed, or you might see a ghost. Others say you must sit in her lap then peer into the mausoleum's keyhole to behold the apparition. A third iteration says that if you sit in her lap, spin around three times, and look directly into her brazen eyes, something strange will soon happen to you.

Down the road from Sleepy Hollow Cemetery is a small wooden bridge that looms over a shallow stretch of creek. Washington Irving described this relic from another time in the scene for which the bridge is now named. It's called the Headless Horseman Bridge, and some people say that they have seen the imposing spirit that inspired Irving's writing. The decapitated Hessian soldier has been spotted riding his midnight-colored mare across the bridge before disappearing into the night. Others have reported seeing the headless horseman make his way through the nearby Old Dutch Burial Ground.

Raven Rock is another location that — along with the ghost that haunts it — made its way into Irving's story.

"Some mention was made also of the woman in white, that haunted the dark glen at Raven Rock, and was often heard to shriek on winter nights before a storm, having perished there in the snow." — "The Legend of Sleepy Hollow"

This seemingly unimportant aside in the tale is based on an actual local haunting that must have been around since Irving's time. The story goes that a woman was out walking when she was suddenly enveloped by an unexpected blizzard. She hid behind a large outcropping of black rock in an attempt to shield herself from the onslaught of snow and wind. Instead, the snow drifts closed her in and buried her at the spot, where she froze to death.

Ever since, people walking past Raven's Rock have heard the distant sound of a woman screaming being carried upon the wind, especially on particularly cold nights. A few witnesses have claimed to see her as well — the hazy figure of a woman who floats past, dressed in all white. It seems to be a residual haunting, the tragic final moments of her life playing out over and over again in a frigid paranormal loop.

The tales of hauntings told around campfires in Sleepy Hollow are numerous, so it's no surprise the town inspired Washington Irving's bone-chilling tale. And it's little wonder that the small village is synonymous with the creepy atmosphere of the Halloween season even to this day.

Terrors of New York State.

Belhurst Castle and Winery | Geneva, NY

Belhurst Castle and Winery, Geneva, NY.

When one thinks of a castle, one is most likely reminded of medieval Europe rather than nineteenth-century New York. In actuality, numerous wealthy immigrants from Europe have built castles and castle-like mansions across the state of New York. Most were originally private homes that have now become hotels, restaurants, or other commercial establishments.

Belhurst Castle and Winery is one such place. This four-story Romanesque Revival style castle sitting on the coast of Seneca Lake was originally built to be the home of Captain Louis Dell Collins and his family. Over the years, it has also been a speakeasy, casino, and supper club. Today, the majestic building hosts a hotel, two restaurants, two ballrooms, a winery, and a spa. According to patrons and employees alike, it also houses an unknown number of very active ghosts.

The original Belhurst Castle building took four years and fifty men to build. One worker fell from the tower during construction and was killed upon impact; it is said that another man "snapped" and went insane while working on the roof. Despite these tragedies in its construction, the resulting home was the epitome of grandeur.

The grand edifice remained with the Collins family until 1932, when a colorful individual named Cornelius "Red" Dwyer purchased the property.

One year later, Red opened it to the public as a speakeasy and gambling hall. Since this was during the Prohibition Era, Red had liquor run down from Canada via the connecting canal system.

In the 1950s, Red was forced by the authorities to stop offering gambling at his establishment, or he was told he would "be stopped." From that moment on, he operated Belhurst as a restaurant only. Ownership switched hands several times over the next fifty years, with lodging and the winery eventually added to Belhurst's offerings along the way, but the castle's resident spirit lingers from the Red Era.

The most famous ghost of Belhurst is an opera singer named Isabella — so famous that the complex's Isabella Spa-Salon is named for her. According to the stories, Isabella had a forbidden lover in her home country of Spain. The couple fled to America and settled in Geneva, New York, where they built a small house and a secret tunnel.

Isabella got a job singing at Red's speakeasy but didn't make enough to live on. They used the tunnel they dug to smuggle in alcohol to sell, which became their main source of income. One day, authorities came looking for Isabella and her lover. They escaped and took the tunnel to their boat waiting on the other side. Her lover made it out, but the tunnel collapsed on Isabella, burying her alive.

While she was never seen alive again, Isabella has been spotted walking the shores of Lake Seneca, an apparition in a white opera dress, as lovely as she is frightening to behold. She wanders the property with an expression of yearning, as if still searching for her lost lover. If one gets close to her, she dissipates into nothingness like so much water vapor evaporating.

Staff members at Belhurst have experienced many strange occurrences that they can only describe as hauntings. Several employees have felt a tapping on their shoulder, only to turn around and see nobody there. This is often followed by a playful chuckle like that of a heavy smoker. Some believe that this is the spirit of Dick O'Brien, former caretaker of the Belhurst Hotel who died in 1972. He was known as a prankster in life, and apparently he remains so in the afterlife.

Other reports from staff members include showers turning on and off on their own and glasses suddenly flying off the shelves in the bar area. Guests of the hotel have reported their share of paranormal activity. Some have heard a lullaby being sung in a soft voice but can never locate the singer. Others have heard children playing — and on a few occasions, screaming — in the next room, only to find out that the room was empty.

One guest complained that they were not able to sleep because of all the noise coming from the floor above: chairs being pushed across the floor and footsteps going back and forth all through the night. Staff apologized but explained that the floor above them was not in use. Secretly, however, the employees knew that the upper floor was where Red's gambling hall used to be, and where sad souls were apparently still losing money.

No one knows exactly how many entities haunt Belhurst, but you're sure to run into at least one if you drop by.

Terrors of New York State.

Utica State Hospital | Utica, NY

Utica State Hospital, Utica, NY.

Asylums for the insane boomed across America in the nineteenth century. Many states began funding the construction of these institutions in an effort to join forces with psychiatry, a relatively new science, with the mission of improving society. New York was no exception; there were almost forty built in the state alone. Unfortunately, what was supposed to be a benevolent endeavor to help us understand and cure mental illness often devolved into overcrowded and understaffed facilities marked by the poorest of conditions and the cruelest of treatments.

Utica State Hospital has such a story… and plenty of spirits to tell it.

New York State Lunatic Asylum at Utica, New York's first state-run psychiatric facility, opened in 1843. Beds filled up so quickly that within seven years of being open, two more wings were built to make more accommodations. The hospital's first director, Amariah Brigham, believed that poor environment was a top contributor to mental illness. The institution emphasized giving patients space, good nutrition, as well as physical and mental stimulation. Brigham would go on to be one of the founding members of the American Psychiatric Association.

The asylum had its own printing house and published the *American Journal of Insanity*, of which Brigham was the editor-in-chief. During the 1850s, the hospital also published a patient-led periodical called *The Opal*. It included articles, poems, and drawings made by patients. Within the pages of this journal, patients discussed their world views and experiences, including what it was like to live in a state-run asylum. *The Opal* gave patients a creative outlet and a voice, with pieces often making social commentary on issues like human rights, restraint and seclusion, medication, oppression, and liberty.

But one patient chose to express himself in a very different way.

In 1852, the first-floor stairway of the main building caught fire, destroying much of the structure and taking the lives of a doctor and firefighter. Four days later, another fire occurred at a barn on the property. At the scene, authorities found William Spiers, a former patient, occasional employee, and convicted arsonist. He admitted to setting both fires, stating that he was simply angry with his supervisor.

Over the years, Utica State Hospital followed the same path as other state-run asylums. The number of patients began outweighing the staff and resources, and conditions worsened over time. Psychiatry was in its infancy, and patients with varying conditions often received similar treatment. Those diagnosed with "sadness" or "religious excitement," people who lived with alcoholism or intellectual disabilities, violent criminals, paranoid schizophrenics — they were thrown together under the umbrella of mental illness and were treated accordingly.

Most of these methods seem barbaric and cruel to our modern sensibilities. Records show that Utica performed electroshock therapy and lobotomies on a regular basis. One of the most infamous treatments became known as the Utica Crib.

This crude device looked like a baby's crib with a lid that could be closed and locked. It was essentially a wooden cage in which "difficult" patients were placed. In the crib, they couldn't get out or even sit up. They would lie in that coffin-sized contraption until someone else decided to provide freedom.

Utica State Hospital hasn't had a patient since 1977 — at least not a living one. Walking past the building today, now used as a records archive for the New York State Office of Mental Health, one can't help but sense that the grounds have been tainted from the cruel events that once took place within those walls.

You can feel the spirits inside, pulling you closer, begging you to ignore the "no trespassing" signs and come in to set them free. Some people have claimed to hear screaming coming from the abandoned parts of the complex. It is believed that this is the agonizing sound of a former patient still living out the cruel treatment they received. Others have seen spectral faces peering through the windows, shadowy figures that stare out sadly as if longing to escape.

One group of paranormal investigators reported several strange encounters while walking around the exterior of the main building. First they seemed to hear the distinct sound of a woman humming an unknown tune. Then one of the investigators became suddenly overwhelmed by the atmosphere of sadness that pervaded the air. Uncontrollable tears streamed down her cheeks for a few minutes, her partners looking on in disbelief.

Finally an apparition was spotted walking the grounds, her details strangely vivid even in the moonlight. She was a middle-aged woman with pale skin and straggly hair who seemed to have dirt streaked down her face. Accompanying this spirit was a strong scent of flowers, so pungent that the investigators could taste it. Somebody captured an audible sigh on an EVP recorder before the ghostly vision and phantom aroma disappeared into the night.

The woman's identity is unknown, but judging by her appearance, the group assumed she was one of countless ghostly patients. Today, the main building is closed off at all times with fences and barbed wire. They used to offer occasional tours but haven't done so since 2018. Perhaps they are taking precaution not to unleash the dark secrets of Utica State Hospital and the countless spirits who harbor them.

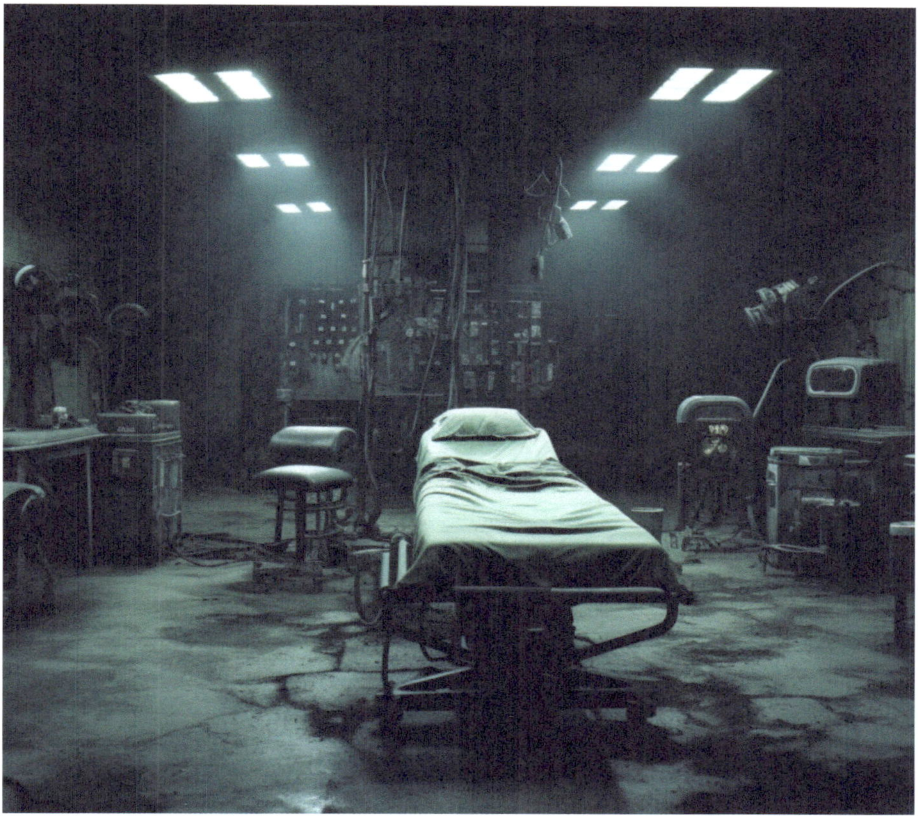

Utica State Hospital, Utica, NY.

Terrors of New York State.

The New York State Education Building | Albany, NY

The New York State Education Building, Albany, NY.

The New York State Education Building has the distinction of being the first building in the U.S. built for the primary purpose of education administration. It's also connected to one of Albany's most disturbing urban legends.

Dr. Andrew Sloan Draper, New York's first Commissioner of Education, was the person who originally suggested a separate building for the state's growing Education Department. The building was designed by the New York City firm Palmer & Horbostel. Construction began in 1908, and the building was dedicated in November 1912. In addition to serving as the headquarters for the New York's Education Department, it also housed the state's Museum and Library until they were moved into a new building in 1976.

Many Albany locals are familiar with the legend behind the Education Building. During construction, a stonemason named Jason was helping a small crew pour concrete for the foundation, which would eventually become the building's basement.

At some point, Jason tripped and fell into the hole that was being filled with concrete. The foreman looked down at Jason, then turned to the other workers and simply said, "Keep pouring." The crew obliged while Jason struggled, limbs flailing until he was completely covered by the concrete.

Some say that the foreman was dissatisfied with Jason's work and gave the command out of anger. Others think that since the foreman was Italian and Jason was Irish, it may have been a racially charged action. Whatever the reason, Jason was sealed up in the building's foundation forever, and his body is still in that concrete today.

Many people believe that Jason's spirit has been trapped, eternally tethered to the location of his horrible death. Due to the traumatic nature of Jason's final moments, the energy attached to the site is usually considered negative and sometimes even dangerous. And it's possible that he is not the only supernatural entity in the Education Building.

Employees have reported an eerie feeling of being constantly watched, especially when no one else is around. Objects have been seen moving across the floor on their own as if pushed by an invisible entity. A few staff members have even spotted dark figures roaming the hallways, shadowy silhouettes that follow closely behind yet seem to vanish as soon as one turns around to face them.

Other activity occurs in the stacks, where volumes of books and department records are stored. Occasionally, lights will flick back on just moments after someone turns them off. Employees have witnessed books mysteriously falling off of the shelves, and it's usually the book they were looking for. Because of the seemingly helpful nature of the ghost in the stacks, it's likely a different spirit, whose identity is not known.

It's much kinder than whatever lurks in the basement…

Employees have taken to referring to the basement as "the dungeon." It's the most haunted area of the building and the closest to Jason's concrete-enveloped corpse. While riding the old steel elevators, employees have felt the presence of another that they could not see. The air in the elevator sometimes grows inexplicably and intensely cold but only for a few seconds. People have seen a man in the basement that they do not recognize. They catch a glimpse of him out of the corner of their eye, but when they turn toward him, he's always gone.

The ghostly phenomena in the New York State Education Building has been frightening enough for a few people to make them leave and never return. For the majority of staff members, however, dealing with the spirits is simply a part of their job. Especially for those who work in the basement, seeing a shadowy figure or feeling the eyes of the dead upon you is just another day at the office.

wejunket.com

Follow **JUNKET** on YouTube, Instagram, Facebook, and Tik Tok to see content, videos, and get the inside scoop about things to do in some of the country's coolest cities. Join us as we travel the country looking for adventures, stories, and the local hidden gems each in America's most historic and iconic places.

You can also check out our latest travel stories and articles about different cities on the Junket Travel Blog: **wejunket.com/blog**

 junketadventures
 junketadventures

 wejunket

wejunket.com/blog

 wejunket

 wejunket

usghostadventures.com

Follow **US GHOST ADVENTURES** on YouTube, Instagram, Facebook, and Tik Tok. You can look forward to content and videos on location at many of these haunted places and watch authentic ghost hunts and clips on our popular channels

You can also check out our latest ghost stories and articles about different haunted cities and the science of hauntings on the US Ghost Adventures Blog: **usghostadventures.com/blog**

 usgadventures

 usghostadventures

 usghostadvntrs

 junketadventures

 USGhostAdventures

 usghostadventures.com/blog

 **usghostadventures**

 usghostadv

#usghostadventures

facebook.com/usghostadventures
usghostadv
usgadventures
usghostadvntrs
pinterest.com/usghostadventures
usghostadventures

usghostadventures.com

Made in the USA
Columbia, SC
16 August 2024

40077305R00202